PROGRAMMING
for
SOFTWARE SHARING

ON INFORMATION SCIENCE

A series devoted to the publication of courses and educational seminars given at the Joint Research Centre, Ispra Establishment, as part of its education and training program. Published for the Commission of the European Communities, Directorate-General Information Market and Innovation.

Additional volumes in preparation.

The publisher will accept continuation orders for this series which may be cancelled at any time and which provide for automatic billing and shipping of each title in the series upon publication. Please write for details.

PROGRAMMING
for
SOFTWARE SHARING

Edited by

D.T. Muxworthy

Program Library Unit, Edinburgh, U.K.

D. REIDEL PUBLISHING COMPANY

A MEMBER OF THE KLUWER ACADEMIC PUBLISHERS GROUP

DORDRECHT / BOSTON / LANCASTER

Library of Congress Cataloging in Publication Data
Main entry under title:

Programming for software sharing.

CIP

(Ispra courses on information science)
Includes index.
1.   Software compatibility.   2.   Electronic digital computers—
Programming.   I.   Muxworthy, D. T.   II.   Series.
QA76.6.P7514   1983   001.64′2   83–8685
ISBN-13: 978-94-009-7147-9   e-ISNB-13: 978-94-009-7145-5
DOI: 10.1007/978-94-009-7145-5

Commission of the European Communities   Joint Research Centre Ispra (Varese), Italy

Publication arrangements by
Commission of the European Communities
Directorate-General Information Market and Innovation, Luxembourg

EUR 8516 EN
Copyright © 1983, ECSC, EEC, EAEC, Brussels and Luxembourg

Softcover reprint of the hardcover 1st edition 1983

Published by D. Reidel Publishing Company
P.O. Box 17, 3300 AA Dordrecht, Holland

Sold and distributed in the U.S.A. and Canada
by Kluwer Boston Inc.,
190 Old Derby Street, Hingham, MA 02043, U.S.A.

In all other countries, sold and distributed
by Kluwer Academic Publishers Group,
P.O. Box 322, 3300 AH Dordrecht, Holland

CONTENTS

PREFACE

Most computer users are familiar with the problems of sharing software with others, and the transfer of programs from one computing environment to another. Software represents an ever-increasing proportion of the cost of computing and these costs tend to nullify all the economic advantages flowing from the wider availability of cheap hardware. Years ago it was hoped that the widespread use of high-level programming languages would help in alleviating the problems of software production, by increasing productivity and by making it simpler for users with similar problems to be able to use the same programs, possibly on different types of machines. It is a common experience that in practice this simple optimism has proved to be unfounded.

It was these considerations which led us in 1979 to organize a two-week course on "Programming for Software Sharing" at the European Community Joint Research Centre, Ispra Establishment (Italy), forming part of the regular series of "Ispra Courses". With prominent invited lecturers, local contributions and through discussion sessions we examined with an audience from many countries the problems involved in the sharing and transfer of software, as well as suggesting ways of overcoming them.

In our local environment we are faced daily with three problems both from engagements in software exchange in the scientific-technical field on a Europe-wide or world-wide basis, and from work with programming techniques and contributions to the international standardization process.

The present volume is however not the proceedings of this course held some years. It is a monograph inspired by that activity. Some contributions are indeed updated versions of material presented during the course, but others are recent papers prepared for the book.

We hope the contributions selected for the book will provide readers with some more insight and understanding of the problems and techniques involved in software sharing. The material should be of value for a wide range of computer users as well as for program developers and implementors.

In presenting this volume our thanks go to lecturers and participants of the Ispra Course, the authors of the contributions to the book and above all to Mr. D. Muxworthy, University of Edinburgh (UK) who undertook the task as editor, and who was instrumental throughout all the plans leading to this monograph.

Many people from the Ispra Establishment have contributed to this publication, which also was inspired by Mr. B. Henry, head of the Ispra Courses. The work and devotion of Messrs. M.D. Dowell and A.A. Pollicini of our Informatics Division is gratefully acknowledged. We also thank Mr. P. De Hoe and his staff from Publications Service of the JCR-Ispra.

Hans Jørgen Helms
Director, Informatics, Mathematics
and Systems Analysis Department

July 1982

INTRODUCTION

David Muxworthy
University of Edinburgh
Edinburgh, UK

A common theme in this volume is that software costs continue to rise whilst hardware costs fall. For many computer installations the true costs of software exceed the true costs of hardware yet while hardware production is based on sound engineering practices, developed over centuries, software production is only very slowly being formalized. The haphazard methods of construction of entities which are to be used in important areas of human activity, from defence systems and macroeconomic systems to areas of more specific potential danger such as the design of motor cars, bridges and chemical plant, would not be tolerated in any other field.

Slowly the methods of producing more reliable software are becoming more widely known. As well as being reliable, good software should be flexible, not only because the problem to be solved commonly changes with time, but also because the facilities available to the software user also change with time and may thus involve several different types of computing systems. Additionally because software production is expensive it is sensible to attempt to achieve economies of scale and to share software with other users with the same or similar problems. Sharing software also implies sharing techniques and a program can contain the distillation of a wealth of experience in a particular problem area. As the users' experience contributors to this volume point out, lack of resources too often means that in practice the choice is between acquiring a shared program and having no program at all.

This book addresses many aspects of sharing software, together with the inextricably linked attributes of good design, reliability and flexibility. Most examples are taken from science and technology but the principles apply to any computer application. More than one author makes comparisons with engineering construction and there are indeed some striking parallels with an industry which developed in the first industrial revolution. It is possible for a railway freight wagon to run throughout much of Europe, or much of North America, and the wheel gauge, loading gauge, couplings and brakes are so standardized that the wagon may be coupled to any appropriate train of almost any railway company. Those who

D. T. Muxworthy (ed.), Programming for Software Sharing, ix–x.
Copyright © 1983 ECSC, EEC, EAEC, Brussels and Luxembourg.

perceived this requirement from the beginning of railways prevailed over those who advocated locally optimal but non-uniform systems.

When the Stockton and Darlington railway was being built in the early 1820's it was not clear whether the primary haulage would be by horse or by locomotive and the track was designed to accommodate both. Later in the decade the promoters of the Liverpool and Manchester railway organized a public competition for locomotives and one, the Rocket, emerged from its Ordeal, a much more expressive word than benchmark, as the winner on each of the counts of power, reliability and efficiency. The building of the London and Birmingham railway in the 1830's is particularly reminiscent of a large modern software project. The work was so big (112 miles of line plus ancillary buildings) that numerous subcontractors were employed. As unexpected difficulties arose the subcontractors fell behind schedule and finally abandoned work as the money ran out. More money had to be raised and costs rose even higher as extra effort was made to catch up on schedule. One particularly intractable problem, a long tunnel through a hill full of quicksand, required either a complete rerouting or, as happened, the hill to be pumped dry. This alone took 19 months and much extra expense. The whole project was completed many months late and costs were well over twice the original estimates. Plus ça change, plus c'est la même chose.

Thus software writers should not assume that theirs is a completely new field but should draw on what is relevant, project management, codes of practice, concepts of design and testing, use of tools and so on from other areas, particularly engineering. Analogies should not be taken too far however. Most users of a new car can drive away without reading any documentation and the user documentation for a bridge is usually non-existent. For software good documentation is vitally important, and is often lacking, and several authors address this point. Unlike physical products, software may be stolen, leaving the original intact and its owner unaware of the fact. The legal state of software affairs is complex and often indeterminate but considerable efforts are being made to imporve matters. Problems of reliable distributed databases affect everyone with a bank account or a credit card and international standards affect all users of computers directly or indirectly. These and other related subjects are covered below.

As editor I have enjoyed reading all the contributions. To guide the reader they have been grouped into three broad categories, namely software development methodology, flexibility, and transfer and sharing. Some authors have made use of the terms "Ada", "UNIX" and "VAX" which are trademarks of the United States Department of Defense, Bell Laboratories and Digital Equipment Corporation respectively. The art of writing shareable software appears to lie in being able to think more abstractly, in so far as is feasible divorcing the design of a program from the language to be used and divorcing the implementation from the actual computer to be used. It might be useful to perceive the computer as malleable in the style of Salvador Dalì, rather than rigid in the style of Canaletto.

I hope readers find the book both interesting and useful.

Software Development Methodology

THE SOFTWARE LIFE CYCLE

Gerhard Goos
University of Karlsruhe
Karlsruhe, Germany

1. INTRODUCTION

The two main criteria for judging principles and methods in programming are the quality of the resulting program and the economics of the production process, the sofware life cycle. In this chapter we overview the phases of the software life cycle. Subsequent chapters treat most of the topics in more detail.

The production of software comprises not only the design, implementation and validation of programs but starts with requirement analysis and ends with maintaining the final program. Altogether we may identify the following phases:

— problem definition and requirements analysis
— design
— implementation and testing
— use and maintenance.

The results of these phases and the problems which we resolve can be seen from table 1.

Usually the phases are not clearly separable in time, neither personally nor functionally. A clear managerial separation is, however, necessary for controlling the progress of the project. Most commonly the phases do not follow in order but difficulties in later phases may require a complete or partial repetition of preceding phases in order to proceed iteratively in the construction process.

An important subgoal of "software engineering" is to keep the number of iterations as small as possible and to keep the span of iteration (i.e. the number of steps which we have to go back during iteration) as short as possible. These are conditions for a time- and cost-efficient project.

D. T. Muxworthy (ed.), Programming for Software Sharing, 3–13.
Copyright © 1983 ECSC, EEC, EAEC, Brussels and Luxembourg.

Phase	Result	Question
	Problem	
Problem definition		
Problem analysis		what?, why?
	Problem specification	
Design		how?
	System specification	
Implementation		by which means?
	Modules, data, tests	
Test		does it work satisfactorily?
	Working system	
Installation and Usage		customer's wish?
	Used system	
Maintenance		necessary improvements
	Improved system	

Table 1

A methodology offering good principles for all phases of the (software-) system development has not been available until now. The differing tasks and levels of abstraction, and the differing qualifications of the people participating cause difficulties. As a consequence software engineering up to now has been a collection of phase- and product-specific techniques. The techniques and phases often are not in harmony with each other. Additionally many of these techniques are rather informal and it may sometimes be difficult to control their systematic application. The rapidly rising demand for software and the even faster growing software costs require the transition to more formal and productive means of software production. This point becomes even more important because of the increasing share of software costs in overall costs of computer systems as can be seen from fig. 1.

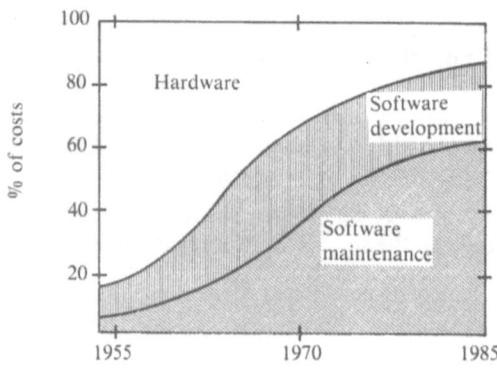

Figure 1: Comparison of Hardware/Software Costs (from Boehm (1976))

2. PROGRAMMING AS AN ENGINEERING ACTIVITY

In the beginning a student of programming will write *throw-away programs.* These programs are written, tested, run and then forgotten. Not only programming exercises are of this type but also many programs written by scientists. They are written for obtaining a certain result and once this result is known they become superfluous.

During his study the novice programmer will learn that certain tasks have to be solved repeatedly. If he is a clever programmer he will single out such tasks and write programs which can be used repeatedly. On the one hand this development leads to the notion of a *program module,* a piece of program which can be reused in different contexts. On the other hand the programmer will learn that the writing of such program modules places additional demands on his programming style: the program must be commented and documented; at least the possible inputs and possible results have to be described. The module must yield acceptable results even with unusual and erroneous input data. The error messages must be understandable not only for the writer of the program because the module may be used by somebody else, etc.

Although program modules are reusable programs, the writer of a module usually does not guarantee the functioning of the program under all commonly met circumstances. Often the structure and the documentation of a program module is not designed such that any further enhancements, modifications and adaptations which the application may require are possible. Finally, program modules, though reusable, are mostly not written such that they may be distributed, installed and used by arbitrary customers; instead at least certain skills are required from the customer. This would be fine if the necessary knowledge would be required for applying the module anyway. Very often, however, it includes details which are not absolutely necessary for applying the program but rather for writing programs of this type. For instance, somebody who would like to take over a text editor for a personal computer must know something about sectoring and formatting of disks, compatibility between the way this editor writes files and the way some compiler expects files, etc. Such knowledge is not a prerequisite for using a text editor in general. It is a prerequisite for using a text editor which is not a standard software product and does not fit into the set of programs with which it has to collaborate. We recognize therefore a third class of programs, called *software products.* They are distinguished from reusable program modules by the following facts: the manufacturer takes responsibility for the functioning of the program; specification of user needs is possible; the program fulfills certain standards, such that distribution and use of the program does not require special knowledge on the part of the customer, except typical application-specific skills.

Throw-away programs, reusable programs and software products are not only clearly distinguishable classes of programs. Their development also requires quite different styles of programming. Throw-away programs can be written by anyone once he has mastered the algorithms and data structures needed for his problem. For reusability the programmer must subject himself to a certain discipline. It is required that the methodology of program development is clearly defined and followed throughout. To transform a reusable program into a software product is a management task: the design and implementation must be supervised so that later development and enhancements of the program are not unduly impeded by programming tricks, etc. Adherence to a given programming methodology and programming standards must be controlled. The resulting program must be evaluated by a third party for establishing its validity. Ease of distribution, installation and use must be tested at selected customers' sites. The software will possibly be modified in order to adhere to the required standard.

These considerations show striking similarities between programming and the situation in other technical areas. As soon as the area of the hobby technician is left we must adhere to certain engineering standards in order to achieve acceptable results. Although the reproduction of software by copying is much easier than the production of technical products by an assembly line, the development of reproducible software products nevertheless requires some management overhead, comparable to what is required in applications of other engineering disciplines. It is therefore quite correct that we should consider programming as an engineering activity as soon as we leave the area of teaching and the area of occasional programming.

The negligence of the fact that programming is an engineering activity has led in the Sixties and Seventies to what has been called the *software crisis:* programming has been considered an easy task for which no particular methodologies and standards are required. The results of this incorrect judgement were and still are underestimates of the cost of software development by factors of from two to ten, corresponding delays in delivery and unacceptable problems of reliability in programs and availability of computer systems. The goal of these chapters is to make the difference between "hobby programming" and "engineered programming" visible and to show how the programming process may be improved by applying sound engineering principles.

The different classes of programs may also be distinguished by considering the economics of the programming process. Let us rate the annual cost of a programmer at US $ 100,000 (salary, social costs, working place, computing time, share of overhead in the company, etc.). It is customary but not fully justified to measure the performance of programming in lines/time unit.

	Statements/Man year
Throw-away Programs	10 - 40,000
Reusable Programs	
— control programs	500 - 700
— compiler/data bank	1,000 - 2,000
— application program	2,000 - 4,000

Table 2: Productivity of Programmers (in accordance with Brooks (1975))

Table 2 shows some commonly quoted figures. From these figures we conclude that the cost per statement (commonly a line in a high-level language) may vary from US $2 to US $50, i.e. by a factor of 25 between throw-away programs and professionally reusable programs. As a rule of thumb the conversion of a reusable program into a software product adds another factor of two to the cost. Hence, in the extreme, we have a factor of 50 between the costs of a throw-away program and a software product. This large factor may cause surprise, but only on first sight. In other engineering disciplines the costs of converting a prototype into a product which can be manufactured in large quantities may even be higher.

In order to diminish the cost of software development it may therefore seem advisable to ask for every phase of the software life cycle what can be done to make that phase cheaper. This method, however, does not lead to the desired effect. The statistics of distribution of costs show that the maintenance phase very often requires 50%, sometimes even 75%, of the total cost. This distribution was not always so as is shown by figure 1.

The leading principle for decreasing the overall cost of software must therefore be to decrease the cost of maintenance. Since these costs are largely dependent on the design and implementation phase, its documentation etc, we must ask in all those phases how we may facilitate the later maintenance even if in this way the cost of the actual phase may be increased.

A discussion of programming as an engineering activity cannot go without considering the rôle of iteration and modification in the program development process. Except when it is written in a ROM nothing is immutable in programming. This fact has mislead many people to believe that it is quite easy and cheap to change programs. Many of the wrong estimates of programming costs stem from this source. As in other engineering disciplines we cannot hope that the requirements, the subdivision of the design, the interfaces, the internal working of modules etc. are established in their final form at the first attempt. Every good design is the result of some good compromises and the factors which have to be traded against each other very often become clear only during the development process itself. Therefore we cannot consider the development process as it is described in subsequent sections as a sequential process. Instead we proceed iteratively: at each stage, even during maintenance, we must be ready to go back in the development process to earlier phases adjusting earlier decisions to newly recognized requirements.

The cost of revising a decision is, however, dependent on the phase to which this decision belongs and the phase in which we recognized that it must be changed. As a rule of thumb the cost of changing a decision will usually be proportional to the square of the span of time for which that decision has lasted; sometimes the costs will depend exponentially on that span of time. This remark shows that the modifiability of software is limited by economic considerations: fundamental decisions of the design process are very soon frozen because it is too expensive to change the decision. On the other hand it may sometimes be cheaper to throw away the complete design or even a finished program and to start the program development from scratch than to make modifications. It is surprising how recklessly decisions are sometimes taken in the vain hope that they can be revised later. It is also surprising that in many cases programs are modified without discussion of whether a complete rewrite would be cheaper.

3. THE PHASES OF THE SOFTWARE LIFE CYCLE

Problem specification and requirements analysis

The writing of software needs a fixed organizational frame. This frame, called a *project,* will provide the necessary organizational structure, personal support, computer access and other technical support. Although discussions about the feasibility, usefulness, etc. of the project will precede, each project must be started by a formal act, the *project foundation*. The project foundation is a managerial decision to assign resources to the project and to take the risk if the project fails. Without this formal act we will have a project without official approval, with no fixed organization, without approved budget, without explicitly assigned project members; each of these points in itself may cause a disaster.

The starting point of a programming process is very often a relatively weak problem statement or idea. The project must therefore start with a step called *problem analysis* or *requirements analysis:* determine the nature of the problem in detail, investigate the goals and the limiting factors of potential solutions. Typical questions which must be answered are the following:

— What are the input and result parameters of the planned program?
— What is the relation between the inputs and the results?
— What constraints are imposed on the input parameters?
— Which permanent data bases are used or updated by the program?
— What is the format of already existing data? How can we convert it for use by the program? Which other programs work on the same data?
— What should happen in case of errors? (break-down of base system, wrong operation, inadmissible or non-available input data, etc.)
— Which resources are available?
— Which performance goals must be met? (time and space constraints, number of users served, maximum amount, complexity and values of input data, etc.)

Except for purely technical computations all computer applications have organizational implications. It is these implications which make requirements analysis a very difficult task. The requirements engineer aims for a system which is embedded. But very often the picture is unsatisfactory because the relationships which form this environment remain unknown and cannot be formalized. Sometimes even the behaviour of the environment will implicitly change depending on properties of the envisaged solution. For example, computer users adapt to the positive and negative properties of a program.

The most difficult problem in requirements analysis is the communication between the requirements engineer and the customer. The customer is often used to thinking in terms which are only very superficially known to the analyst, or which are completely unimportant for the planned software product. The converse of this statement is also true: the customer is very often unable to understand the relevance of questions of the requirements engineer or has no suitable answers at his disposal for such questions.

Incompletely stated requirements and misunderstandings between the requirements engineer and the customer are the most frequent sources of errors of the final software product (c.f. Bell et al (1977)).

Many people have made attempts to circumvent such difficulties by more formalized aids for requirements analysis. Systematic techniques for interviewing the customer, the use of questionnaires and formalized languages for representing the results of requirements analysis are the most common means. Hommel (1980) gives a comparative overview of such methods for requirements specifications by applying them to the specification of a packet switching station in a post office.

The result of requirements analysis must be a precise *problem specification* which forms the basis of the subsequent design phase. It may also form the basis for a contract between the customer and a software company. Before the problem specification is finalized a *feasibility study* is usually required by which possible ways for solving the problem are explored. The feasibility study must guarantee that the problem specification is not contradictory, and forms the basis for estimating the amount of time, the resources and the costs involved in the project.

Curiously enough requirements analysis and even the precise problem specification are missing in many projects, especially in the academic environment. They are replaced by ad hoc decisions during the design. The reasons for this mistake include the fact that in programming courses the problem specification very often goes unnoticed because the problem is mathematical in nature and its specification is quite easy. For the same reason the novice software engineer also tends to believe that his program will solve the given problem if he has satisfied the problem specification. Common experience, however, shows that many or even the majority of errors cannot be detected by this method because already the problem specification does not properly reflect the intention of the customer.

Design

The problem specification state *what* should be done. The design phase must answer the question *how* the given problem should be solved. The design does not result in the software product itself but only in the technical description of the intended program. This description must also include reasons why the design decisions have been taken in the given way, which alternatives have been considered and why they have been found less useful.

Only for simple problems may the design phase lead to the final program. In most cases, however, the design phase is "programming-in-the-large" (De Remer and Kron, 1975). Its goal is the subdivision of the given problem in subproblems such that each subproblem corresponds to a module of the final program and such that the complete solution consists of the combination of all such modules. There are several questions concerning this modularization which must be answered:

— How can we derive a suitable modularization from the given problem?
— Is the intended modularization also suitable for distributing the workload amongst several programmers?
— Is the intended modularization "stable", i.e. can the modularization easily be adapted to possible changes for the requirements?
— Is the design correct, i.e. do the intended modules actually solve the given problem?

There are many *design methodologies* for developing and documenting the design of software. The most common one is the method of top-down design: the solution is developed in a hierarchic fashion. First a module is written for solving the given problem on the basis of an "abstract machine". Then modules are designed for the operations and data structures of this abstract machine. These modules may work on the basis of another abstract machine and the process is continued until we arrive at the level of the actually given base system. Other methods, especially for the design of concrete programs, include Jackson's method (Jackson, 1975) and the method of Composite Design (Myers, 1975). If the complexity of the problem is characterized by a great many cases which may partially overlap then the technique of decision tables may be useful.

Most of these techniques not only lead to a modularization of the intended software but also help in validating the design. This is best illustrated in the case of the top-down design method. Here the solution of the given problem is examined for correctness on the assumption that the underlying abstract machine is working correctly. The design of the implementation of this abstract machine is examined afterwards in the same fashion.

Besides the overall structure the interfaces between the modules are the most important result of the design phase. They must be specified so that it is possible to assign the implementation of different modules to different programmers without running into trouble because of misinterpretations of the interfaces. The validation of the design also depends on a consistent interpretation of the interfaces.

For documenting the result of the design phase many people have proposed so-called design languages but none of these proposals have been widely used in practice other than what has been called *pseudo-code:* an arbitrary (but usually block-structured) programming language is used for describing the resulting software. Pieces which have not yet been designed or implemented are replaced by comments describing the desired effect.

The documentation of the design by help of pseudo-code or any other means is used not only as basis for the subsequent implementation. It is also used for validating the design against the problem specification, for estimating the expected performance of the software, and for a first examination as to whether the design meets the requirements of the customer. For the latter application very often also less formal specifications (the *external specification*) are used in order to facilitate understanding on the part of the customer.

Implementation

The implementation transforms the system specification resulting from the design into the modules of the system. Hence implementation means what usually is understood as "programming".

Implementation consists of three tasks:

— Transform a system specification into a program
— Generate code for the program in a computer
— Validate the program.

The implementation decides the efficiency of a program. This efficiency may be achieved on two levels:

— on the algorithmic level
— during the conversion of the algorithm into machine statements.

The possible gains in efficiency correspond to this hierarchy: the possible gain by an efficient algorithm usually is larger by orders of magnitude compared to what can be achieved by efficient coding of the algorithm. This fact is often not sufficiently recognized.

The choice of the implementation language is dependent on the availability of compilers and the level of detail which must be controlled by the programmer. The use of machine oriented languages leads to a refined specification of the program compared with a high-level programming language. In deciding the level of the language we trade the programming time against a possible gain in code efficiency (time and space efficiency). Additionally every refinement of a specification, i.e. a transformation from one level of abstraction to a lower one, may possibly introduce new errors and have to be validated again.

Tricks must be avoided in programming. If they are necessary for achieving maximum efficiency in critical phases then they should be documented in such a way that every programmer can understand them.

Experience shows that a good design may considerably shorten the implementation and the subsequent testing. Nevertheless most program properties are very much determined in the implementation phase.

An important part of the implementation phase is program verification. It is the checking of whether the program really fulfills the specification. A complete formal verification of a complex program is impossible with today's verification methods. Nevertheless critical algorithms and the global flow of control should be formally verified (under the assumption that all modules are working correctly). A weak but very useful form of verification is code inspection. The program is read by people different fom the original programmer. It is checked for understandability and whether it conforms to the specification. Code inspection is helpful not only for verifying a program but also for preparing for the maintenance phase: not only the program text but also the documentation are scrutinized much in the same way as will be necessary for maintenance. Hence omissions and documents and program modules which are not understandable can be detected at a time when the programmers who created the problem are still available for help.

Testing

In the testing phase a program (or a module) is executed with inputs for which the results or the behaviour of the computation are known in advance. The actual computation is compared to the expected results. But even if a program has been formally verified it still must be tested for validity. If the verification was by pencil and paper there may be writing errors in the machine readable version of the program. Or a compiler may have introduced errors by generating incorrect code. Or the program may be functionally correct but its time or space requirements may exceed some given limitations. Or the test cases may reveal that the specification and hence the program do not conform to the intentions of the customer. Finally the behaviour of the program in the case of erroneous input, mistakes by the operator or malfunctioning of the base system can only be seen by applying appropriate robustness tests.

Altogether testing serves the following purposes:

— enhancement of verification (function test)
— checking whether the specification and the program conform to the intentions of the customer
— performance test
— test of robustness.

Testing occurs in steps simultaneously with the implementation. First test cases are applied to single modules (module test). To this end the modules must be embedded in a suitable test bed. The test bed supplies the necessary base functions, calls and inputs for the module; it also records the results and may support the evaluation of the test cases. For example in the case of top-down testing the base functions may not yet be available; in this case they are replaced by operations which simulate their effect to the extent necessary for the test. A successful module test is followed by integration tests where gradually more and more modules are put together until the complete software system is under test.

Testing, the development of test cases and the writing of testing aids is not an add-on feature which can be considered after the software has been written. It has to be planned in the design phase and the test cases and testing aids must be developed simultaneously with the system specification and the implementation.

Installation and Acceptance Test

Installation places the product in the intended environment where it has to perform its task. In many cases adaptations and conversions are necessary for getting the software working; e.g. the input data must be converted to the format required by the new software, programs for processing the results must be adapted to new output formats, the working of the environment must be adapted to making optimal use of the new system etc. Very often intense training of the users is required, so installation is primarily an organizational problem.

After installation the customer has to accept the system. Acceptance is a formal action: the customer declares his satisfaction with the delivered system (and specifies any necessary improvements). He takes the responsibility for paying for the system. Acceptance ends the development of the system and the period of warranty, if any, starts. Acceptance very often is based on a series of *acceptance tests,* e.g. test cases which are specifically designed for checking the proper working of the system within the customer's environment. Because of the implications these test cases are developed very early in the project and form part of the contract between the customer and the contractor. They can never be invented ad hoc during the installation phase.

If the application requires uninterrupted operation then the old and the new system must be operated in parallel until the new system is found satisfactory. Such parallel operation places a particularly heavy burden on all the people involved. Very often additional hardware is required to allow simultaneous operation, to store data in distinct formats etc.

Maintenance and Distribution of Costs

Maintenance is the last phase in the software life cycle. It accompanies the software product throughout its use. Strictly speaking, maintenance only means improvements and repair necessary for removing errors which were either contained in the original product or introduced by using the product. Since software does not deteriorate by use the latter case cannot happen. The amount of time and money which has to be spent on maintenance is completely determined by the preceding phases.

It is very difficult to get reliable figures about the distribution of labour and costs among the phases of the life cycle. Zelkowitz et al (1979) and Daly (1977) quote the following:

Requirements analysis and specification:	6-15%
Design, implementation and documentation:	12-35%
Validation:	13-16%
Maintenance:	34-67%.

The main conclusion which we have to draw from these figures is that maintenance always occupies an unbelievably high percentage of the overall cost. One must also realize that this percentage is determined in advance by the decisions taken in the design phase and the care spent on the development. An attempt to decrease the cost of a software development must therefore always consider the question of how to minimize the maintenance costs, never how to minimize the costs of coding, testing or documentation. This point is frequently overlooked, especially when delivery dates are pressing or the efficiency of the program is not satisfactory.

REFERENCES AND READING

Bell T.E., Bixler M.E. and Dyer M.E. (1977), An extendable approach to computer-aided software requirements engineering. IEEE Trans, Softw. Eng. Vol. 3 No. 1.

Boehm B.W. (1976), Software Engineering. IEEE ToC C-25, 12, pp. 1226-1241.

Brooks F. (1975), The Mythical Man-Month: Essays on Software Engineering. Addison-Wesley Publ. Co.

Daly E.B. (1977), Management of Software Development. IEEE Trans. Softw. Eng. Vol. 3 pp. 230-242 (May 1977).

De Remer F. and Kron H. (1975), Programming-in-the-large versus Programming-in-the-small. International Conference on Reliable Software, Los Angeles. Also in SIGPLAN Notices, Vol. 10, No. 6, pp. 114-121.

Hommel G. (ed.) (1980), Vergleich verschiedener Spezifikations-verfahren am Beispiel einer Paketverteilanlage. Teil 1. KfK-PDV 186, August 1980.

Jackson M.A. (1975), Principles of Program Design, London: Academic Press.

Myers G.J. (1975), Reliable software through composite design. New York: Petrocelli/Charter.

Weinberg G.M. (1971), The Psychology of Computer Programming. New York: Van Nostrand Reinhold.

Zelkowitz M.V., Shaw A.C. and Gannon J.D. (1979), Principles of Software Engineering and Design. Englewood Cliffs: Prentice-Hall.

DESIGN OF PROGRAMS

Gerhard Goos
University of Karlsruhe
Karlsruhe, Germany

In this chapter we are concerned with programming-in-the-small, that is with the design of algorithms and the corresponding data structures. We first present the ideas of structured program development. We then give a short introduction into the programming language Pascal concluding with a lengthier example.

1. STRUCTURED PROGRAM DEVELOPMENT

A fundamental problem in designing programs is the limited human ability to comprehend complicated situations. Psychology teaches that humans are normally unable to relate more than 5-7 subjects at the same time. The size and complexity of a task therefore constitutes an additional problem superimposed on the difficulties related to the contents. The reduction of complexity to a manageable size is an important issue in program design.

We study this question in terms of the decomposition of an algorithmic transformation into steps on the level of a programming language. We use for this purpose the programming language Pascal.

Decomposition of Control

An algorithm A expresses the mapping of certain input data onto some output data. We characterize the properties of the input data by some predicate P, the *precondition* of the algorithm, and the properties of the output data by some predicate Q, the *postcondition* of A. The predicates are also called assertions. The fact that A transforms data satisfying P into data satisfying Q is expressed by the formula

$$\{P\} \; A \; \{Q\}.$$

The transformation of preconditions into postconditions by an algorithm is very similar to the deduction of a theorem Q from some assumptions P according to the

D. T. Muxworthy (ed.), Programming for Software Sharing, 15–34.

rules of formal logic. In this case we write $P \Rightarrow Q$. The validity of the deduction will be guaranteed by a proof which will normally compose the required deduction from simpler ones. It is therefore natural to look into the possibilities for such subdivisions and to carry them over to the decomposition of algorithms. We find five such decomposition principles which for algorithms are called

— sequential decomposition
— collateral decomposition
— distinction of cases
— induction
— abstraction.

SEQUENTIAL DECOMPOSITION

Sequential decomposition corresponds to the law of transitivity

$$\frac{\begin{array}{c} P \Rightarrow Q \\ Q \Rightarrow R \end{array}}{P \Rightarrow R}$$

in logic (The formulae represent a metadeduction: when the formulae above the line are valid then the formula below the line is also valid). When we replace the arrows by algorithms we obtain

$$\frac{\begin{array}{lll} \{P\} & S_1 & \{Q\} \\ \{Q\} & S_2 & \{R\} \end{array}}{\{P\} \ S_1;S_2 \ \{R\}}$$

The semicolon indicates that the two steps S_1, S_2 are applied one after the other. This sequence corresponds to the fact that in the logical deduction we have first to establish Q before we can infer R by $Q \Rightarrow R$.

In general the method of sequential decomposition in programming says:

Given a state satisfying the precondition P. Then we can achieve a state satisfying the postcondition R if we can find intermediate assertions $A_1,...A_n$ and statements $S_0,...,S_n$ such that

$$\begin{array}{llll} \{P\} & S_0 & \{A_1\} & \\ \{A_i\} & S_i & \{A_{i+1}\} & i=1,...,n\text{-}1 \\ \{A_n\} & S_n & \{R\} & \end{array}$$

These conditions yield

$$\{P\} \quad S_0; \ S_1;...;S_n \quad \{R\}.$$

COLLATERAL DECOMPOSITION

Collateral decomposition corresponds to the conjunctive law of logic:

$$\frac{P_i \Rightarrow Q_i \qquad i=1,...,n}{P_1 \& P_2 \& ... \& P_n \ \Rightarrow \ Q_1 \& Q_2 \& ...Q_n}$$

The corresponding principle in pogramming would be

$$\frac{\{P_i\} \ S_i \ \{Q_i\} \qquad i=1,...,n}{\{P_1 \& P_2 \& ... \& P_n\} \ \text{COBEGIN} \ S_1,S_2,...,S_n \ \text{COEND} \ \{Q_1 \& Q_2 \& ... \& Q_n\}}$$

where COBEGIN ..., ... COEND indicates that the actions are executed collaterally, i.e. in arbitrary order, merged in time or strictly in parallel. The principle of collateral decomposition is, however, not invariably true as we can see from the simple example

$$
\begin{array}{lll}
\{ x = 3 \} & x := x + 1 & \{ x = 4 \} \\
\{ x = 3 \} & y := x + 2 & \{ y = 5 \}
\end{array}
$$

$$\{x = 3\} \text{ COBEGIN } x := x + 1, y := x + 2 \text{ COEND } \{x = 4 \ \& \ y = 5\}$$

The conclusion $y = 5$ is true only when we assume that the value of x is fetched before the new assignment takes place but this assumption is in contradiction to collateral execution which leaves the order of fetching the value of x and the new assignment unspecified. Hence in this example we can neither conclude $y = 5$ nor $y = 6$, both assertions may hold depending on the order of evaluation.

Owicki and Gries (1976) have studied these matters in detail and found that the principle of collateral decomposition is valid when we additionally require that all conclusions $\{P_i\} \ S_i \ \{Q_i\}$ are "interference-free". The simplest way to guarantee non-interference is by forbidding shared variables, i.e. if during execution of S_i the variable x is inspected then no S_j, $j \neq i$, is allowed to assign to x. This very crude method may be refined by requesting that the assertions used in verifying $\{P_i\} \ S_i \ \{Q_i\}$ remain invariantly true during the execution of the S_j, $j \neq i$.

As an example consider an iterative process

$$x^{(m+1)} := A \, x^{(m)} + b$$

for computing the solution of a set of linear equations. A is a square matrix and $x^{(m)} = (x_1^{(m)}, \ldots, x_n^{(m)})$, $b = (b_1, \ldots, b_n)$ are vectors. Traditionally we use the scheme sequentially, one equation after the other. The newly computed $x_i^{(m+1)}$ are either reused immediately (successive replacement) or are only used after an iterative step has been completed (simultaneous replacement). We could also compute all $x_i^{(m+1)}$ collaterally, e. g. by assigning each equation to one of n special processors. If we then reuse the $x_i^{(m+1)}$ immediately the process converges to the required solution if we can prove convergence independently of whether in computing $x_i^{(m+1)}$ for x_j, $x_j^{(m)}$ or $x_j^{(m+1)}$ is used, i. e. if the proof of convergence does not interfere with the computation of any particular x_j.

Our current programming languages do not allow for expressing collaterality. But modern hardware allows for splitting a computation into several streams of operations. Therefore compilers must be able to detect under which conditions a sequential computation may be split using the rules for collateral decomposition. This possibility depends on the sometimes rather arbitrary order in which the programmer has put his assignments.

DISTINCTION OF CASES

Another powerful aid in mathematical proofs is the distinction of cases. It allows the addition to an assumption P of further assumptions C_i in order to deduce R. The proof must then be carried for several cases C_i, $i = 1, \ldots, n$ and we must have

$$P \Rightarrow (C_1 \text{ OR } C_2 \text{ OR } \ldots \text{ OR } C_n).$$

The disjunction of cases must be true if the main assumption P holds. In programming this principle leads directly to Dijkstra's guarded commands (Dijkstra 1975 or Dijkstra 1976):

If $\{P \ \& \ C_i\} \ S_i \ \{R\}$ $i = 1,...,n$ and $\{P \ \& \ C_i\}$ holds for at least one index i, $1 \le i \le n$ then

$$\{P\} \ \text{IF} \ C_1 \to S_1$$
$$\square \ C_2 \to S_2$$
$$...$$
$$\square \ C_n \to S_n \ \text{FI} \ \{R\}.$$

In the IF-FI construct we have the conditions C_i *(guards)*. A statement S_i is only executed when its guard is true. The construct is indeterministic: several C_i may be true at the same time; in this case an arbitrary statement S_i with valid guard C_i is executed. We have required that at least one C_i holds; otherwise the effect of the construct is undefined.

In conventional programming languages like Pascal indeterminacy is removed from the construct by guaranteeing that at most one alternative has a valid guard. We have two forms:

The conventional (two-sided) conditional statement follows the rule

$$\frac{\{P \ \& \ C\} \qquad S_1 \qquad \{R\}}{\{P \ \& \ \text{NOT} \ C\} \qquad S_2 \qquad \{R\}}$$
$$\{P\} \ \text{IF} \ C \ \text{THEN} \ S_1 \ \text{ELSE} \ S_2 \ \{R\}$$

Since C OR NOT C is a tautology, always precisely one of the two conditions holds. If in one of the two cases no action is required we may replace the execution of S in our rule by logical deduction. This yields the one-sided conditional statement of Pascal:

$$\frac{\{P \ \& \ C\} \qquad S \quad \{R\}}{P \ \& \ \text{NOT} \ C \ \Rightarrow \quad R}$$
$$\{P\} \ \text{IF} \ C \ \text{THEN} \ S \ \{R\}$$

The second form of the distinction of cases in Pascal is the general case statement. Here the condition is restricted to comparing the value of an expression with some constant values c_i. In contrast to the conditional statement it is the responsibility of the programmer to guarantee that $e = c_i$ for some index i, $1 \le i \le n$. The rule for the case statement is then

$$\frac{\{P \ \& \ e = c_i\} \quad S_1 \quad \{R\}, \qquad\qquad\qquad\qquad i = 1,...,n}{e \ \epsilon \ [c_1,...c_n] \qquad\qquad \text{The value of e is contained in set } [c_1,...,c_n]}$$
$$\{P\} \ \text{CASE} \ e \ \text{of} \ c_1:S_1; \ c_2:S_2;...;c_n:S_n \ \text{END} \ \{R\}$$

Examples for applying these constructs are:

$$\{n \ \text{integer}\} \ \text{IF odd (n) THEN } n:=n+1 \ \{n = 2^* \ ((n+1) \ \text{DIV} \ 2)\}$$
$$\{n \ \text{integer}\} \ \text{IF odd (n) THEN } y:=x \ \text{ELSE} \ y:=1 \ \{y = x^n \ \text{MOD 2}\}$$

where DIV denotes integer division and MOD the remainder function:

$$a = a \text{ DIV } b + a \text{ MOD } b, \quad 0 \le a \text{ MOD } B < 1 \text{ for } a, b > 0$$

$\{1 \le \text{month} \le 12\}$ CASE month OF

jan, mar, may, jul, aug, oct, dec:	days: = 31;
apr, jun, sep, nov:	days: = 30;
feb:	IF year MOD 4 = 0
	THEN days: = 29
	ELSE days: = 28;

END {days = number of days in month}

It may come as a surprise to the inexperienced programmer that a distinction of cases always ends with a state described by one single postcondition R and not several postconditions corresponding to the number of cases. This requirement is, however, quite natural: our program maps the input data onto one unique set of output data independent of the number of conditional statements in the program. Moreover, we would be unable to get any insight into the effect of the successor statement of a conditional or case statement if there is no uniquely defined precondition for that statement.

INDUCTION

The principle of mathematical induction says: given an ordered set M with initial element i_0 and a successor function

$$i_{k+1} := \text{succ}(i_k) \qquad k = 0, 1, 2, \ldots$$

which enumerates M, if for a predicate P over M

$P(i_0),$
$P(i) \Rightarrow P(\text{succ}(i))$, for arbitrary $i \in M$

then P holds for all $i \in M$, especially for the last element if there is any.

In programming we are interested in this principle only for finite sets M; otherwise our algorithms will not terminate. M therefore corresponds to an interval [0,n] of the integers or, more generally, we characterize M by a condition C which is true for all $i \in M$, but false for other elements of the universe under consideration. Under these assumptions we replace the deduction arrow by the execution of a statement S and obtain two programming principles depending on whether S is expressed as a function of i or not, as follows.

In the first case we have the rule for the normal for statement of Pascal:

{P(0)}
$$\frac{\{P(i-1)\} \; S(i) \; \{P(i)\} \qquad i = 1, \ldots, n}{\{P(0)\} \text{ FOR } I := 1 \text{ TO } n \text{ DO } S(i) \; \{P(n)\}}$$

For example if:

$$P(i): \qquad s = \sum_{j=1}^{i} a_j$$

then the assignment
$$s: = 0$$

yields P(0) and

$$\{P(i-1)\} \; s: = s + a[i] \; \{P(i)\}$$

Hence we have with empty precondition

$$\{\ \} \quad s:=0;$$
$$\text{FOR } i:=1 \text{ TO n DO } s:=s+a[i] \ \{P(n)\}$$

Similarly, if

$$P(i) : c_j = a_j + b_j \text{ for } 1 \le j \le i$$

then P(0) is always true and

$$\{P(i\text{-}1)\} \ c[i]:=a[i]+b[i] \ \{P(i)\}$$

Hence

$$\{P(0)\} \text{ FOR } i:=1 \text{ TO n DO } c[i]:=a[i]+b[i] \ \{P(n)\}$$

In the second case the statements S must contain assignments which guarantee that we successively consider all elements of M. We do not care how this is done in detail. As soon as M is exhausted the condition becomes false. Furthermore, if P is a predicate which is true for all considered elements of M then P must be true in the beginning (no elements considered) and

$$\{P \ \& \ C\} \ S \ \{P\}$$

where the precondition C indicates that M is not yet exhausted and the postcondition says that P is true also for the element considered by executing S. These pieces together give the rule for the while statement

$$\frac{\{P \ \& \ C\} \ S \ \{P\}}{\{P\} \text{ WHILE C DO S } \{P \ \& \ NOT \ C\}}$$

which holds provided the loop terminates. The condition P is called a *loop-invariant*. From the verification point of view our rule is not the most general rule which we can apply for proving properties of loops. Dijkstra (1976) gives a more general rule. But for most practical applications our rule which is due to C.A.R. Hoare is appropriate.

To prove that a loop actually terminates is not a theoretically decidable problem. Also in practical cases it may cause difficulties. For example it is unknown whether the loop

$$\text{WHILE } n>1 \text{ DO IF odd(n) THEN } n:=3*n+1 \text{ ELSE } n:=n \text{ DIV } 2$$

terminates for arbitrary initial values $n>0$. We very often succeed by constructing a strongly monotone integer function of the number of iterations which is bound so that the number of iterations must be finite because otherwise the bounds would be exceeded. Note that it does not matter if our bounds actually grossly overestimate the number of iterations. For proving termination it is only necessary to know that the loop will finally halt.

As an example we try to compute the least common multiple lcm(a,b,c) of three positive integers $a,b,c>0$. Normally we would use the asymmetric formula:

$$\text{lcm}(a,b,c) = \text{lcm}(\text{lcm}(a,b),c)$$

and $\text{lcm}(a,b) = a*b \text{ DIV hcf}(a,b)$. For a symmetric solution we observe that lcm(a,b,c) is the minimum of the intersection of the sets of all multiples of a,b, and c respectively. Hence we have to generate all multiples of a until we find a value which is as well a multiple of b and c. Generation of multiples could be done by addition:

$$\{A = p*a\} \quad A := A + a \quad \{A = (p + 1)a\}$$
$$\{B = q*b\} \quad B := B + b \quad \{B = (q + 1)b\}$$
$$\{C = r*c\} \quad C := C + c \quad \{C = (r + 1)c\}$$

When we start iteration with A = a, B = b, C = c then we know that initially

$$A, B, C \leq lcm(a,b,c)$$

If one of these values, say A, is strictly less than another one, say B, then

$$A = p*a < B \leq lcm(a,b,c)$$

Hence

$$A + a = (p + 1) a \leq lcm(a,b,c)$$

since lcm(a,b,c) is a multiple of a. We are therefore allowed to increase A by a without violating the condition A $\leq$ lcm(a,b,c). If, however, neither A > B nor B > C nor C > A then

$$A \leq B \leq C \leq A$$

i. e.

$$A = B = C$$

and we have found a common multiple. Since still A,B,C $\leq$ lcm(a,b,c) this multiple is the least one.

These considerations lead to the following program

```
{a,b,c > 0, integer}
A := a; B := b; C := c;
WHILE A ≠ B OR B ≠ C
DO
    {loop invariant: A,B,C are multiples of a,b,c respectively and A,B,C ≤ lcm(a,b,c)}
    IF A < B THEN A := A + a
    ELSE IF B < C THEN B := B + b
    ELSE {we know now C < A}
            C := C + c
{A = B = C = lcm(a,b,c)}
```

To prove termination of this loop we observe that the values of each of A,B,C cannot exceed a*b*c. A + B + C is therefore a suitable monotone integer function: it increases monontonically in each iteration by min(a,b,c) and it is bounded by 3*a*b*c.

ABSTRACTION

The most important means for simplifying the presentation of complicated situations consists in defining new entities which represent a group of related entities, formulae etc. in the foregoing presentation. In this way we reduce the number of entities with which we have deal with at the same time. The method is well known in all sciences. Whenever we define a new term in mathematics, physics, chemistry, etc. we essentially do this to condense our description of some situation and in the hope that by this condensation the description will become more lucid.

A simple application of this principle in programming is the grouping of statements into a compound statement, a block or a procedure. It expresses that we consider this group of statement as a unit. In terms of pre- and postconditions we have for a compound statement

$$\frac{\{P\} \ \ S \ \ \{Q\}}{\{P\} \ \text{BEGIN S END} \ \{Q\}}$$

where S is a sequence of statements, i. e. the grouping does not influence the meaning. But seen from the outside we have introduced a barrier BEGIN - END so that we are no longer able to split S into its components. We have "abstracted" from these details.

By abstracting from certain details we do not declare these details irrelevant or unimportant. We only express that the desired overall effect of the unit may be achieved in an arbitrary manner which is of no interest to the outsider. This view becomes particularly apparent when we add declarations to a block. Let D be a sequence of such declarations and let H be an assertion describing the properties of the entities introduced in these declarations.

We have then for a block

$$\frac{H \ \Rightarrow \ \{P\} S \ \{Q\}}{\{P\} \ D; \ \text{BEGIN S END} \ \{Q\}.}$$

This rule says that D; BEGIN S END will guarantee postcondition Q starting from precondition P if we can prove $\{P\} \ S \ \{Q\}$ under the assumption H.P and Q themselves must not refer to any of the entities declared by D. For all constant declarations, e.g.,

> CONST pi = 3.1415926

H contains the defining equation;

For variable declarations, e.g.,

> VAR x : REAL

the assertion is "there is an object x to which the operations for reals may be applied with the usual axioms".
For a type definition, e.g.,

> TYPE complex = RECORD re,im:REAL END

the assertion describes the properties which we associate with objects of this type.

The same rules as for blocks apply to parameterless procedures. The only additional effect is the introduction of a name which serves as a substitute for a procedure body. For procedures with parameters the situation is a little bit more complicated. Lack of space forbids us to go into more details. The interested reader is referred, e.g. to the book by Gries(1981).

The details from which we abstract describe the implementation of the transformation in which we are interested. Even more important is the abstraction from implementation issues in the case of data structures and data types. For example when dealing with real numbers we are interested in precision and range but not in the particular arrangement of mantissa and exponent within a word. Similarly, the arrangement of the components of a multidimensional array in storage does not matter when we deal with matrix problems. The representation of an array in storage or the representation of any other type must, however, be known for constructing the access function to individual elements or for any other operation with objects of the given type. On the other hand the details of the access function are unnecessary if we only want to use it; in this case we only need to know what the arguments and results of such an operation are and how executions of (the same or different) operations on the same data are interrelated. The key idea in constructing a useful data abstraction is therefore to consider the data representation not by itself but together with the operations which we want to perform with these data. When we abstract from representational issues then we abstract at the same time from the implementation of these operations. We retain only the external description of the value range of the data type, in the case of arrays, e. g. the possible shapes, dimensions and sizes of arrays, and the operations together with the rules which these operations obey. In the case of integers the operations are the usual basic arithmetic operations together with the axioms known from mathematics: commutative, distributive, associative laws, etc. A data type together with its operations and the associated rules is called an *abstract data type*.

Whenever we consider the instruction set of a computer, its data structuring facilities and its basic data types from the applications point of view we abstract from the implementation of these instructions, be it by microprogram, hard-wired or simulated by software. A uniform level of discourse such as that provided by the hardware-software interface of a computer is called a *level of abstraction*. Every programming language provides us with such a level of abstraction. In principle we could build for any language such as Algol, Fortran, Pascal a computer with the basic operations, control structures, data types, scope rules, etc. of that language as instructions, data types and storage structure. Examples of where such attempts have been successful include the design of the Burroughs 5000 series as an Algol-machine in the early sixties and the newly developed P-code microcomputer which more or less possesses Pascal as its machine language. In general, however, we implement such languages by software, an interpreter for APL implementing the APL-machine being a typical example. A collection of abstract data types and control structures such as the quoted interpreters or the interface of an operating system is therefore also called an *abstract machine*.

Up to now we have explained abstraction as a"bottom-up" principle, forming new units from smaller one. But the principle also works the other way around. From the point of view of program design the resulting "top-down" strategy is even more important. It consists of two steps:

(a) Build a solution to the specified problem from steps and data which may be considered as the basic operations and data of an abstract machine.
(b) Implement the abstract machine either by mapping it directly to hardware facilities or by mapping it to an already implemented abstract machine, e.g. by a compiler or by repeating steps (a) and (b) for further refinement.

We will study this process in an example in section 3.

2. A SHORT INTRODUCTION TO PASCAL

In this section we will briefly summarize the main features of the programming language Pascal which we use for examples. For a more detailed introduction and for a complete language description the reader is referred to Jensen and Wirth (1974).

The language Pascal designed by Niklaus Wirth in 1968 - 71 is remarkable for its facilities for structuring data and control, being at the same time a very small language. Pascal is a language based on Algol 60. It is now available on almost all commercial computers including many microcomputers. Many implementations are based on the "P-code compiler", a portable compiler developed at the ETH Zürich translating Pascal into a machine language, called P-code, for an abstract stack computer.

A Pascal program has the form

>   PROGRAM programname (list of file names);
>   declarations
>   body.

DECLARATIONS

Declarations are constant, type, variable, or subprogram declarations and appear always in this order. They introduce new names and ascribe properties to them. These names may then be used in the body which is a sequence of statements parenthesized by BEGIN-END. Every name appearing in a statement must be explicitly declared; there are no implicit declarations. All declarations and statements are separated by a semicolon.

The constant, type and variable declaration sections are introduced by the keywords CONST, TYPE and VAR respectively. In case of constants and types there follow equations

>   constantname   = formula;
>   typename   = type description; {see below}

which assign the value or type resulting from the right hand side to the name on the left. The formulae in constant declarations are evaluated at compile-time. Variable declarations take the form

>   variable_name_list : type

and introduce new variables of the given type. The name list is a list of identifiers separated by commas.

PROCEDURES and FUNCTIONS

Subprogram declarations have the form

>   PROCEDURE produrename   parameter-list;
>   declarations {optional}
>   body

or

>   FUNCTION functionname   parameter-list : typename;
>   declarations {optional}
>   body

In the first form the subprogram delivers results via parameters. A function delivers a result of type typename. A result is specified as in Algol 60 by assigning a value to the functionname within the body.

The parameter-list is optional. It consists of a sequence of variable declarations enclosed in parentheses. In the case of the specification

>   FUNCTION f (a,b:integer; c:real) : Boolean;

the parameters are transmitted by call-by-value. Value parameters are input parameters. The parameters names a, b, c are local variables of the subprogram initialized with the corresponding actual parameter. In the specification

> PROCEDURE p (a:integer; VAR b,c:integer; d:real; VAR x:real);

b, c and x are "VAR-parameters" transmitted by call-by-reference, i.e. whenever we refer to the formal parameter in the body of the subprogram the address of the corresponding actual parameter is substituted. VAR-parameters are suitable as result and transient parameters.

Pascal requires that the type of parameters and function results always be given by a typename. Specifications such as

> PROCEDURE p (VAR a : ARRAY [1..n] OF real);

are forbidden and must be replaced by

> TYPE ...
>   vector = ARRAY [1..n] OF real
>   ...
> PROCEDURE p (VAR a : vector);

In order to simplify our presentation we will sometimes ignore this restriction.

Both procedures and functions may be called recursively.

The declarations in a subprogram, if any, declare local entities of the subprogram. The scope of the names and the life-time (extent) of the objects are restricted to the subprogram. In particular, local variables do *not* retain their value between successive calls of a subprogram. As in Algol 60, subprograms may also access the entities declared in the environment in which the subprogram declaration appears. Such entities are termed global parameters (global constants, global variables, etc.). In order to prevent misunderstandings and undesired side-effects it is advisable to avoid using a global parameter at the same time as an actual VAR-parameter; in functions assignment to global parameters and VAR-parameters should be avoided.

TYPES

Pascal distinguishes scalar types and structured types. Scalar types comprise the predefined types Boolean, integer, real and char. Additionally a new scalar type may be defined by enumerating the possible values as in

> day = sunday,ponedelnik,mardi,Mittwoch,jueves,venerdi, sawwato

The enumeration imposes an order on the value set. The values are denoted by identifiers. Additionally we may restrict the range of values of an already known type by specifying a subrange as in:

> working day = ponedelnik .. sawwato
> day of month : 1 .. 31

Enumeration types are particularly useful for value ranges where the actual coding of the values is irrelevant but a non-numeric coding increases readability. Subranges inform the reader, both the human and the machine, that the values of some variables are expected not to exceed certain bounds. The run-time system will check that this assertion is true.

There are four constructors for constructing a structured type out of one ore more component types:

```
ARRAY [index bounds] OF component type
RECORD field declarations END
FILE OF component type
SET OF base type
```

An array constructor defines usual arrays. Index ranges are arbitrary scalar types (except real) or subranges thereof. This fact implies among other things that Pascal only allows for arrays with static bounds. The rules are even more restrictive than in Fortran since also array parameters have statically fixed bounds. Strings are considered as array of characters of suitable length. Indexing is achieved by writing a[index] or, in case of a multidimensional array a [index 1,...,index n]. The indices are arbitrary expressions of the appropriate index type.

A record type

```
person = RECORD Christianname, lastname: string;
               birthday : RECORD year : —3000..2000;
                                 month: 1..12;
                                 day: 1..31;
                          END;
               sex : male, female
         END
```

specifies a structure consisting of fields of possibly differing types. The fields are selected by identifiers, e. g. Christianname, lastname, birthday, sex. As the example shows nesting of record types is possible. If we introduce a variable

```
lecturer : person
```

then the fields are named

```
lecturer. Christianname,...,lecturer.birthday.year,etc.
```

There is a special statement, the WITH statement which allows for shortening the naming of fields. In

```
WITH lecturer
DO BEGIN sex := male; birthday.month := 8 END
```

or

```
WITH lecturer, lecturer.birthday
DO BEGIN sex := male; month := 8 END
```

we have "reopened the scope of the field declarations for the components of the records listed in the beginning". Hence sex refers to lecturer.sex and month refers to lecturer.birthday.month.

The last field specification in a record type may be a distinction of cases for specifying several variants of records. In our example we could replace the last field specification by

```
CASE sex: male, female OF
male     : (salary : real);
female   : (maidenname : string;
              numberofchildren : 0..maxint)
```

The fields in a variant are allocated depending on the values of the tag field appearing in the case clause. At different times several variants may occupy the same place in storage.

File types specify sequences of elements of their component type. They are used for representing sequential files as defined by the operating system. Of particular interest are files of type

   text = FILE OF char

There are two standard files called "input" and "output" of type text which represent the standard input and output medium (card reader/printer or terminal). Except for these two files every file must be declared as a variable. Additionally all files must be listed in the program heading.

To each file f there is a buffer variable f↑ of the component type of f declared. (Since ↑ is not available on most printers the marks ^ as in rôle or @ are used instead.) The following operations for files exist:

Function	eof(f):	A boolean function indicating that f is at the end of file position.
Procedure	put(f):	Provided eof(f) is true the value of f↑ is appended to f.
	get(f):	Advances the current file position and assigns the value of the next component to f↑. If no such component exists eof(f) becomes true.
	reset(f):	The file is positioned to its first component and its value is assigned to f↑.
	rewrite(f):	The file is emptied and eof(f) becomes true.

For text files additionally the following subprograms exist:

Function	eoln(f):	true if the file position is advanced to a line boundary.
Procedure	read(f,x):	x is a variable of type char, integer or real. Reads from f one character or the longest string which represents a number, depending on the type of x, and assigns the value to x. In the case of numbers leading blanks and line boundaries are skipped.
	readln(f):	advances the read position to the beginning of the next line.
	write(f,v):	prints the value v of type char, Boolean, integer, real or string starting at the current file position. The width m of the printing area may be specified by writing v:m.
	writeln(f):	skips to the beginning of a new line.
	page(f):	skips to the beginning of a new page.

Further possibilities and simplifications in using the procedures read, readln, write and writeln are explained in Jensen and Wirth (1974).

A set type has the powerset of its base type as its range of values. The base type must be a scalar type. Most implementations restrict the maximum number of elements of the base type. Usually SET OF char is allowed but this is near to the maximum. For sets we have the operations union (+), intersection (*), set difference (-) and membership (IN); the relational operators test for set inclusion.

For representing recursive data types like binary trees or directed graphs, Pascal allows for pointers. A pointer is a value v "pointing" to some object w of type t. The type of v is then denoted by ↑t; t is usually a record type. The objects w cannot be normal variables but are anonymous,dynamically created objects of unrestricted lifetime. NEW (v) creates a new object w of type t and assigns to variable v a pointer to w; the type of w is derived from the type of v. Each pointer type includes the value NIL which does not refer to any object. If v is a pointer variable and its value is not NIL then the "referenced variable" v↑ designates the object w to which v is pointing. If for example we want to create a linear list of length m_0

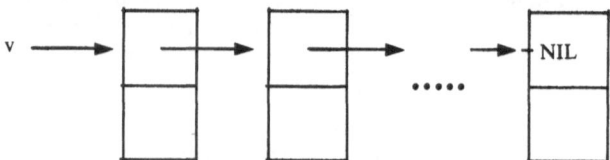

we write

```
TYPE t = RECORD p:↑t; i:item type END;
VAR v,vl:↑t;
...
v: = NIL; m: = m₀;
WHILE  m > 0
DO {loop invariant: v points to a list of lenght m₀-m}
      BEGIN vl: = v;
            new(v);        {creates a new first element}
            v↑.p: = vl;    {assign the pointer to the tail}
            m: = m-l
  END
```

Note that t contains a field of type ↑t; hence t is called a recursive type.

EXPRESSIONS

Expressions are built from values, operators and parentheses in the usual manner. Values are constants, variable names, field designators, indexed and referenced variables, file buffers or function calls. The operators in order of ascending priority are:

=, < >, <, < =, >, > =, IN	(< > denotes inequality)
+, −, OR	(unary and binary)
*, /, DIV, MOD, AND	
NOT	

Note that OR, AND and NOT have higher priority than the relational operators.

STATEMENTS

There are eight kinds of statements most of which we have already seen in the preceding section.

The assignment statement

> x := f

assigns the result of the expression f to the variable x. The proof rule for assignments is C.A.R. Hoare's famous axiom of the assignment

$$\{P_{f \to x}\} \ x := f \ \{P\}$$

In words: after the assignment the assertion P holds if f is evaluable (no division by zero, etc.) and before the assignment a condition $P_{f \to x}$ holds which we deduce from P by replacing x by f everywhere. Instead of $P_{f \to x}$ often P^x_f is written.

The goto statement is written

> GOTO label

where labels are represented by integers. A label is defined by prefixing the appropriate statement by

> label :

Additionally labels must be declared in the declaration part of the main program or a subprogram depending on where the label definition occurs. Labels are declared by

> LABEL list of labels

This must be the first declaration in the corresponding declaration part.

Jumps do not change the state of the computation and hence do not occur in the decomposition of a problem. In fact, Pascal programs do usually not contain any jumps and label definitions at all. The only cases where they are needed are error situations and premature termination of loops.

Procedure and function calls are written

> $p\ (ap_1,...,ap_n)$

where p is the subprogram name and ap_i are the actual parameters in order. Parameterless calls are just written

> p

We know already compound statements and blocks, the WITH statement, conditional statements (IF and CASE statements), and two forms of the loop. In addition to the WHILE DO loop and the FOR loop with an ascending count Pascal allows for a loop

> REPEAT statement sequence UNTIL condition

and a FOR loop with descending count:

> FOR count : = initial value DOWNTO final value DO statement

The proof rule for the REPEAT UNTIL construct is

> {P} S {Q}
> Q AND NOT C ⇒ P
> _____
> {P} REPEAT S UNTIL C {Q AND C}

The statement sequence S is always executed at least once. Termination of the loop must be proved separately.

The proof rule for the FOR DOWNTO loop is similar to the rule for the ascending case in the preceding section.

3. AN EXAMPLE: SORTING BY SELECTION

We consider the following problem. Given a sequence $S = (v_1,...,v_n)$ of values v_i from an ordered set M, find a permutation $(v_{j1},...,v_{jn})$ of the values such that

> $v_{j1} \leq v_{j2} \leq ... \leq v_{jn}.$

This statement is already an appropriate problem specification provided we know the intended range of n. For our discussion we assume n so small that a sorting method with complexity $O(n^2)$ is adequate.

Before we develop a solution we need a precise definition of the term sorted: a subsequence $R = (s_1,...,s_k)$ composed from elements of S is ordered if $s_i \leq s_{i+1}$ $i = 1,...,k-1$; it is sorted if it is ordered and does not contain a gap with respect to S. This may be expressed formally as:

$$C(s', s): \quad \text{IF } s \leq v < s', \quad s, s' \in R, v \in S$$
$$\text{THEN } v \in R$$

For example if S = $\{26,94,41,54,108,65,57,78,27,103,80,38,11,43,39,92\}$ then $T = (11,26,41,43)$ is ordered but not sorted with respect to S because 27 is missing.

Sorting by selection is a sorting method based on the idea:

Select the minimal element s from S and append it to the sorted sequence R.
If $|S| > 1$ then apply the step again to S-{s}.

We start from a initial sequence $S = S_0$. The initially empty sequence R yields at the end the sorted sequence.

This idea may be schematically reformulated as a procedure

```
PROCEDURE sortl (VAR S,R : sequence);
{precondition P: R is sorted and for all r∈R,s∈R:r≤s
                 and S₀ = R ∪ S
  postcondition = precondition}
VAR m:M;
BEGIN IF S not empty
    THEN
        m := minimum of S;
        remove m from S;
        append m at the end of R;
        sortl(S,R)
    END
END {sortl}
```

Sortl is to be called in the context of the statements

```
S := S₀;
R := empty sequence
```

Obviously this text is not yet a Pascal program. It is a program for an abstract machine A with M as basic data type and "sequence" as a type constructor. Furthermore the following operations must be available:

test if a sequence is not empty
detemine minimum of a sequence
remove (m,sequence)
append (m,sequence)
assign empty sequence.

For a machine with these properties our program can be proved correct.

Theorem:
(1) The procedure sortl terminates and is partially correct.
(2) Under the assumption that the test, remove and append operations require a constant amount of time the time complexity of sortl is $O(n^2)$.

Proof:
(1) During each call one element is removed from S; hence the procedure sortl is recursively called at most n times and the recursion terminates. The precondition P is true initially since R is empty. By induction we see now: if P is true before a

call of sortl and S is not empty then we have for all $r \in R$, $s \in S$, $m = min(S)$

$$r \le m \le s$$

Hence appending m to R does not destroy the sorting of R. Also $S_0 = R \cup S$ holds at the end of sortl again. Altogether we see that P is true at the end of sortl if it was true initially. When S becomes empty we have therefore R sorted and $R = S_0$ as requested.

(2) It is well-known that the minimum of n elements can be determined by accessing each element once but not with less accesses. The number of comparisons is n-1. Hence the amount of time for a single call of sortl with $|S| = n \ne 0$ is

$$C(n) = c*n + c' + C(n\text{-}1)$$

where c and c' are constants, and for $|S| = n = 0$ we have $C(0) = c''$. Summing up yields:

$$C(n) = \sum_{i=n}^{1} (c*i + c') + c''$$
$$= c*n(n+1)/2 + n*c' + c''$$
$$= O(n^2)$$

(Note that from this consideration also the termination of the algorithm follows.)

We are now left with a program which is correct provided we can implement the required data structures and operations.

Before we try the implementation we observe that our procedure body schematically has the form

PROCEDURE p; IF C THEN BEGIN S; p END

Such a procedure can always be transformed into

PROCEDURE p'; WHILE C DO S

The precondition of procedure p serves as loop invariant in p'. Taking the initialization into account we therefore arrive at

```
PROCEDURE sort2 (VAR R,S: sequence);
VAR m:M;
BEGIN R := empty sequence;
    WHILE S not empty
    DO {invariant: P} BEGIN
        m := minimum of S;
        remove (m,S);
        append (m,R);
    END
END {sort2};
```

This procedure is to be called with

sort2 (R,S_0)

in order to get S initialized. The sequence S_0, the input parameter, will be emptied since it is transmitted as a VAR parameter.

We have not to establish the correctness and complexity of sort2 again. Such properties follow immediately from the corresponding properties of sortl and the systematics of our transformation. Such transformations exist in several forms.

Another example is

PROCEDURE p; BEGIN S; IF C THEN p END

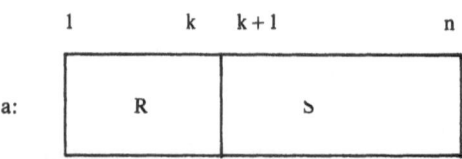

PROCEDURE p'; REPEAT S UNTIL NOT C

Again the precondition of p and the loop invariant of p' are the same.

All operations which we have to implement deal with the representation of R and S. Since we assumed $n = |S_0|$ to be small we could represent both sequences by arrays of length n. This decision requires 2n storage places. But only n of these will be occupied since always $|R| + |S| = n$. To save space we put R and S together in an array a with n elements:

1	k	k+1	n

a:

| R | S |

In the beginning we set k := 0. This implies S = a, R empty. If $a[k+1] = min(S)$ after the search for the minimum, then the assignment k := k+1 implements remove (m,S) and append (m,R). Together with a suitable algorithm for finding the minimum we have the final program

```
PROCEDURE sort3 (VAR a : array[1..n] OF M);
{precondition: a contains S₀
 postcondition: a contains R = S₀ sorted
 The type M must be such that comparison of values is allowed.}
VAR m : M;
    h,i,k : integer;
BEGIN
    k := 0;                  {R := empty sequence}
    WHILE k < n-1   {|S| > 1}
    DO {loop invariant: a[1..k] sorted and for i≤k, k<j: a[i]≤a[j]}
      BEGIN k := k+1;
              {find minimum}
              m := a[k]; h := k;
              FOR i := k+1 TO n
      DO IF a[i]<m THEN
         BEGIN m := a[i]; h := i END;
         {exchange m=a[h] and a[k]}
         a[h] := a[k]; a[k] := m
    END {k loop}
{A[1..n-1] sorted and the loop invariant yield a[1..n] sorted}
END {sort3};
```

The application of this procedure shows the following table. The stairway separates R and S.

26	11	11	11	11	11	11	11	11	11	11	11	11	11	11	11
94	94	26	26	26	26	26	26	26	26	26	26	26	26	26	26
41	41	41	27	27	27	27	27	27	27	27	27	27	27	27	27
54	54	54	54	38	38	38	38	38	38	38	38	38	38	38	38
108	108	108	108	108	39	39	39	39	39	39	39	39	39	39	39
65	65	65	65	65	65	41	41	41	41	41	41	41	41	41	41
57	57	57	57	57	57	57	43	43	43	43	43	43	43	43	43
78	78	78	78	78	78	78	78	54	54	54	54	54	54	54	54
27	27	27	41	41	41	65	65	65	57	57	57	57	57	57	57
103	103	103	103	103	103	103	103	103	103	65	65	65	65	65	65
80	80	80	80	80	80	80	80	80	80	80	78	78	78	78	78
38	38	38	38	54	54	54	54	78	78	78	80	80	80	80	80
11	26	94	94	94	94	94	94	94	94	94	94	94	92	92	92
43	43	43	43	43	43	43	57	57	65	103	103	103	103	94	94
39	39	39	39	39	108	108	108	108	108	108	108	108	108	108	103
92	92	92	92	92	92	92	92	92	92	92	92	92	94	103	108

4. STRUCTURED PROGRAM DEVELOPMENT USING FORTRAN

Program development as in the foregoing section essentially depends on the availability of a language such as Pascal which allows for easy formulation of recursive procedures, while loops, complicated data types etc. The understanding of an algorithm is very much eased if we have elegant and concise formulations for these constructs at our disposal. Otherwise it may happen that our programs become twice as long and we loose the overview of the development. This situation will invariably lead to errors.

The question arises what we shall do if we do not have Pascal or a similar language at our disposal but for some reasons must use Fortran, Cobol, etc. The answer is demonstrated by the transition from a recursive formulation of our sort procedure to an iterative one: although recursion is not available in Fortran the loop is not too difficult to formulate.

The lesson which we learn is: we should use Pascal or a similar language during the design. As soon as we arrive at a final formulation we use Fortran, or what we have, as the coding language and hand-translate the program into this language. This translation will follow fixed rules similar to the transformation rules of the preceding sections. We leave it to reader to establish these rules. The most complicated situations arise from recursions which cannot easily be transformed into loops and from storage management problems. In these cases the translation will have to simulate the stack and heap techniques by which Pascal is implemented.

Looking at the programming language in this way reveals that we have actually used Pascal as a design tool and Fortran as a coding language. The design ends with the final program if a suitable programming language is available. Otherwise a separate coding stage follows. This is the reason why we have put design and implementation together in the software life cycle and did not introduce two steps as many other authors do.

Our discussion shows that it is not the actual use of Fortran which contradicts structured program development techniques but the use of Fortran as a design tool. This idea may even be extended: when we design a compiler, a data base system or any other large program, it may turn out that Pascal too is a poor design tool. We should choose our design tools according to the needs of the problem; the question whether the tool is implemented or not is of secondary importance.

LITERATURE

Dijkstra E.W. (1975), Guarded Commands. Nondeterminacy and Formal Derivation. CACM 18, pp. 453-457.

Dijkstra E.W. (1976), A Discipline of Programming. Prentice-Hall.

Gries D. (1978) (editor), Programming Methodology. A Collection of Articles by Members of IFIP WG2.3. Springer Verlag.

Gries D. (1981), The Science of Programming. Springer Verlag.

Horowitz E. and Sahni S. (1978), Fundamentals of Computer Algorithms. Computer Science Press .

Jensen K. and Wirth N. (1974), Pascal - User Manual and Report. Lecture Notes in Computer Science, Vol. 18.

Owicki S. and Gries D. (1976), An Axiomatic Proof Technique for Parallel Programs. Acta Informatica 6, pp. 319-340. Reprinted in Gries (1978).

PROGRAM STRUCTURE

Gerhard Goos
University of Karlsruhe
Karlsruhe, Germany

Every program consists of statements and is therefore structured by definition. We are, however, not interested in arbitrary structures but in a structural decomposition into modules which may be used as the basis for

— distribution of work among programmers
— program verification
— modification and maintenance.

We claim in this chapter that algorithms and abstract data types are the means best suited for modularization of a program. We discuss how to express modules and the resulting program structure in some programming language and we consider hierarchic program structure as it arises from program development by step-wise refinement.

1. PROGRAM MODULES

Several Notions of Modularity

Modularity is one of the catchwords of informatics with several, not necessarily consistent meanings. We may consider:

— syntactic modularity: a piece of a program forming a syntactic entity such as a subprogram or block.

— physical modularity: a separately compilable piece of a program.

— a piece of a program with "minimal" interaction and interface to the remaining program.

— conceptual modularity: a piece of a program which may be designed and verified independently of its use starting from a specification of the interface only: conversely such a module should be usable without knowledge of the details of its implementation.

D. T. Muxworthy (ed.), Programming for Software Sharing, 35–47.
Copyright © 1983 ECSC, EEC, EAEC, Brussels and Luxembourg.

— functional modularity: a piece of a program which is functionally closed, i.e. auxiliary data and functions are contained within the module itself; the module does not use global data unless they are to be considered as part of the underlying base system.

From these notions only the last two show some similarity with the notion of a module as it occurs in other engineering disciplines. They are also the only notions which lead to some insight into how we should modularize a program. for example in the third case, we even do not know when an interface should be considered minimal.

The most serious drawback of these notions is, however, that they cannot be used to guide the design process. They do not tell in advance what functions or data should be put together into a module. All they can be used for is to judge a posteriori whether a proposed modularization is suitable or not.

Modularity in programming serves various purposes. We build programs from smaller units, the modules, and reduce the overall complexity by this step. An appropriate modularization is also an important means for easier maintenance, portability and similar properties of programs. Verification is based on a modular decomposition of programs.

The Specification of Program Modules

The introduction of program modules as intermediate units splits the construction of a program into two steps: the building of the program from modules as basic building blocks and the construction of the modules themselves. We may split these steps again by repeated application of this subdivision. For each module we need a specification interfacing the two steps. The specification on the one hand describes the desired properties of the module as seen by the user. On the other hand it describes the required properties as seen by the implementor.

The specification of a module must describe the possible calls of the module, the input parameters, their admissible ranges and relationships, the possible ranges of the results and their dependence on the input parameters. Part of the effect of a call of the module may be a change of the internal state of the module which may influence the results of subsequent calls of the module. A module can only be used reliably if the actions taken in case of incorrect inputs or of malfunction of the base system are also specified. This requirement is usually very difficult to fulfill and is one of the sources of problems during maintenance.

In practice, specifications are usually given informally. The reasons mostly lie in the difficulty of constructing more formal specifications. These, however, are necessary if we wish to apply verification or other validation techniques. Parnas (1972a) showed how to specify the interdependence of different function calls without mentioning the concept of a state of a module. A completely formal specification could for instance describe each operation in terms of pre- and post-conditions (Wulf et al., 1975). Liskov and Zilles (1975) give an overview of several formal specification techniques. All currently known formal specification techniques still contain certain pitfalls limiting their applicability. The most used technique at the moment seems to be the algebraic specification technique, see e. g. Guttag and Horning, (1978). Note that the use of states of a module in an external specification usually results in an overspecification. It suggests that state variables as used in the specification, actually exist in the implementation which may not be the case. It also violates the principle of information hiding (Parnas, 1971).

A specification is a document accompanying the module during the whole of its lifetime. The module may be designed for reusability in other environments. Hence, its functions and data might be more general than actually required in the first instance. It is therefore not sufficient to guarantee that the specification adequately describes the properties of the module as seen in the first application. It should cover every aspect which could become relevant for its use in arbitrary applications. The step from an external view of a module to the view of an implementor often corresponds to a substantial change in the conceptual view of a module and in the interests and goals of the people involved. This change is particularly significant if it corresponds to a change of level in a hierarchic system. A prominent example is the difference between the views of a user and a system designer on the functions provided by an operating system. Another example are error messages from a compiler. They are often given in terms of states of the parser. The designer of the compiler has obviously forgotten that the user has another picture of the compiler than he has: states of the parser are internal details which do not occur in the external specification of the compiler and thus cannot be understood by the user.

2. PROGRAM MODULES AND DATA STRUCTURES

Data Structures as Abstract Data Types

In what follows the notion of an abstract data type as introduced earlier will play a fundamental rôle. An abstract data type consists of a set of operations, some axioms and a set of values. The data type is called abstract because in formulating the ingredients of an abstract data type, the possible implementation is of no importance. The axioms describe the meaning of the operations but they do not say how the operations may be implemented. There may be several representations of the data and several possible algorithms for performing the operations which are equivalent from the abstract points of view.

Abstract data types may be viewed as algebras. This view leads to the algebraic specification method (Guttag and Horning, 1978) which we will shortly describe. Clearly, any kind of data is interesting only if we know how to interpret these data and what the effect of operations on these data will be. The algebraic specification of an abstract data type exhibits this behaviour by specifying only the operations and the axioms but not the range of possible values. The values are implicitly specified as sequences of operations applied to some constant values (functions with zero arguments) which can not be simplified. Operations (or functions) are described in the form of algebraic mappings:

$$f : T_1 \times ... \times T_m \to T_o$$

describes a function with m arguments belonging to the data types $T_1,...,T_m$. Axioms are written in the form

$$x := y \text{ (the meaning of x is y)}$$

where x and y are formulae built from the previously defined operations.

As a simple example we specify the abstract data type Boolean:

[data type Boolean]

true:		→ Boolean
false:		→ Boolean
not:	Boolean	→ Boolean
and:	Boolean × Boolean	→ Boolean
or:	Boolean × Boolean	→ Boolean

For all x, y ϵ Boolean

A1	not (false)	$:\equiv$ true
A2	not (true)	$:\equiv$ false
A3	and (false, false)	$:\equiv$ false
A4	and (false, true)	$:\equiv$ false
A5	and (true, false)	$:\equiv$ false
A6	and (true, true)	$:\equiv$ true
A7	or (x, y)	$:\equiv$ not (and (not(x), not (y)))

In this simple example obviously all expressions can be reduced to either true or false. Hence these two functions are the only possible values.

More complicated examples are stacks, queues and sets. A stack is characterized by the fact that we can push objects on it which then will hide previously pushed objects. Only after removal of the last pushed object is the previous object visible again. This description leads to the following formal specification of a stack with objects T:

[data type stack (T)]

create:		→ stack
push:	stack × T	→ stack
pop:	stack	→ stack
top:	stack	→ T
empty:	stack	→ Boolean

For all Sϵstack, xϵT

A1	empty (create)	$:\equiv$ true
A2	empty (push(s, x))	$:\equiv$ false
A3	pop (push(s, x))	$:\equiv$ s
A4	top (push(s,x))	$:\equiv$ x

By induction we may prove that all stacks may be represented in the form

$$\text{push (push (... push (create,} x_1),...,x_{n-1}), x_n), n \geq 0$$

which usually is shortened to

$$\text{push (create; } x_1,...,x_n).$$

Because of this property push and create are called constructor operations.

The above specification is parametrized with the component type T. No particular assumptions about T are made. Furthermore we observe that the specified stacks have unlimited depth. The introduction of a maximum depth would go along with the introduction of a stack overflow exception.

The data type queue describes a sequence to which we may append elements at one end and remove elements at the other end (enqueue and dequeue respectively):

[data type queue(T)]

create:		$\rightarrow$ queue
enq:	queue $\times$ T	$\rightarrow$ queue
deq:	queue	$\rightarrow$ queue
front:	queue	$\rightarrow$ T
empty:	queue	$\rightarrow$ Boolean

For all $q \in$ queue, $x \in$ T

A1	empty (create)	$:\equiv$ true
A2	empty (enq(q,x))	$:\equiv$ false
A3	deq (enq(q,x))	$:\equiv$ IF empty(q) THEN q ELSE enq(deq(q),x)
A4	front (enq(q,x))	$:\equiv$ IF empty(q) THEN x ELSE front (q)

The values of type queue can be represented in the form

$$\text{enq (create; } x_1...x_n), \ n \geq 0.$$

Clearly, the specification is completely independent of whether we implement the queue as a linked list or put it into an array. These details become interesting for the user of such a module only when he is considering questions of time and space complexity. The independence from implementation decisions and its formality are the main advantages of the algebraic specification method. There remain, however, many problems to be solved until the method will become useful also for large practical problems, cf. Majster (1977).

Classification of Program Modules

Subsequently we consider functional modules. We may classify such modules into five categories. One extreme is a function without permanent data, the other extreme is a set of data without associated functions.

The first category consists of modules providing one single function without any relationship between distinct calls. Most mathematical functions and numeric algorithms belong to this class. Typical examples are modules for computing exp(x) or for computing the zeroes of a function using Newton's iteration.

The second category consists of single functions whose results depend on common data. Typical examples are random number generators. Their results depend on state variables whose values were modified in previous calls.

Sets of several functions operating on common data belong to a third category. The results of such functions may depend on preceding calls of some other functions of the set. Modules of this category are used to structure programs by building groups of functions which solve problems of the same area or provide a set of basic operations for the next higher level of abstraction. Examples are the symbol table module in a compiler with functions for coding and decoding identifiers, or an interpreter for a command language.

The characteristics of modules of the fourth category are nearly the same as those above. However, the conceptual view is more oriented towards data than based on the functional aspect. Such a module defines a class of objects together with the applicable operations. An example for this category is the stack module providing the usual operations for manipulating stacks. It represents an abstract data type. If we also consider modules of the third category as types then typically only one object of such a type is needed. However, the number of objects belonging to a class of the fourth category is conceptually not restricted.

The last (fifth) category consists of modules for which the data type aspect is dominating. Implicitly defined functions exist for accessing the value of objects and their components. Other functions are not directly related to the module definition. These modules correspond to record definitions in the Pascal sense.

This classification of modules is based mostly on their external specification and their conceptual usage. From a purist's point of view the first and the fourth category are the most important classes. All other classes may be derived from simple functions or from abstract data types.

A similar classification may be based on the implementation of a module. The differences between the categories are much more significant in this case because different implementation techniques are applicable to different categories. In many cases this classification will put a module in another category. For example, sin(x) and cos(x) are independent functions when seen from the outside. They may, however, be implemented by two routines which, after range reduction, use the same polynomial with the same table of coefficients.

Program Modules in High Level Languages

Language constructs for expressing modules of both the extreme categories are well known and exist in several high level languages. Procedures and records in Pascal may serve as an example. Constructs for expressing more general modules do not exist in these languages. For discussing such constructs we shall first compare the usage and the implementation of procedures and records.

A procedure call dynamically leads to the creation of an activation record containing the local data of the procedure. There is only one function operating on this record, namely the procedure itself. If the procedure is non-recursive, there exists at most one instance of the activation record at a time; otherwise the lifetimes for recursive invocations are nested. Storage may be allocated by stacking the records.

On the other hand the number of instances of an arbitrary record and their lifetimes are not given by the definition of the record type. They are determined by the usage of the objects. Because the number of objects and their lifetimes are generally unpredictable, dynamic creation and deletion of records may cause technical problems with storage allocation and garbage collection. Other difficulties may arise if functions associated with a record type are additionally bound to some environment, i.e. they use data from that environmnent. In that case we must guarantee that the function is applied neither to nonexistent records nor outside the specified environment.

Language concepts for expressing all categories of modules discussed above may now be derived from the following considerations:

A module consists of several functions associated with a record describing the commonly used data objects. For modules of category 1 to 3 the number of invocations in a given context and their lifetimes are statically fixed. The number of instances of such modules may dynamically vary only by creating or deleting new contexts. These modules are used for structuring a program.

On the other hand modules of category 4 represent abstract data types. The rules about (dynamic) creation and lifetimes of such objects as well as the naming conventions should be the same as for all other data types. Finally, records of category 5 are of interest as building bricks for modules of all other categories. We need them for representing activation records of procedures as well as for representing the nodes of an arbitrary graph (as an example of an abstract type).

For clarity of programming, ease of compilation, and run-time organisation it will be useful in a concrete programming language to distinguish explicitly between modules for structuring a program and for building objects.

Modules in Some Current Languages

We discuss in this section the formulation of modules in Simula (Dahl et al., 1971), Ada (Ichbiah et al., 1981) and Fortran.

Simula provides procedures and classes as syntactic structuring concepts. Classes behave like procedures except that their activation record is retained after the call and their local entities (variables, procedures) may be accessed from the outside. Procedures are useful for representing category 1 modules. All other categories are modelled by classes. The class concept is fully dynamic. We may call a class arbitrarily often; each time a new object is created. Thus, classes are truly category 4 modules. The other categories are modelled by making restricted use of the power of the concept. The price which is paid for this generality consists of some overhead at run-time: for all objects — activation records and classes — storage is allocated on a heap; a garbage collector collects the space of objects which are no longer accessible. Simula does not distinguish between globally visible data and functions and those which are for internal use only. It therefore does not provide for the desirable security, preventing the user from accessing implementation dependent entities.

Ada provides functions, procedures, packages, tasks and records as syntactic structuring concepts. Functions and procedures represent category 1 modules. Packages are category 3 modules. They may also be used to represent category 2 modules. Tasks represent separate sequential processes, a topic which we did not include in our discussion. Records are category 5 modules. Abstract data types (category 4) must be represented by defining a package containing a type declaration and all the operations for the abstract type. The type declaration specifies the representation of the objects of the abstract type. We may then create arbitrarily many objects of this type by normal declarations.

Ada requires the splitting of the definition of a module into a specification and a body. The specification contains all the externally visible information while the body describes the implementation. When the implementation changes no change in the specification is necessary.

Fortran only provides functions and subroutines together with COMMON zones. According to the standard, functions and subroutines are category 1 modules. Most implementations, however, retain the local data between successive calls. In such a case functions and subroutines may be used also as category 2 modules. Category 3 modules must be implemented by a collection of subprograms communicating via a common COMMON zone. With respect to security we note that nobody can prevent other subprograms from accessing this COMMON zone although it only contains the local data of the module. Fortran does not have any good means for implementing abstract data types. The operations may be formulated as subprograms, but for dynamically allocating objects we must take the storage from arrays and explicitly program the allocation strategy. There is also no way for grouping objects together in a record except by using arrays.

Hierarchic Program Structure

The method of step-wise refinement or top-down design for constructing algorithms solving isolated problems is demonstrated in Goos (1982 a) and Goos (1982 b). For the design of larger systems we generalize the method for controlling the complexity arising from the bigger size of the problem.

Step-wise refinement as used in constructing the algorithm for sorting by selection started from a simple program which we could easily prove correct. We then refined the solution by replacing the operations "find minimum", etc. by appropriate implementations. The final program showed the operations of the foregoing abstract program merely as comments.

When we apply this technique to larger problems we find three characteristic difficulties:

— In a larger system we find it difficult to accept that at the very end the levels of abstractions through which we have gone during the design are not, or are only insufficiently, represented in the final program. This behaviour renders the methodology as an aid of design only. It fails to support maintenance since the design steps can only be retrieved with difficulty and the program is hard to understand. Especially we must expect that after a certain period of maintenance the levels of abstraction have been rendered meaningless, a situation quickly leading to all kinds of messy behaviour of the system. This is not to say that we should try to replace the methodology by any other one but it should be improved.

— Straightforward application of step-wise refinement leads to a tree-like decomposition. It ignores a basic principle of engineering, namely the minimization of basic building blocks. If, for example, abstractions like stacks, queues or sequences occur at several places in a system design with similar performance characteristics then we should implement these data structures by a common package. But top-down design does not enforce this commonality.

— When we consider the major steps even in a sequential program, for example a compiler, we find that such phases as lexical analysis, parsing, semantic analysis and code generation have a much more complicated interface than can be represented by a single procedure call. They behave more like abstract data types. Correspondingly the design of the highest level of abstraction, the control program invoking all these steps, no longer determines the interface of the modules completely. There are additional interactions, e. g. via the error handling routines.

The solution to the first problem consists in more rigid methods for representing the structure of the design in the structure of the final program. The proper isolation of program modules as discussed in the previous section is the key issue in this respect. The second problem may be attacked by generalizing the tree-like structure resulting from step-wise refinement to an acyclic directed graph:

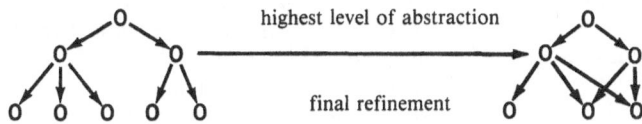

To this end we must explicitly define the possible relationship between modules even those which do not stem from the same step of refinement, and we must introduce the search for such a relationship into our methodology. To guarantee that we do not run into circular dependencies we must restrict ourselves to unidirectional, "hierarchic" relations. For the last problem we must admit that the abstract program does not determine all relations between the modules of the underlying abstract machine. The modules are not as isolated as they may appear from above. In practice very often the relationships detected later may even lead to a redesign of the control program.

Hierarchic Relationships

Parnas (1974) has called a system hierarchically structured by a relationship or predicate A>B if the system consists of parts such that we can define levels by saying

(1) Level 0 is the set of parts A such that there does not exist a B with A>B

(2) Level i is the set of parts A such that
    (a) there exists a B on level i-l with A>B;
    (b) if A>C then C is on level i-l or lower.

This definition characterizes precisely those relationships represented by acyclic directed graphs.

As Parnas further points out the term hierarchic structure is not consistent in the literature. The difference is mostly one of the relation " >". In particular, Parnas has identified the following relationships:

— The "uses" hierarchy: the correct working of module A depends on module B, "A uses B". This relationship is the most common and the most important one. As a matter of fact, it coincides with the relationship "A delegates work to B". B may be called by a subprogram call, for example, the call of a mathematical function. But also the converse situation occurs. The start of a user program by the operating system is a subprogram call, but the user program uses the operating system, not conversely.

— The "call" hierarchy: "A calls B". As noted this relationship does not always express a conceptual dependency of A on B.

— The "access" hierarchy: "B may access A". This relationship defines rings of production: The lowest layer is protected against accesses from the outside but it may access all other ones.

— The hierarchy of ownership: "A may use resources owned by B". This relation often goes along with the relation "B is more privileged than A".

Parnas discusses these relations in the context of operating systems: the T.H.E. system (Dijkstra, Habermann), the MULTICS system (MIT) and the RC 4000 system (Brinch Hansen). The different relationships may lead to distinct structures of a system. As a matter of fact, it is usually wrong or even impossible to impose the same hierarchic structure with regard to different relationships. This raises the question: what is the "right" relationship? This question cannot be answered in isolation. Hierarchic structure is not a virtue in itself but a means to reduce complexity and to ease the understanding of a system. It therefore primarily depends on other goals of a system design what relationship suits the needs best.

Also the other question cannot be answered: is a hierarchic structure always superior to non-hierarchic structures? H. A. Simon (1969) notes that hierarchic structures as observed in biological, social, economical and technical systems belong to the most common and the most stable structures. But similar to what we can see in social systems, we observe that in programming the strict obeyance of a hierarchic discipline often leads to huge overheads in transmitting information from one member of the system to another. This overhead may be sometimes be deadly to the purpose of the system. (It is of course questionable whether such an overhead is a consequence of imposing a hierarchy at all or merely a hint that an unsuitable relationship has been used in establishing the hierarchy.)

Abstract Machines

By strengthening the relationship of the "uses"-hierarchy such that if A uses B and A is on level i then B is precisely on level i-1 (but not lower), we get the relationship between abstract machines which we considered earlier. We may illustrate this structure by the following example.

Given a problem which we solve by writing a Pascal program. We then must additionally supply an implementation of Pascal on our computer. Hence our Pascal program is only a reduction of the original problem P_0 to the problem P_1, the implementation of a compiler and a runtime system for Pascal. On a microcomputer the runtime system may be implemented directly, incorporating routines for storage allocation, storage access, e.g. addressing of multidimensional arrays, input/output and standard functions. In a multiprogrammed environment we may run programs written in several high-level languages simultaneously. Thus we have to implement several runtime systems. Each of these reduces a problem of type P_1 to the problem P_2 of implementing a resource allocation scheme for distributing the available resources among the submitted programs and their runtime system. P_2 is solved by the operating system.

This example exhibits the following properties:

— The original problem P_0 is solved not by one program but by a number of program layers L_1, L_2, L_3: Pascal program, runtime system, operating system.

— Each such layer L_i solves a problem P_{i-1} on the basis of some programming tools. These tools together constitute an abstract machine and are described as problem P_i. The final abstract machine P_3 is given by hardware.

— Except that every layer implements the tools for the foregoing one, the layers are independent from each other. As long as we do not consider detailed questions of efficiency we are not concerned about the implementation of the runtime system when we write a Pascal program. Conversely, when writing an operating system or a runtime system we are not concerned with properties of the Pascal programs for which we are supplying the tools.

The input data and commands for our original program L_1 appear in this context as the "program" which we run on the abstract machine P_0. This view, as strange as it may seem initially, is quite sound on many occasions. The uninitiated user wants to use the computer including its programs as a black box, as a machine which he may "program" by submitting data for solving his external problem. The fault is not on the part of this user but very often on the part of the programmer who forces the user to deal with internal details in which he is not interested.

Additionally we see that hierarchies of abstract machines may be nested. By considering the operating system or the whole computer including programs as one layer we do not preclude a more detailed view in which this layer is subdivided by intermediate interfaces representing additional abstract machines.

The Order of Design Decision

A hierarchic decomposition of a problem often is difficult to obtain. It may need several steps to arrive at it. Up to now we have suggested top-down design, the technique of starting at the problem and ending at the base system after several steps of refinement. We could, however, equally well start at the bottom level building the hierarchy from below.

Top-down design requires a precise specification of the problem, the definition of the topmost abstract machine. There are two difficulties with this approach. Firstly it may sometimes be very difficult in the beginning to specify the problem completely. For example, how can we define the detailed catalogue of system calls for an operating system before we have an idea of what the system will look like? Secondly some experience is necessary to define the intermediate abstract machines such that we actually can implement the last but one machine on the predefined base system. On the other hand top-down design is preferable if the base system is not yet completely fixed at the beginning of the design phase.

The second approach, bottom-up design, requires a precise specification of the base system on which we successively build higher abstract machines. In this case we may satisfy a variety of requests on the upper levels at once providing a suitable range of data structures and functions. In principle it does not matter when we have supplied more tools than actually needed by the next higher layer. Bottom-up design is therefore preferable if the problem statement still contains some degrees of variability which are only fixed later in the design. In a bottom-up design it is, however, much more difficult and requires much more experience to guarantee that an abstract machine is actually complete, i. e. it contains all structures and operations which are later on needed on the next level.

From the point of view of program validation it appears that top-down design is the obvious method for formally verifying a program. For testing and debugging the top-down approach requires that we are able to simulate the functions of the (not yet designed) underlying abstract machine for running a certain layer. The bottom-up approach on the other hand requires driving routines for testing a layer. The writing of driving routines is always possible while the simulation of an abstract machine is sometimes very costly. If, however, the simulation is possible then normally it is preferable over the bottom-up approach because it more easily allows to construct test cases.

Taking altogether it becomes clear that neither top-down nor bottom-up design is the best in all cases. In practice an approach known as "middle-out" is used: On the basis of previous experience a rough draft of the complete solution and its decomposition is made. This draft design is then detailed and verified in a top-down fashion. (For this reason everybody advocates top-down design.) Finally coding and testing proceed top-down or bottom-up depending on the problem and the available tools.

REFERENCES AND READING

Dahl O.J., Myhrhaug B. and Nygaard K.(1971), Simula 67 Common Base Language. Norwegian Computing Center, pub. S-22.

DeRemer F. and Kron H. (1975), Programming-in-the-Large versus Programming-in-the-Small. International Conference on Reliable Software Los Angeles.
Also: SIGPLAN Notices 10, 6, pp. 114-121, 1975

Goos G. (1972), Hierarchies.
In: F. L. Bauer (ed.): Software Engineering. An Advanced Course. Lecture Notes in Computer Science 30, Springer Verlag.

Goos G. (1982 a), The Software Life Cycle. (This volume).

Goos G. (1982 b), Design of Programs. (This volume).

Goos G. and Kastens U. (1978), Programming Languages and the Design of Modular Programs.
In: P.G. Hibbard, S. Schuman (eds.): Constructing Quality Software. Proceedings, North-Holland.

Guttag J.V. and Horning J.J. (1978), The Algebraic Specification of Abstract Data Types.
Acta Informatica 10, pp. 27-52.

Ichbiah J. D. et al. (1981), Ada Reference Manual. Lecture Notes in Computer Science, Vol. 106, Springer.

Liskov B.H. and Zilles S. (1975), Specification Techniques for Data Abstractions. International Conference on Reliable Software Los Angeles.
Also: SIGPLAN Notices 10, 6, pp. 72-87, 1975

Majster M.E. (1977), Limits of the "Algebraic" Specification of Abstract Data Types.
SIGPLAN Notices 12, 10, pp. 37-42.

Parnas D.L. (1971), Information distribution aspects of design methodologies.
IFIP Congress 1971, Ljubljana

Parnas D.L. (1972a), A Technique for Software Module Specification with Examples.
CACM 15, 5, pp. 330-336.

Parnas D.L. (1972b), On the criteria to be used in decomposing Systems into Modules.
CACM 15, 12, pp. 1053-1058.

Parnas D.L. (1974), On a "Buzzword": Hierarchical Structure.
Information Processing 74, North-Holland.

Simon H.A. (1969), The Science of the Artificial. MIT Press.

Wulf M., London R.L., Shaw M. (1975), Abstraction and Verification in Alphard.
In: S. Schumann (ed.): New directions in algorithmic languages.
IFIP WG 2.1 Working Conference Munich. Published by IRIA, Rocquencourt, 1976

Wulf W.A. (1976), Structured Programming in the Basic Layers of an Operating System.
In: F.L. Bauer, K. Samelson (eds.): Language Hierarchies and Interfaces. Lecture Notes in Computer
Science 46, Springer Verlag.

PROGRAMMING LANGUAGES AND STYLE

Peter Poole
University of Melbourne
Parkville, Australia

1. INTRODUCTION

The main function of a programming language is to encode the algorithms developed during the design process as a program which can be executed by the computer to produce the desired results. Another but no less important function is to enable algorithms to be communicated amongst people in as precise and exact a manner as possible. Programs must be understandable by people as well as by machines. The early programming languages were rather close to the language of the machine and proved to be very error prone so that achieving a high degree of reliability was extremely difficult. Programs written in such languages were hard to comprehend and programmers had to make extensive use of comments in order to transmit their algorithms to other people. Modern assembly languages still suffer from these defects. With the development of the high level language based on well defined syntax and semantics, programmers were provided with a tool which, in addition to increasing productivity, enabled them to create more reliable and understandable programs. Unfortunately not all languages are equal in allowing these goals to be achieved. Thus, the language chosen for a particular project and the way in which it is used can have a considerable impact on the quality of the final product.

Programs written to be shared by a community of users on a number of different machines must be of the highest quality, in particular, they must be reliable, portable and easy to understand and maintain. Too often, a language is used in a particular project for reasons other than to achieve these qualities, for example, assembly language to maximize efficiency, some high level language because it happens to be available on the local machine and the programmers are familiar with it. That is not to say that programmers should not be well skilled in the use of the language adopted for the project but it should only be one of the factors taken into account when the choice is made - it should not be the overriding one. If portability is a major objective, then the existence of compilers on machines other than the one

D. T. Muxworthy (ed.), Programming for Software Sharing, 49–68.

on which the software is to be developed must be taken into consideration; if highly reliable software is required, a language which enhances the ability of programmers to write correct programs should be the preferred one; if it is expected that the software will have a long lifetime and be frequently modified and enhanced, then the ease with which programs expressed in the language can be understood by other people will be of primary concern. The choice of a language for the development of shared software is not an easy one and requires very careful consideration.

The manner in which a language is used can impact greatly the quality of the final program. If programmers have not developed an acceptable style, then the resulting programs will be far less understandable than they should be and much more likely to contain residual errors. Good style can be developed through education and exposure to the work of others whose style is considered of a sufficiently high quality to serve as model in much the same way as one teaches students to develop an appropriate style for using a natural language. To some extent, the style used by an individual programmer may be improved by ensuring that the appropriate software tools are available. Some tools can help a programmer to develop a good style; other tools can be used to reject code where the style is unacceptable.

2. CHOOSING THE LANGUAGE

The choice of the language used for a particular project is influenced by many factors, some of which may be outside the control of the programmer. However, in selecting a language, consideration must be given to the following qualities and characteristics.

(a) *ease of learning:* if programmers are to write reliable programs, then they must be thoroughly conversant with the language they are using. They must understand every construct and know what behaviour to expect when it is incorporated in a program. This implies that the language should be simple and well supported by programming texts and language manuals. "Large" languages such as PL/I or Ada with a multiplicity of features require programmers to have had considerable experience in using the language before they can master it completely. Even then, the probability of introducing an error through the misunderstanding of a particular construct is much higher than for a smaller language such as Pascal.

Another factor which impacts the ease of learning a language is the orthogonality of the language design. The more orthogonal the design, the fewer the restrictions a programmer has to remember about what he can or cannot do with a particular construct. For example, in Fortran, any subroutine may call any other subroutine except itself; the number of dimensions of an array is restricted to 3 (in Fortran 66) and the programmer cannot exceed this limit even though the algorithm to solve a particular problem quite naturally makes use of arrays of more than 3 dimensions; while arrays of reals or integers are permitted, arrays of arrays are not; the assignment of a value to an index variable in an assigned GOTO statement must be carried out via an ASSIGN statement and not with the normal assignment operator. None of these restrictions apply in Pascal — recursive use of procedures is supported; there is no restriction on the number of dimensions of an array; the elements of an array may be arrays or records as well as variables of primitive types; values are assigned to the selection variable of a CASE statement using the assignment operator. Thus the design of Pascal is more orthogonal than that of Fortran and a programmer has to remember fewer restrictions. That is not to say that Pascal is completely orthogonal — there are irritating restrictions in that language as well. For example, one can read and write integers, reals, booleans and characters but not variables of enumerated type: arrays may be assigned and compared but not input or output without statements which use the dimensions of the structure explicitly.

The ease with which a programmer learns a language and acquires mastery over its constructs can depend on the way in which he has been introduced to the art of computer programming and the languages with which he is already familiar. Thus Fortran programmers can become very irritated and uncomfortable with the verbosity of Cobol: programmers trained in Cobol can become confused with the mathematical notations and restrictions of Basic. There is now considerable observational evidence to suggest that the most appropriate introductory language for the teaching of programming is Pascal and most educational establishments throughout the world have adopted this practice. Programmers trained initially in Pascal will write "better" Fortran and Cobol when faced with these languages in a real world situation. Unfortunately, the reverse is not true. When Fortran programmers are confronted with Pascal, they tend to write "Fortral", that is, Fortran constructs expressed in the Pascal language. They must be re-educated in order to be able to take full advantage of the unfamiliar but more powerful features of that language. The same probably holds true in any situation where a programmer moves from one high level language to another more powerful one.

(b) *fault avoidance:* some languages are much more error prone than others. High level languages by virtue of a well defined syntax and semantics are less likely to allow a programmer to write erroneous code than an assembly language where there is little or no restriction on what the programmer can do. Amongst high level languages themselves, there are variations with regard to how easy it is to make an error. Fortran for example by not enforcing the rule that a variable must be declared before it is used permits subtle errors to be introduced which can be quite difficult to detect. The COMMON and EQUIVALENCE facilities of that language are other examples of constructs which are a prolific source of errors. Although one can justify their introduction into the language on the grounds of efficiency of memory utilization, the situation which exists today, in view of the falling hardware costs, is such that the dangers associated with using them are no longer warranted.

Some of the newer languages have been designed with a view to improving reliability. Pascal, for example, permits the programmer to express the intent of what he wants to do much more rigorously than does Fortran. In this language, it is possible to define new types in addition to the primitive types provided in the basic definition. Thus, the type definition

TYPE DAYSOFWEEK = (MON, TUE, WED, THUR, FRI, SAT, SUN)

defines a new scalar type which may then be used in variable declarations. Variables of type DAYSOFWEEK may only take on the values enumerated in the list above. The only operations permitted on such variables are comparison and assignment.

Although Pascal provides programmers with greater protection than other languages against making mistakes, it is not without its deficiencies. For example, a semi-colon is used as a statement separator rather than as a terminator. This apparently trivial difference in a rule can lead to orders of magnitude difference in the number of errors. Some programmers find it exceedingly difficult to decide whether to include a semi-colon or not. Of course the errors are usually minor ones and quite easily removed at compile time. Nevertheless it is another source of faults. These lessons about terminators versus separators have been well-learned and, in Ada, the semi-colon is used as a terminator. Other problems arise with the assignment operator ": = ". People are used to writing " = " in mathematics and Fortran and there is therefore a tendency to use this symbol for assignment. Other problems can occur because of operator precedence. Thus it would appear to be quite natural to write a boolean expression of the form:

$$a < 3 \text{ and } b > d$$

However, this would be invalid in Pascal since the binding of "and" is higher than that of relational operators. To be acceptable, the relations must be enclosed in parentheses. In a language like APL where there is a wealth of operators and expressions are evaluated from right to left, prior experience with other languages on the part of the programmer can be detrimental to the writing of correct expressions. There is some experimental evidence (Gannon and Horning 1975) which suggests that familiarity with left-to-right evaluation and operator precedence can make it extremely difficult to find expression evaluation errors in languages which adopt some other convention.

(c) *fault detection:* one of the many advantages of using a high level language is that checks can be applied at compile time and errors detected before the program enters the run time phase. The earlier an error can be detected during the development of software, the easier and cheaper it is to correct. Consider the example given in the previous section. If STARTDAY and FINISHDAY are variables of the above type, then the expression

STARTDAY * FINISHDAY

is meaningless and would be flagged at compile time as an error. Now, it is obvious that we could have mapped the days of the week onto integers in Fortran and still performed comparisons and assignments. However, the above expression, now involving variables of type INTEGER, would be compiled and executed, perhaps giving rise to some erroneous results. The philosophy behind the design of languages such as Pascal and Ada is that as many mistakes as possible should be detected at compile time as syntax errors, rather than at some later stage. A certain amount of redundancy is required in a language to facilitate this error checking. Thus variables must be declared before they are used and their types specified. Spelling errors in identifiers or attempts to apply illegal operators to objects of a given type can then easily be detected. The gains in productivity using a typed versus a non-typed language have been demonstrated in a number of experiments. Gannon (1977) found that twice as many runs were required to complete programs for relatively simple tasks when these were written in a typeless language compared with a typed language. There were also fewer errors in the submitted programs in the typed case.

Redundancy does not always help with error detection. Since it tends to lengthen a program, it increases the chance of introducing an error somewhere in the text. Thus there must be a trade-off so that redundant features are advantageous and do not cause more errors than they prevent. Redundancy has sometimes been introduced into a language more as an aid to the compiler writer than the programmer. Thus the COMMON feature of Fortran and the external attribute of PL/1 require the programmer to duplicate information in order to support independent compilation of procedures. Such information is redundant but if the programmer makes an error in duplicating the information, then the fault may not be observed until run time. Ideally such declarations and type specifications should only be made once, irrespective of how many separately compiled procedures refer to them.

While it is preferable to detect errors at the compile time if possible, run time checks may also be used to report on faults. Again some languages have better support for these facilities than others. Consider the subrange definition in Pascal

TYPE INDEX = 0..63

This implies that variables of type INDEX will never take on values outside the range 0 to 63. Thus the assignment statement

SELECT := 64

where SELECT is a variable of type INDEX will cause the compiler to generate a syntax error. On the other hand, the statement

SELECT := SELECT + 1

cannot be checked at compile time since there is no way of determining the value of SELECT before the addition is performed. It may be the result of some other calculation or it may have been read in from input. However, the compiler can generate code to check at run time that the value of SELECT does not fall outside the specified limits. Similarly array subscripts can be checked to be within array bounds and case selectors within case bounds. The cost of run time checks can be very high and many millions of operations may have to be carried out before an error is detected. Some compilers enable these checks to be turned on or off as required. Whether the overhead is warranted will depend on the degree of reliability required and the cost of a fault occuring. A possible strategy is to use run time checks during program development and deactivate them when the software is placed in production. The decision as to whether to continue with such checks or not will probably depend on economic considerations.

(d) *understandability:* programs should be written in such a way as to facilitate communication with people as well as with machines. It is not sufficient to have an algorithm expressed as a program which will compile and execute correctly but which is incomprehensible to other programmers. The need to be able to understand programs arises from two main requirements:

(i) errors in a program can be much more readily detected by humans reading the text if the program can be easily understood.

(ii) a program may have a life perhaps of many years and during that time it is unlikely to remain unchanged. Thus persons other than the originator of the software may have to make enhancements, correct errors, etc. and for this purpose, they must be able to read and comprehend the program text.

Many of the features of programming languages which determine the readability of programs expressed in it are discussed later in the section on programming style. Length of identifiers, manifest constants, user-defined types, data structures, modularity, program layout, powerful control structures, all contribute, if used properly, to making a program comprehensible to others. Suffice to say, that programs written in Pascal or Ada are more easily understood than those in Fortran or Cobol which in turn provide better facilities for writing understandable programs than assembly languages. One might be led to conjecture that the more powerful a language, the more easily one can understand an algorithm expressed in it. However, such is not always the case. APL, for example, which contains many operators and enables complex data structures to be manipulated very easily can be used to construct very obscure programs. APL addicts take a great delight in creating ''one-liners'' which although extremely powerful are often almost incomprehensible. There is an obvious analogy with natural language. The meaning one derives from a piece of text is not necessarily a function of its brevity, the complexity of its sentences and the size of the words used. The structure, the logical organization of the arguments, the careful choice and use of words are much more important in conveying meaning to the readers. Programs should be as readable and as understandable as a book. They should contain the equivalent of sentences, paragraphs, chapters, table of contents and a cross reference index. Intelligent use of a programming language supplemented where necessary by natural language in the form of comments can help to achieve this goal.

(e) *maintainability:* the influence of a programming language on maintainability is primarily through understandability. The more comprehensible the program, the easier it will be to correct residual errors or add new features providing the program structure can readily support enhancements. However, the programming language can impact maintainability in other ways; for example, a language which supports a constant declaration mechanism provides the programmer with a very safe way of contructing his program so that it can be easily modified simply by changing the value of a constant. Type definitions of languages like Pascal and Ada also facilitate maintenance. Thus values can be added to or removed from an enumerated type list without requiring a remapping of values. The layout of a record can be altered simply by modifying the record definition. Data structures which depend on this definition are all adjusted automatically by recompilation. However, in a language such as Fortran, if the data structure required naturally to solve a problem is an array of records, then this would have to be mapped onto perhaps a number of arrays. An alteration to the layout of the record would undoubtedly require much more substantial changes to the code.

Another important facility to simplify the task of maintenance is independent compilation of modules. ''Standard'' Pascal does not support this and although the feature has been added to most versions of the language, nevertheless, in principle, if one wished to modify a program written in Pascal, then the whole of the program would need to be recompiled. While not impossible, it could be expensive and time consuming.

The most advanced language with regard to maintenance is Ada which not only supports independent compilation but also permits the specification of a module to be separated from the module itself. Such a structuring unit is called a ''package''. Providing the package body always conforms to the specification, then it may be changed without any changes being required to the calling sequence or even requiring that the using module be recompiled. Typically, a package consists of data structures and the procedures which provide access to the data. The specification describes the facilities provided by the package and the body is the implementation of those facilities. As an example, consider a package for manipulating stacks. A possible specification might be

```
package stack is
      procedure push (x:real);
      function pop return real;
end;
```

This provides access to the subroutines "push" and "pop" which place an item on a stack or take one off respectively. Nothing is specified as to how a stack is implemented. This depends on the package body. It might be that the stack is implemented as a linear array with an index defining the current top of stack or as a linked list or even via basic hardware instructions if the machine architecture supports such a facility. The module which uses the package need not concern itself with the method of implementation; its view of the package is simply as a mechanism for manipulating a stack data structure.

(f) *efficiency:* attitudes towards efficiency have varied tremendously over the years, influenced largely for the falling costs of hardware and the significant increases in resources available on a given machine. Thus, the goal of the original programmers was to write code as efficiently as possible in order to maximize the utilization of a scarce and expensive resource whether it be CPU time or memory. The only choice was machine language and indeed the initial developments of high level languages like Fortran were resisted strongly by some people who felt that the resultant programs would be too wasteful of machine resources. Today we have a situation where hardware is cheap but software is expensive. Thus we should choose languages to minimize the software costs and be less concerned about maximizing hardware utilization. Assembly language should be avoided since it is now well recognized that it is the most expensive language to use even if it produces the most efficient programs. There are of course circumstances where speed is still of the essence, for example, in real-time systems where it may be necessary to guarantee that an interrupt can be serviced in some minimum period of time. Here it may still be necessary to use assembly code but only for those time-critical sections. The remainder of the system should be written in some high level language chosen for other reasons.

There is usually an inverse correlation between the power of a language and the efficiency of the resulting object code. The more complex a particular language construct, the more difficult it is for the compiler writer to generate efficient code. The mismatch between the abstract machine defined by the language and the real machine is too great to permit efficient mapping. In some cases, for example APL, the mismatch is so great that the abstract machine has to be interpreted rather than be mapped directly. One has to pay for the power of the language by using more machine cycles. However, the situation is one which is changing all the time as new machines appear. Many of the newer architectures contain hardware facilities specifically designed to support high level language constructs efficiently - recursive procedure calls, stacks, access to records, vector operations etc. There exist machines which are designed to support specific languages. The most well known of these is the Burroughs range of computers which was designed with the Algol language in mind. The new Intel 32-bit microprocessor is reported to have been designed as an efficient machine for the execution of programs written in Ada.

(g) *portability:* for software to be shared effectively, it must be portable, that is, it must be capable of operating in environments different from the one in which it was developed initially. This includes different machines and hence rules out the use of assembly languages except through interpretation. This has the disadvantage that there is a considerable overhead associated with simulating one computer on another. Thus the portability of software written in a high level language depends upon the availability of the appropriate compilers on the target machine or at least on the existence of a compiler which is itself portable and which can be moved easily to new machines at a cost far less than that required to produce it initially.

If portability js an overriding consideration for a given piece of software, particularly where the target machines are not known, then the most appropriate language is probably Fortran in spite of its deficiencies in other areas. Fortran compilers exist for a wide range of machines, from micros to main frames and across all manufacturers. If the language used is a subset of standard Fortran and certain features which are known to vary slightly from one implementation to another are avoided, then the probability of being able to transport such a program to a large number of different machines is very high. Such is not the case for Pascal partly because it is a much more recent language and partly because no international standard for the language exists as yet. Thus there are many variations of the Pascal language and this impacts portability. However the situation is improving all the time. An ISO standard for Pascal is expected to be adopted in 1982-83 and the number of implementations of Pascal compilers is increasing. As many of these are based on the original compiler developed by Wirth on the CDC6600, there are fewer differences between the various implementations than would be the case if all compilers had simply been developed from the language definition by independent compiler groups.

Many of the problems encountered when software is moved to a different machine occur in the interface between the programs and the operating system, i.e. the run time environment. Although the program might compile successfully, correct execution is not possible because of the way it is linked to the remainder of the system. Input-output is one particularly troublesome area. One solution to the problem is to make the operating system itself portable. Two highly successful projects of this type are UCSD Pascal and UNIX. The former is written almost entirely in Pascal with the compiler producing an intermediate language called P-code which is interpreted on the host machine. All that is required to move the system to a new machine is to implement an interpreter in machine language for the P-code. Once this is operational then the whole of the operating system, compilers, utilities and applications software can be moved. Since most of the implementations are designed for single user operation on a micro, the penalties incurred by interpretation are acceptable. The UNIX system on the other hand is designed for multi-user operation and hence efficiency is an important consideration. About 95% of the operating system together with the associated software is written in C, a high level language developed for systems programming. The C compiler itself is portable and can be implemented on a new target machine by rewriting the code generator phase, an exercise which requires a few man months of effort. After this has been completed, the operating system kernel must be implemented before the remainder of the system is moved. Again the effort involved is of the order of a few man months. Originally developed for the PDP11 range of machines, UNIX has been ported to the VAX 11/780, Perkin Elmer 3200 series and the Z8000 and

M68000 micros amongst others. The C compiler itself is even more widespread and the C language is one which must be considered if portability is a goal particularly for systems type applications or where the target machine is a micro. It offers many of the advantages of other high level languages whilst still enabling the programmer to access low level features of a machine, e.g. bit manipulation, operations on registers. When using C in UNIX, one has access to a superb set of tools for the development of software, e.g. editors, symbolic debuggers, filters, file utilities and software management systems. It represents one of the most advanced development environments available today.

An interesting question as yet unanswered is how portable programs in Ada will be? Since the language was developed primarily for the implementation of embedded systems, that is, computers which function as part of some more complex system, the problem of cross compilers had to be faced from the very beginning. Since Ada is such a large language, a reasonably powerful machine will be required to support a compiler for it. Clearly considerable attention has been given to the requirements of portability in the design of the language. The environment enquiry facility means that a program can adapt its own behaviour to the characteristics of the machine on which it is operating; the package concept means that low level modules can readily be replaced without affecting the remainder of the system; the properties of the support environment have been defined in some detail and this will facilitate the development of such systems over a range of machines with identical functional characteristics; the comprehensive validation suite being developed in parallel with the first compilers will mean that compiler implementations can be very thoroughly checked out; subsets and language variations have been forbidden or at least cannot be called Ada. In theory, programs written in Ada should be extremely portable - it remains to be seen what will happen in practice.

3. USING THE LANGUAGE

Once the language for a particular project has been selected, it is still necessary to ensure that it is used correctly in order to achieve the desired goals. It must be stressed, however, that no matter how powerful the language and how skillfully it is used, nothing can compensate for poor design or incomplete specifications. The encoding of the algorithm is the final stage in the software development process to achieve something which at least can be tested on a computer. If the requirements analysis and specification have not been carried out correctly or if the design has not been formulated in a logical and consistent manner, then the resultant program is unlikely to meet its acceptance criteria. The main factors which affect the way a language is used correctly are

      (a) familiarity with the language

      (b) programming style

      (c) use of tools.

Language Familiarity

It may seem like stating the obvious to say that programmers must be completely familiar with a language before they can use it to develop software which is destined to be shared. Unfortunately, all too often, "familiarity" means being conversant with the characteristics of the language as defined in the manufacturer's programming manual. The ignorance displayed by the programming community about the existence of language standards is appalling. Organizations such as the American National Standards Institute (ANSI) and the International Standards Organization (ISO) publish language definitions which have been accepted world wide. International standards exist for Fortran and Cobol; standards are currently being developed for Pascal and a draft version has been published. Awareness of a standard and familiarity with what it contains can help to make software more shareable in a number of ways.

(i) *Avoidance of language extensions:* Most manufacturers add extra facilities to their language processors which, although often quite useful in allowing the programmer to exploit the particular features of their machines, usually cause problems when the software is moved to another environment. Such extensions render the language non-standard and familiarity with the standard will enable the programmer to avoid them, irrespective of how attractive they might be. Often, non-standard features will simply fail to compile on a different machine. However, sometimes the error is much more subtle so that the program compiles and executes in the new environment but produces the wrong results. As an example, consider mixed mode in Fortran which is not permitted by the standard. Suppose a program which makes use of mixed mode is developed on a system where the compiler, when evaluating an arithmetic expression, only converts from integer to real when it encounters a real operand. If this program is moved to another environment where the compiler first scans an expression to determine the dominant mode, then the results obtained from executing the program may differ from the original ones. The reason for the discrepancy may be very difficult to determine.

(ii) *Avoidance of "undefined" features:* Sometimes standard documents are rather vague about a particular feature in a language or omit discussion about it altogether. The compiler writer must then make a decision during implementation as to how the feature will be handled by the compiler and this may vary from one implementation to another. An excellent illustration of this problem is the computed GOTO in Fortran. The standard states that the value of the index variable cannot exceed the number of statement numbers in the GOTO. However, it says nothing about what action is to take place when the index variable is outside the allowed range. Myers (1976) reports that five compilers from different manufacturers generated five different actions for the statements

        I = 5
        GOTO (11, 12, 13, 14), I

One compiler generated a wild branch, two others generated branches to statements 11 and 14 respectively, a fourth skipped to the statement after the GOTO, while the fifth treated the situation as an error and terminated the program. Programs developed in any of the first four systems would have produced different results when executed on one of the others, thereby affecting reliability. Since the standard gives no guide as to what to do when the index is out of range, the programmer must take steps to check for that situation by inserting the appropriate code so that the behaviour of the program is the same whatever course of action the compiler takes.

Familiarity with a language being used to develop portable software also implies some knowledge about how a feature not described in the standard but essential to any implementation is implemented in a variety of different systems. Care can then be taken in using such a facility so that modifications to make the software operate on another system are relatively straightforward to carry out. Familiarity can also mean some idea of the cost of using a particular facility. Whilst efficiency must not be the overriding concern nevertheless some idea of the overheads incurred in using a particular construct might make the software less expensive on machine resources and more acceptable to other users. For example, recursion is a particularly powerful and elegant programming construct which can be less prone to error than iteration. On the other hand, there can be very extensive overheads associated with recursive calls of procedures. An iterative solution to the problem may be far more efficient without being all that more difficult to understand and program reliably.

Programming Style

Programming style is often considered to be a matter of personal choice. However, over the years, various guidelines and recommendations have been developed and there is a growing consensus of opinion that anyone who follows these is less likely to make errors and hence more likely to write reliable code. Some of these proposals are discussed below.

(i) *Identifiers:* Careful choice of identifiers can greatly improve the readability of a program and hence increase the probability of locating an error or facilitate the addition of extra features. Names should be chosen to be meaningful and understandable, not too short and not too long. A recommended range is from 4 to 12 characters. Sometimes this is not possible since the language itself restricts the length of an identifier, as for example in Fortran; sometimes too long an identifier may give rise to a subtle error when the program is moved to a new environment. If the language definition specifies nothing about the length of identifiers, then the compiler writer must make a decision as to how many characters will be examined to determine whether the identifier is unique or not. In the CDC Pascal compiler, only the first 10 characters of an identifier are considered significant; in other Pascal compilers on byte oriented machines, identifiers are often distinguished on the basis of the first 8 characters. Thus, for a program developed on a CDC computer, identifiers which only differ from the ninth character onwards will be treated as identical when the program is compiled in another environment. The moral is to avoid using similar names which make programs difficult to read anyway and can lead to coding errors. When selecting meaningful names, one should ensure that there is a high degree of dissimilarity particularly in the first 6 - 8 characters.

The choice of a meaningful name sometimes leads quite naturally to the inclusion of digits in the identifier. The numerals "0" and "1" should be avoided since they are all too easily confused with the letters "O" and "I"; care must be taken if the numerals "2" and "5" are used not to have them mistaken for the letters "Z" and "S" respectively. As a general rule, if digits are to be included, they should be placed at the end of the identifier and not in the middle.

Finally, never under any circumstances should a language keyword be used as an identifier irrespective of how appropriate it might be for the particular application. For example, the Fortran statement

    10 FORMAT(1) = J(1)

could be a valid assignment statement and not just an invalid FORMAT statement as one might expect. Use of keywords as identifiers defined by the user just confuses the reader.

(ii) *Constants:* A constant in a program is an object whose value does not change throughout the course of the computation. Some are true constants in the sense that their value is always the same, e.g. **pi**, **e**, etc. In other cases, the value may alter during the lifetime of a program, e.g. the size of a table. All too frequently, programmers embed constant values in the body of a program and these can be widely distributed. When the value has to be changed because of some new requirement, it is necessary to scan the text carefully changing all such occurrences. This is a potential source of error since either some occurrences will be overlooked or, alternatively, some other constant with the same value will be altered erroneously. It is good practice to gather together all constants used in a program at one particular place in the text and assign an identifier to each value. When a change has to be made, it only has to be carried out once and one can remain confident that the desired effect will occur at all relevant places in the code. Some languages such as Pascal and Fortran 77 provide facilities for defining constants and guarantee that no constant value will be changed during execution; Fortran 66, on the other hand, has no such constructs. However, DATA statements do permit values to be associated with names although there is no protection against inadvertent alteration.

Writers of portable software must take special precautions to ensure that machine dependent values are declared as named constants and clearly marked and documented as such, so it is a simple matter to alter the value when the program is moved to a new machine. Where appropriate, constant identifiers should be used in declarations as well as in executable statements, for example, when declaring the size of an array. There may be limitations imposed by the hardware on the size of such structures in a particular environment and it is essential that the program can be modified easily and safely.

(iii) *Variables:* A frequent source of errors in Fortran programs comes from the fact that variables do not have to be declared. Thus, a spelling error in a variable identifier causes a new variable to be defined although this situation can usually be detected if one uses a cross-reference generator. Sometimes it can give rise to extremely subtle errors. All variables should be declared at the beginning of the module in which they are to be used, even in Fortran. Further, the type of all variables should be stated explicitly; using the implicit typing of Fortran dependent on the first letter of an identifier is not a recommended practice. In languages such as Pascal which permit the programmer to define new types, an effort should be made to take full advantage of this facility, thereby improving the probability of detecting errors at compile time rather than at run time. The readability and understandability of the program are also greatly improved.

Use of explicit type definitions can also help to avoid problems which arise from the way a particular data type is mapped onto a machine word. Suppose a program developed on a machine where the compiler generates 32-bit integers is moved to one where integers are only 16 bits long. If the program now fails, it may be suspected that the different representations for integers are the cause of the trouble. In Fortran, all integer variables are candidates for examination. However, if a Pascal programmer has made sensible use of integer subrange types, then only those variables which could take on values outside the capacity of the 16-bit machine need to be checked. What is more, Pascal provides the programmer with a convenient way of utilizing fault detection techniques in such a situation by making available the maximum value an integer variable may take in a particular system.

The manner in which data aggregates such as arrays and records are mapped onto the memory of the machine and accessed may also affect reliability. In some systems, the COMMON variables in Fortran are mapped in ascending order of addresses whilst in others descending order is used. Thus a program which makes implicit assumptions about the order will fail when moved from one system to another. In Pascal, the problem can be easily handled by ensuring that run time checks on attempts to access outside the bounds of an array are activated.

Another problem area connected with the use of variables is initialization. Very few systems have facilities for detecting uninitialized variables. Thus, a program which behaves unpredictably from one run to another or when moved to a new environment may contain a variable which is never set initially and whose value depends on whatever was left in the corresponding memory location by the previous program. Some operating systems clear memory to zero before loading a program whilst others do not. Thus a working program which behaves unreliably when operating in a new environment may be responding to the effects of a variable whose initial value is being set randomly. Some software tools exist which will analyze a Fortran program to determine whether a variable occurs in the left-hand side of an assignment operator or in an input statement before its value is used in an expression. This can give a warning about the possible occurrence of an uninitialized variable. A somewhat similar probem can arise with local variables in a Fortran subroutine where the variable is initialized the first time the routine is called. The language definition states that on exit from the subroutine, local variables shall become undefined. However in most implementations, the variable retains its value and there is nothing to stop the programmer from making use of it during subsequent executions of the subroutine. If this program is then moved to another environment where the underlying storage allocation mechanism is different, then unreliable behaviour may occur.

Questions of efficiency can influence the way variables are used in a program, sometimes to the detriment of reliability. Thus, programmers are often tempted to economize on the storage required by using the same variable for two different purposes. Apart from the fact that the identifier is likely to be meaningful for only one of the instances, the practice increases the chance of introducing an error when modifying the program. Using special values of a variable to indicate special situations such as a failure is not recommended. In a similar vein, using the same store space with different names as, for example, in Fortran via an EQUIVALENCE statement, is to be avoided wherever possible. The saving in storage may not justify the extra effort required to debug the program. Desire to improve execution efficiency sometimes leads programmers to make such heavy use of temporary variables that the algorithm is obscured and difficult to comprehend. Temporary variables reduce readability since they introduce more detail into the program which the reader must deal with in order to understand the algorithm. The few micro-seconds saved are often not worth the increased complexity.

Another aspect of the usage of variables which must be taken into account in the creation of reliable and understandable programs is scope. For example, excessive and unnecessary use of global variables is considered detrimental to achieving these qualities and hence poor programming style. A global variable is highly visible and can be accessed from any routine in a program. Thus, if an error occurs because a global variable contains an incorrect value, then all procedures are candidates for examination to determine the source of the faulty code. If, on the other hand, the scope of the variable can be restricted to just that part of the program where it is required, then the size of the region to be searched is reduced. This is an example of "information hiding" (Parnas 1972) which states that a variable should only be accessible to those parts of the program which depend on it. Unnecessary accessibility merely increases the probability of introducing an error. Unfortunately, in a language such as Fortran, which has no block structure or hierarchy of procedures, one is forced to make far more extensive use of global variables than is really necessary. A subroutine can only access its own local variables or global ones - it cannot access variables local to other subroutines. In Pascal where one can declare nested procedures, access to variables can be made to ones local to the procedure in which the procedure containing the reference is declared, i.e. references outside the procedure are not restricted to global variables alone. Thus one is not forced to declare shared variables as global. The appropriateness of the position where a variable is declared is determined by the module structure of the program. The principle of information hiding has been a guiding one in the design of the Ada programming language. The package construct ensures that the writer of a module need expose to the calling environment only those variables which are required to use a module correctly. The need for global variables is thereby greatly reduced.

(iv) *Expressions:* In most languages, the evaluation of expressions occurs from left to right and takes into account operator precedence. Unfortunately the precedence relations differ from one language to another and thus it is easy for a programmer to become confused. A simple rule is that, whenever there is any doubt, parentheses should be used to remove any possibility of ambiguity.

Certain types of arithmetic operators can produce different results on different machines and programmers should take extra care in such situations. Integer arithmetic provides a good example. The expression:

$$2 * I / 2$$

where I is an integer may or may not be equal to I depending on whether the compiler generates the code for the multiply operation before that for the division. If the division is executed first, the expression will only be equal to I if I is even. Operations on real operands may also have to be handled with care if there is a possibility that the program will be moved. Thus the expression

$$A * (B - C)$$

may produce on a particular machine a very different result from

$$(A * B) - (A * C)$$

if B and C are nearly equal in value whereas on another machine with a higher accuracy the two results would be the same.

In evaluating boolean expressions involving AND and OR, a compiler on one machine might generate code to cause all of the operands to be evaluated completely whereas, in another system, the code may include a conditional transfer of control to bypass further evaluations once the final value of the expression is known. Thus, an operand involves a call to a function with side-effects, different results will occur in the two cases. While it is recommended that creating functions with side-effects should be avoided, nevertheless in some situations, they can be quite useful and hence any time they are incorporated in a program, great care must be taken to guard against possible errors.

The dangers of using mixed mode have already been mentioned in relation to language extension. However, even when permitted as a standard feature of the language, they should be avoided. Thus a programmer who introduces a boolean variable into an arithmetic expressions because he knows that true is represented by 1 and FALSE by 0 on a particular machine, is simply asking for trouble. Another compiler may generate a completely different representation. Similarly, although we know that characters are usually represented internally by small integers, arithmetic operations on characters variables should never be performed unless any underlying assumptions about the collation sequence are clearly stated. Languages such as Pascal provide standard functions to enable a program to convert from integer mode to character mode and back again. By using such functions, a programmer has some guarantee that his program will be invariant across machines.

(v) *Statements:* The assignment statement is a common feature of programming languages and generates few problems. It can be susceptible to side-effects when the left-hand side is an array element whose subscript is altered by a function called from the right-hand side. The address calculated to store the value will differ depending on whether it is computed before or after the right-hand side is evaluated. Mode conversion is also permitted in some languages. Pascal allows integers to be converted automatically to real before being stored but not the reverse; Fortran allows both. The question is then what value to store when a real is assigned to an integer? Unless the language specifies what happens exactly, it will be left up to the implementor of the compiler. Some writers express the view that excessive use of assignment statements can have a destructive effect on a program and tend to obscure its meaning. This point should be considered when one is contemplating the use of temporary variables to improve efficiency. Unnecessary and indiscriminate use of assignment statements is not considered to be good style.

Problems with selection statements have already been mentioned in relation to the computed GOTO in Fortran. Similar remarks apply to the Pascal CASE statement. Algol 68 on the other hand permits the programmer to nominate a statement to which control will be transferred if the selector is out of range. The arithmetic IF in Fortran is well known as a troublesome statement since it is very easy to make a mistake with it. Although the Fortran logical IF is not a particularly powerful statement, it should be used in preference. In Pascal and Algol 68, the IF-THEN-ELSE construct provides a much more powerful way of controlling program flow but it is not without its problems. Since there is no limitation on the statement following THEN, an ambiguity can arise due to the so-called "dangling ELSE". Although the language definitions resolve the conflict, nevertheless, care must be taken with reading and interpreting such constructions. Some writers suggest that for every THEN there should be a corresponding ELSE even if it followed by the null statement just to show that the alternative has been considered. There has also been some criticism about using deeply nested IF statements on the grounds that such "structured" programs are as complicated as their "unstructured" counterparts. To determine under what conditions a statement in the middle of such a construct is executed can be quite difficult. Thus considerations of good style dictate that such constructions should be avoided. Usually a nested IF can be replaced by a CASE statement which should be used for preference.

Problems with repetition statements can stem from the way in which the compiler implements them to obtain efficient operation. If the iteration variable of a DO or FOR statement is placed in a register before execution of the loop is initiated, then a subsequent attempt within the body of the loop to modify it may not be successful. In another situation where registers are not used, the alteration could take place. Thus, as a general rule, even if the language permits it, no attempt should be made to alter value of the iteration variable within the loop. The DO statement of Fortran 66 can give rise to some difficulties in understanding an algorithm since in most implementations it is always executed at least once even if the exit conditions are satisfied initially. Other languages provide a more logical construct which can cause execution of the controlled statement zero or more times, e.g. the FOR statement of Pascal and the DO statement of Fortran 77.

There has been a great deal of discussion in the literature in recent years about the merits of structured programming and the evils of using GOTO statements. This has led some programmers to attempt to write GOTO-less programs, in the process producing something which is quite difficult to comprehend. Indeed the use of the GOTO should be avoided wherever possible but not to the point of absurdity. In some situations, the GOTO is the only natural statement to use and programmers should not be frightened of including it. However, there is no doubt that in the past it has been used far too frequently and, in many cases, unnecessarily leading to a "spaghetti-like" structure in many programs. Where the language provides the appropriate control structures, they should be used in preference to explicit transfer of control; where it does not as, for example, in Fortran, then a systematic use of GOTO can still produce a structured program which is comprehensible to the reader. Structure in a program is something that comes from the design and not just from the avoidance of the GOTO.

Input-output statements are a particularly troublesome area in program portability. The best advice that can be given in relation to style is that wherever possible, one should encapsulate them in small procedures which can be readily changed to compensate for the differences between environments.

(vi) *Procedures:* Intelligent use of procedures is a key factor in producing well structured programs. Problems with respect to reliability arise mainly from the parameter passing mechanisms. For example, in Fortran, if a numeric constant is supplied as an actual parameter to a subroutine where the corresponding formal parameter occurs on the left-hand side of an assignment statement, then in some systems the value of the constant will be altered permanently; in other systems, it will remain unchanged. Thus, a program developed in the latter type of environment is likely to prove unreliable when moved to the former one. Good style therefore requires that assignment should never be permitted to formal parameters for which a constant could be an actual parameter. In Pascal, the problem does not arise, since it is necessary to declare variable parameters explicity and the error would be detected at compile time. Functions with side-effects have already been mentioned in several contexts as a potential source of trouble and good programming style dictates that they should be avoided if possible.

One aspect of the use of procedures which is influenced by style is the number of formal parameters. In most programming languages, the correspondence between actual and formal parameters is determined by position. Thus the more formal parameters in a procedure, the greater the probability of an error due to a transposition of actual parameters. Most language definitions say nothing about the maximum number of formal parameters permitted. The choice is left to the compiler writer who, if he imposes a limit, sets it well in excess of anything that reasonable programmers are going to need. A knowledge of what this limit is should never be exploited by a programmer since in addition to increasing the chance of introducing errors, there could also be an impact on portability, i.e. the compiler on the machine to which the software is being moved might use a smaller limit and the program would fail to compile. There is no recommended upper limit on the number of formal parameters that should be declared in a procedure. The situation is simply the more one uses, the higher the probability of an error occurring in a procedure call. Some languages are safer than others. Thus Pascal in requiring a user to declare the type of a formal parameter and whether it is input or input-output is safer than Fortran or Cobol. Further the number of formal parameters required can often be reduced by defining a suitable record without any loss of understanding. Since the type definition will only occur once, transposition errors cannot occur. Ada goes even further than Pascal by requiring a programmer to declare whether a formal parameter will be input or output or both. In the first case, the parameter acts as a local constant whose value is that of the corresponding actual parameter; in the second case, it acts as a local variable whose value is assigned to the corresponding actual parameter as a result of executing the procedure; in the last case, both access and assignment to the corresponding actual parameter are permitted. In the case of functions, only input parameters are allowed. Thus, by forcing the programmer to state very explicit how a procedure will use actual parameters, the probability of introducing errors is decreased. Further, as well as providing the conventional calling notation dependent on position, Ada allows the names of formal parameters to be associated with actual parameters in the procedure call. This redundant information not only improves the understandability of the code but also enables the programmer to guard against transposition errors. However, there is one aspect of the Ada procedure calling mechanism which does not contribute to improved reliability, namely, the ability to provide default actual parameters in the procedure heading. Thus, the number of actual parameters in the call does not have to equal the number of formal parameters in the declaration - default values are supplied for those omitted. Whilst this may be a convenience to the programmer, it is also a potential source of error since the fact that a programmer has omitted actual parameters cannot be detected at compile time. All default mechanisms suffer from this defect - reduced reliability in return for programmer convenience.

(vii) *Comments:* Assembly language programs need to be documented profusely in order to make them understandable; for programs written in a high-level language, the best documentation is a clearly visible structure with meaningful identifiers. Too many comments can be harmful since they tend to distract the reader and perhaps give him an incorrect understanding of how the code is actually working, i.e. they may say what the programmer intended to write and not what he has actually written. However, comments can be particularly valuable at the start of a procedure since they can be used to describe what the procedure does, what parameters it requires, what results it produces and what the meaning of each variable is.

Understanding the data structures in a program is the key to understanding the program itself.

(viii) *Structure:* The outcome of the application of a good programming style should be a "well-structured" program, readily understandable by man as well as machines. With regard to control structures and data structures, this, implies the repeated use of a small number of fundamental structures to create more complex ones. The main basic structures are:

(a) concatenation:	statement sequences, declaration lists, procedure sequences.
(b) selection:	conditional statements, variant data types.
(c) iteration:	for, do and while loops, vectors, lists.
(d) encapsulation:	blocks, records, packages.
(e) abstraction:	subprograms, data types.

A program which can be decomposed into these basic units is considered to be "well-structured"; one that cannot is likely to contain more residual errors and certainly will be less comprehensible to human readers. In addition to this logical structure, there is also a need to ensure that the program is "well-structured" with regard to appearance. If the visual structure reflects the underlying control and data structures, then the reader's ability to comprehend the underlying algorithm will be greatly enhanced.

Use of Tools

Correct use of a language is largely a matter of self-discipline on the part of the programmer. One cannot force someone to adopt a good programming style unless he is convinced that the results of his efforts will be the better for it. Education and exposure to the work of others considered to have a good style are the best means of ensuring that the members of a programming team will procedure programs of an acceptable level of quality. There are however some software tools which can assist in this process:

(i) *text editor:* a powerful text editor particularly one with repetitive facilities can be a very useful tool for the production of well written programs. Tasks for which it can be used are conversion of short identifiers into meaningful ones, checking for duplication of identifiers, updating of comments to ensure that they stay consistent with the code, rearranging the order of procedures so that logical groupings are maintained. The main function of such a tool is to assist the programmer in maintaining a program in as readable and understandable a form as possible.

(ii) *standard verifiers:* being familiar with a standard does not necessarily guarantee that a programmer will not make use of non-standard features - standard documents are often very difficult to read and interpret. Where appropriate, use can be made of software tools to check that the language used to write a program conforms to the standard. For example, some compilers have a standard check option which, if activated, will cause any non-standard feature to be flagged as an error. Another possibility is to use a standard verifier such as PFORT (Ryder, 1974) which will check any program to determine if it is written in standard Fortran. Since the verifier itself is written in standard Fortran, it is readily portable and available on many systems.

(iii) *program text formatter:* since the understandability of a program is enhanced if the layout of the text reveals the structure, a number of software tools have been developed for structured languages such as Pascal, C, etc. which will format the program text using an appropriate set of rules to control indentation. Even for Fortran, there exist programs which will improve the readability of the text for example, by reorganizing statement labels so that they are in ascending order within a subroutine and hence easily located. In other software tools, the facilities of editors and formatters are combined so that changes to the program can be carried out without disturbing the desired layout. Such tools are language dependent since they are controlled by the syntax.

(vi) *preprocessor:* since the choice of a language for a project may be constrained by considerations other than understandability, another approach to providing programmers with a more suitable language is to use a preprocessor or program generator. The language used for expressing the algorithm initially can then be translated into the final one. The most well known example of this approach is the RATFOR system (Kernighan, 1975). RATFOR standing for Rational Fortran is an extended version of Fortran which supports structured programming constructs as well as a number of cosmetic improvements. A preprocessor is used to translate programs written in RATFOR into standard Fortran. This can then be distributed to sites which have the appropriate compiler. Since the preprocessor itself is written in Fortran, it is also portable and software can also be distributed in the original form if so desired. This approach is not without its drawbacks since the preprocessor cannot detect errors in the original form of the program and any unrecognizable construct is transmitted unchanged through to the Fortran version. Thus the programmer faced with an error at this level has to deduce what is wrong with the RATFOR code. However, since preprocessors are usually relatively cheap to produce, the advantages of placing a more powerful language in the hands of a programmer far outweigh the disadvantages of the system. Program generators exist for other languages, particularly Cobol, again often to support structured programming.

4. CONCLUSION

High level languages are the best means that we have available today for expressing algorithms to solve problems on computers. Unfortunately, we are now only too well aware of their inadequacies - too complex, difficult to master, error-prone, insufficient redundancy, non-orthogonal, poor support of modularity, easily abused, non-existent fault tolerance and little support for reasoning about correctness. The Algol derivatives (Algol 60, Algol 68, Pascal, Ada) are better languages than those based on Fortran (Fortran IV, Fortran 77, PL/1) which in turn are superior to Cobol. Assembly language comes a bad last in the programming language stakes. What of the future? As the power of computers continues to increase, mankind will attempt to solve more and more complex problems. Given the rapidly increasing costs of producing software, it is only too clear that programming languages as we know them today will be incapable of supporting such developments. Since they are not easy to use, at least to produce reliable software, they necessitate the employment of highly skilled professional programmers who in some sense stand between the users and the information they wish to obtain. Apart from the fact that the requisite number of skilled personnel is unlikely to be available, a possible solution to the problem is to place much more power in the hands of the end user so that he can access the information he requires directly. Development of such "fourth generation" languages is currently underway as exemplified by the high level query languages becoming available for accessing databases. The ultimate goal must be a situation in which the user describes the problem to the computer in a specification rather than an algorithmic language. The computer can then generate the program to solve the problem. It is no longer science fiction to conjecture that ultimately natural languages could be used for this purpose.

REFERENCES AND READING

Gannon J.D. and Horning J.J. (1975), Language Design for Programming Reliability, IEEE Transactions on Software Engineering, SE-1, No. 2, 179 - 191.

Gannon J.D. (1977), An Experimental Evaluation of Data Type Conventions. CACM, 20, No. 8, p. 584-595.

Horning J.J. (1979). Programming Languages. Computer Systems Reliability. (Ed.), Anderson T. and Randell B., Cambridge University Press, p. 109.

Kernighan B.W. (1975), RATFOR - a preprocessor for Rational Fortran. Software - Practice and Experience, Vol. 5, p. 395.

Kerninghan B.W. and Plauger P.J. (1974), The Elements of Programming Style. McGraw-Hill.

Myers G.J. (1976), Software Reliability. Wiley and Sons.

Parnas D.L. (1972), On the Criteria to be used in Decomposing Systems into Modules. CACM, Vol. 15, No. 12, p. 1053.

Ryder B.C. (1974), The PFORT Verifier. Software-Practice and Experience, Vol. 4, p. 359.

van Tassel D. (1975), Programming Style, Design, Efficiency, Debugging and Testing. Prentice-Hill.

PROGRAM VALIDATION

Peter Poole
University of Melbourne
Parkville, Australia

1. INTRODUCTION

The function of the validation phase of the software development cycle is to demonstrate that the software is reliable. The dictionary defines the word "reliable" to mean "that which may be trusted". To say that a piece of software is reliable is to imply that it can be depended upon to carry out the functions for which it was constructed. All software is developed to achieve some goal whether it be a small square root subroutine for other users to incorporate in their programs or a large real-time system supporting hundreds of simultaneously active terminals. The dependency or trust is on the part of the user who expects that the correct result will be returned when the square root routine is called or that an appropriate response will be output by the online system within an acceptable period of time after a query has been made. However, "reliability" does not imply just "correctness" alone. To say that a program is "correct" means that it conforms exactly to its functional specifications. Given a set of valid inputs, a correct program will behave as expected and produce correct output. However, such a program may not necessarily be a reliable one. For example, in the unlikely event that the designer of the square root subroutine had not allowed for negative arguments and the routine returned some spurious result, then the user would deem the routine unreliable even though it always returned the correct result for positive arguments. If the real-time system functioned perfectly during periods of light usage but failed under conditions of heavy loading, then it would be classed by its users as unreliable, at least by those who were continuously inconvenienced by its failures. The fact that the designer had not allowed for such a situation would not save the system from being criticized. Thus correctness is not enough to guarantee reliability. If a correct program is operated in a less than optimum environment, it may produce incorrect results. Another aspect of reliability is, therefore, "robustness" i.e. the ability of a program to withstand unexpected demands or to continue operating in an imperfect environment and still produce a minimum level of service. The square root routine must not only detect negative arguments and take an appropriate course of action

D. T. Muxworthy (ed.), Programming for Software Sharing, 69–86.
Copyright © 1983 ECSC, EEC, EAEC, Brussels and Luxembourg.

but also ensure that a correct result is returned when operating on such values as the smallest or largest positive numbers that can be represented on the particular machine. The real-time system must degrade gracefully when subjected to excessive load, first by increasing the response time for all users and finally by refusing to accept further requests which would reduce the service below an acceptable level. This level must be part of the original specification and one of which users are aware. To be considered reliable, software must match up to user expectations which in turn are geared to an understanding of what the software is expected to do. Unexpected behaviour is not a characteristic of reliable software irrespective of the operating conditions.

It may be argued that the inability of software to handle unexpected situations is simply due to a less than adequate specification and indeed there is some truth in this view. If the specification is complete and the final program is correct, then it should be reliable. Unfortunately, specification is probably one of the least well understood processes in the software development cycle and often the one to which the least attention is paid. It seems to be an inordinately difficult task to specify a complex software system completely and to envisage all the possible adverse situations that might arise when it is put into service. A poor specification guarantees unreliable operation. However, all the other phases in the development cycle have their effect on reliability and the software developer must be aware of the tools and techniques which can be used to improve quality. Failure to use a methodical approach to the design of the system, lack of forward planning to detect and correct errors, poor choice of programming language, scant attention paid to programming style, inadequate testing procedures, insufficient documentation, unawareness of the importance of maintenance, all will contribute to reducing the reliability of the final product. Reliability is not a property of software which can be injected after the program has been constructed. It must be a desired goal from the very outset of the project and one aimed for during all phases of development.

If software is to be shared, then there is an even greater need to achieve high reliability. If a failure occurs in an environment other than the one in which the program was developed, then either the user is faced with the task of locating the error in code with which he is not familiar or the writer must debug the software at a distance, at best, a very difficult and frustrating task. The more error free the program is before it is distributed, the less the likelihood that the originator will be besieged with queries and complaints about unexpected behaviour. Since the objective of producing shared software is to reduce overall costs by preventing unnecessary duplication of effort, users must have confidence in the programs imported from other environments so that they are discouraged from developing similar ones. There is a feeling prevalent amongst programmers that it is easier to develop one's own programs than it is to make the effort to understand how to use someone else's software, an attitude all too often reinforced by bad experiences with unreliable software developed elsewhere. There is nothing more irritating, after one has made the effort to import and implement a software package, than to be faced with unexpected behaviour which deviates from that described in the accompanying documentation. If sharing of software is to become an accepted practice throughout the industry, then it is essential, above almost all else, that such software be highly reliable.

The most obvious way of reducing the number of residual errors in a piece of software is not to make them in the first place. This is the optimal strategy for improving software reliability. Unfortunately, it is easier said than done. Given the current tools and techniques, programmers seem capable of generating errors with consummate ease. It has been suggested that the tendency to refer to mistakes as "bugs" is an attempt on the part of the programming community to preserve its own sanity in the face of so many errors by attributing their existence to some external agency. Nevertheless, fault avoidance seems to offer the best hope of producing reliable software and many of the topics discussed in this book are aimed at just this objective. At each phase in the development cycle, there is a potential for introducing errors. By using the appropriate tools and techniques, one can attempt to avoid making errors in a particular phase or at least detect them so that they are not transmitted through to the next one. The further an error is allowed to propagate, the more difficult and the more expensive it is to detect and correct. The basic principles of fault avoidance are minimization of complexity coupled with a systematic and methodical approach to the development process.

Even if fault avoidance techniques are practiced rigorously, there is still a likelihood that errors will exist in the software when it is put into service. Attention must therefore be given to the possibility of fault detection while the program is executing. This is particularly important for shared software operating in an environment remote from the one in which it was originally developed. The more information that can be transmitted back to the originator of the software, the more likely it is that he can determine the cause of the error and correct it. Another advantage is that the amount of damage caused by the error can be minimized. Note that fault detection has connotations with regard to hardware as well as software reliability. Redundant code introduced to detect a fault may enable one to distinguish between a hardware or a software failure. As an example, consider a filing system whose basic structure involves blocks set up as a linked list. If a link becomes corrupted and the error is not detected, then the longer the situation is allowed to exist, the more severe will be the damage and greater the loss of information when the filing system has to be returned to a previous state. If, however, the operating system periodically initiates a process which checks the link structure and notifies the operator when an inconsistency is detected, then corrective action can be taken to minimize damage. An analysis of the frequency and types of faults may indicate whether they are due to hardware or software.

The main techniques used to validate software are testing and proving. The former implies execution of the program or module with the objective of finding errors; the latter uses mathematical reasoning to deduce that the program is correct on the basis of some formal definition of the input and output specifications. Associated with these activities is that of debugging, which refers to the process of locating the cause of the error so that it can be corrected and testing or proving resumed.

There is a great deal of confusion in the industry about the distinction between testing and debugging. Programmers are often heard to state that after they have finished writing a program, then the next step will be to debug it. Now it may be on the basis of past experiences that they know that there is a very high probability that the program will contain errors and that debugging will be required. However, first they must test or analyze the program to demonstrate that errors exist. It must be clearly recognized that testing can only show the presence of bugs, never their absence. If the program happens to be correct, testing will still be required but, as no errors will occur, debugging will not be initiated. However, on the basis of testing alone, we cannot say that the program is correct, although we may be able to infer something about its ultimate reliability. All we can really say is that for the given set of inputs, no errors were detected when the program was operating in a particular environment. How reliably the program will operate in its intended environment will depend upon the number of residual errors not detected by the testing, their effect on the operation of the program and the degree of similarity between the real and test environments.

2. TESTING

There are various levels of testing through which a software system must pass during its development cycle. First the individual routines must be tested before being combined to form the program or module. In turn, each module must be tested to confirm that it is functioning according to its specifications. Next, the modules must be integrated, with testing being performed at each level of integration until the full system is assembled and operational. At this point, the system can be checked to see if it functions according to its external specifications. Testing to this level is often referred to as *verification* since the software is executing in a test or simulated environment as opposed to a real one. At the next stage the system is tested to see if it meets its original objectives. This is the process of validation if a real environment is used; otherwise it is still verification. Finally, the system is installed in its working environment and acceptance testing is carried out to determine whether it meets user requirements or not. For software designed for sharing, validation must be carried out each time the system is moved to a new environment. Thus, the test data and test procedures used to validate the system originally must be carefully preserved for later use in other environments.

The importance of the testing phase should not be underestimated, at least, given the current state of the art of constructing software. Although the goals of software engineering are to improve reliability by using better tools and techniques in the earlier phases of the development cycle, nevertheless, at the moment, inadequate testing will lead to unreliable software in the field and a continuation of the high cost of maintenance. It is generally accepted that about 50% of the cost of developing software goes into the testing, debugging and maintenance phases. The later an error is detected, the more expensive it is to fix, apart from whatever costs are incurred because the software failed to function correctly. Thus, the testing phase is the last one in which an error can be detected before it can do real damage. Since economics enters into the situation, we must also consider how to carry out cost-effective testing. Simply exercising the program on a large number of test cases and hoping that errors will be detected is not of much value, since there is a high probability that errors will remain. What is required is a good testing strategy and the application of systematic and well planned testing procedures, making use wherever possible of automated testing tools.

Testing Strategies

The testing strategy chosen will depend upon the way in which the various modules are written and integrated. Choosing the right strategy is an important decision which must be made early in the life of the project. Possible strategies considered here are top-down, bottom-up and one which combines elements of both of these approaches.

Top-Down Testing: This strategy attempts to parallel the top-down design methodology. After the program has been designed, the main module is written first and tested. Since it will call lower level modules and these do not yet exist, it is necessary to create stubs. These are dummy modules which perform sufficient of the functions of the real ones to enable the main module to be tested. Thus, a stub for an output routine may merely print a message to the effect that it has been entered, before returning control to the caller, perhaps after performing some validity checks on the input parameters. An input stub could return values which simulate the behaviour of the real input module. Once the main routine is thought to be working, then the modules at the next level are coded and used to replace the corresponding stubs. In turn, new stubs are created to enable the whole program as it exists at that moment to be tested. The process is repeated at each level until the modules at the lowest level have been written and incorporated to form the whole program which can then be tested in its entirety.

The approach appears to have many advantages, not the least of which is the systematic way in which the program is written and tested almost in parallel. Further, once the input modules have been constructed, any test data can be retained and used to check out modules at lower levels. Thus as each new module is added, the program can be tested to see that no undesired interaction with code at a higher level has occurred. The disadvantages of the approach arise from the fact that sometimes it can be just as difficult to write the stub as it is to write the module itself and the more complex the stub, the more likely it is that the stub itself will contain errors. Another disadvantage is that the module is rarely tested as thoroughly as it ought to be since this would require the creation of quite complex stubs. What is actually tested are those paths which are activated in calling the stub and processing its outputs. Paths which require a more sophisticated stub often remain inactive with the programmer telling himself that he will return and test these once the stub has been replaced by the real module. Unfortunately, all too often he forgets. Top-down testing has sufficient disadvantages that programmers should be very wary of using this strategy on its own.

Bottom-Up Testing: As its name implies, this is the reverse strategy to the previous one. Coding and testing start with the lowest level modules. However, as each module is written, it is also necessary to write a driver program and create suitable data to test it. Once the module has been tested, then it can be incorporated in the next level and called as required. However, the driver program and test data are of no value at this level and new ones must be created. The old ones of course will be retained in case it is found necessary to modify the associated module on the basis of subsequent testing carried out at a higher level.

The disadvantage of the approach is that it is not as systematic as top-down and requires the development of more software. It is usually much more complicated to write drivers than it is to write stubs and there is therefore a possibility that the module will not be adequately checked out because of an error in the driver. Nevertheless, there is a good chance that the module will be exercised when it is integrated into the next level although any errors may then be more difficult to locate. Bottom-up is an acceptable strategy providing the extra effort is available to write the drivers. If a number of programming teams are working on the project, then a good approach is to assign one team to write the driver programs for modules produced by another team on the basis of the module specifications alone. Providing it passes such a test, then one could integrate it with higher level modules with some degree of confidence.

Combined Testing: The most satisfactory testing strategy is one which combines both the bottom-up and top-down approaches. As mentioned above, one of the advantages of top-down testing is that once the input module is working, then subsequent test data can be retained to exercise the program as modules at lower levels are integrated. However, often the I/O modules are at the lowest level in the design hierarchy and would only be integrated into the program at the last step, thereby nullifying the postulated benefits. The objective should be to incorporate these modules as soon as possible. Thus, an appropriate strategy is to start testing top-down from the main module and bottom-up from such key modules as input-output with the objective of meeting somewhere in the middle. Once this degree of integration has been achieved, then the remainder of the testing can be carried out top-down as the program is expanded out to its full extent. Any test data generated at the first point of integration can be reused at later stages. Thus, one retains the advantages of having a skeletal working program while ensuring that higher level modules that call critical low level ones are more thoroughly tested than would be the case if only stubs were used.

Testing Procedures

The procedure for testing a module involves designing a test case, executing the module to carry out the test, monitoring its behaviour, examining the output and comparing it with the expected output. If an error is detected, the module is debugged to find the cause, modifications are made if required and the test is repeated; if not, then the next test case is tried. The process continues until all the planned test cases have been executed, whereupon the module is ready to be integrated with other modules or phased into the next level of the development cycle.

Designing Test Cases: The key to effective testing is the design of the test cases. However, this is not an easy task. As an example of the difficulty of designing tests, Myers (1976) quotes results from experienced data processing students in a class on software reliability who were asked to develop test cases for a program which reads 3 integer values representing the lengths of the sides of a triangle and prints a message whether the triangle is scalene, isosceles or equilateral. About 50% of the students failed to check that the three input numbers could form a valid triangle at all and only one-half of those who did checked all three possible permutations. All students tested for an equilateral triangle and most for an isosceles triangle but again one-half of the latter failed to check the three possibilities. The results to say the least are enlightening and are indicative of the problems that must be overcome to train programmers to test their programs properly.

There are no hard and fast rules for designing test cases except to point out that if the program works with one set of test data, there is no guarantee that it will work with another. The more test cases used, the better. However, volume testing is no answer. A square root routine which has been tested with 1000 positive numbers may still fail when given a negative number as an input parameter. Good test case design requires creativity, experience, a clear understanding of what the program is supposed to do and even a somewhat destructive attitude to the whole process. It has often been suggested that programmers should not be allowed to test their own program. Instead, the task should be given to other programmers, preferably ones with a great deal of experience. Since the objective of testing is to expose errors, there can be a strong psychological block on the person who wrote the code to construct appropriate test cases. It is difficult to be destructive of one's own creation and people do not like admitting even to themselves that they have made a mistake. Sometimes because they have fallen behind schedule, programmers are tempted to cut short the testing phase and convince themselves that a module is working in order to make up time. Further, a misunderstanding of the specification which leads to an error may be reflected in the design of the test cases so that the error goes undetected. A different viewpoint might, on the other hand, result in the error showing up during testing. This is not to say that someone else should test a module or routine as soon as it has been written. Programmers should do a certain amount of their own testing if only to learn the type of mistakes they make. However, before a module is integrated with another one, it should be subjected to testing by someone other than the writer. Certainly, the more complex the module (or collection of modules), the more critical it is to use testers other than the originators of the code.

There are some guidelines available to help in designing test cases. Firstly, the input requirements of the module must be examined closely so that test cases can be created for both valid and invalid input data. Valid inputs should be chosen to include typical cases as well as extreme ones at the limits of the input range. Cases which might produce some pathological behaviour should also be incorporated. Thus, to test a square root routine, one might use some positive numbers chosen at random, some perfect squares, the largest and smallest positive numbers that can be represented by the machine, zero and a negative number. A terminal input routine which specifies a maximum length of line might be tested with a typical line, a line of length equal to the maximum, lines whose lengths are one more and one less than the maximum, the null string, as well as perhaps a line which contains invalid characters. Output specifications should also be analyzed so that appropriate test cases can be designed to check them in a similar manner to the input requirements. A second guideline is to ensure that each code sequence in the module is exercised at least once. Repetitions should be tested for zero iterations, one iteration and the maximum number of iterations (if this is reasonable). In general, any section of the code that the programmer suspects might be a source of problems should be exercised thoroughly. This aspect of testing can be greatly facilitated by forward planning, for example, by including comments in the code or in supporting documentation to remind the writer to test this particular section.

Executing the Tests: Once the test cases have been designed, then the test data can be created and the module exercised. The data can be provided as direct input or as values supplied by a driver program or stub. The output can either be printed and inspected by eye or checked by the driver program which can then report success or failure. In the case where output is printed, it should also be stored in a file so that when the module is thought to be working correctly, there will exist a file of valid output. If, at a later stage, changes are made to the module which should not affect the output, then one simply needs to compare the two output files using an appropriate tool to verify that the same results have been obtained in both cases. It should be noted that the fact that the expected output has been obtained is still no guarantee that the module is working correctly. There may be some internal change occurring which will only manifest itself as a failure after many more inputs than exist in the test data. For this reason, it is often sensible to produce extra output in the way of partial results and values of key variables as part of the test run.

Appropriate parameterization of the code can also be extremely helpful in executing test runs to ensure that the module is exercised thoroughly. For example, a module which manages the allocation of buffers might initially be tested with only one buffer available to ensure that, after its resources are exhausted, it can handle the situation correctly. The number could then be increased as the level of confidence in the reliability of the module rises. When it is placed in service, the number of buffers available will depend on such factors as the amount of memory, the desired response time, etc. and the parameters can be set accordingly. An added advantage of parameterization is that test case situations can readily be reproduced at any stage in the life of the module if it is suspected that it still contains residual errors.

Another form of testing is system testing as opposed to module testing. The various modules have been integrated to form the final system and it is now necessary to determine how well it meets the original objectives. For this reason, it is important that these objectives be well documented. Answers are required to the following questions:

(a) Does the system function as described in the user documentation?
(b) Can the system withstand heavy loads, for example, large volumes of data or a high transaction rate?
(c) How well does it perform under various loading conditions, e.g. response time and throughput rates?
(d) What demands does it make on storage, both main and secondary, and processor time, and how well do these match up to those predicted?
(e) What configurations are required to support the system?
(f) How secure is the system against penetration by unauthorized users?
(g) How difficult is it to install and, in the case of portable systems, how much effort is required to move it to another environment?
(h) How reliable is the system and what is its expected availability?
(i) How compatible is it with previous systems if such exist?
(j) How easy is it to recover from an error, either hardware or software?
(k) How difficult will it be to maintain, i.e. what is the quality of the support documentation?
(l) Is the user image likely to be acceptable to the proposed user community?
(m) How difficult will it be to integrate the system if it is simply another component in an even larger system?

Again, there are no hard and fast rules for system testing. Creativity, experience, thoroughness, attention to detail and a determination to find errors are essential characteristics of members of the system test groups. Certainly, system testing should not be carried out by the development team although there should be good lines of communication between the developers and the testers. If there is one piece of advice that should be followed by all software developers, it is this: use your own product first in a production environment before releasing it on an unsuspecting and long suffering user community.

Testing tools

Since testing is such a difficult task, yet one which is of vital importance to the reliability of the final product, it is surprising that so little has been done to automate the testing process. Certainly, testing tools are nowhere as numerous or widespread as debugging aids. Testing aids fall into three main classes: those which enable test data to be generated in a systematic, convenient and reproducible manner, those which analyze or augment the program text and those which monitor the execution of the program at run time.

As discussed previously, testing in a bottom-up manner requires the creation of driver programs which supply test data to a module and check its output. One type of testing tool of the first class is a program which generates such drivers from specifications supplied by the programmer. The module together with its driver can then be compiled and executed. Another type of testing aid will generate input data to exercise a specific path on the basis of information gathered from an analysis of the program text. Test file generators fall into this class since they can be used to simulate input coming from a file, thereby obviating the need to set up actual physical files in order to test the program. This can reduce both programmer and computer time requirements considerably. For the testing of real-time systems, simulators which generate the input transactions in a controllable and reproducible form are an invaluable aid. If a fault is timing or load dependent, then it may be extremely difficult to locate if input is being generated by a number of human users. A very common form of simulator is one which simulates interactive terminals. Often it is set up on a completely separate computer to the one on which the system under test is executing. The action of each terminal is directed by a scenario which is a set of actions that a human operator may perform in order to accomplish some specific functional task. Usually such sequences of actions can be described in a high-level programming language.

The second class of testing aids includes tools which will analyze the program text with a view to determining its structure and saying something about possible errors. For example, the DAVE system (Osterweil and Fosdick, 1976) carries out a data flow analysis of Fortran programs and reports on data flow anomalies. Commonly occurring errors which can be detected by this system are referencing uninitialized variables, failing to use a computed value, unused parameters in parameter lists, omission of COMMON declarations. Another useful tool in this class is the code auditor which checks a program to see if it conforms to the standards of some specified programming practice. Obviously program proving systems fall into this class also since they operate directly on the program text. Finally, there are those programs which augment an existing program without disturbing its logical properties by adding extra statements which will provide useful information when the program is executed. One example is a preprocessor which will detect assertions supplied by the programmer as comments and generate code to test the logical condition at run time. Another is one which will insert a series of subroutine calls at appropriate points in the program so that the flow of control is visible at run time. A count of the number of times each basic block is executed can also be obtained from such a system. Obviously these testing tools have application in the debugging phase as well.

The final class of testing aids are the run time tools which interact with the program during execution. These can generate statistics about the number of times each statement is executed or each branch of a conditional statement is taken, the frequency with which each subroutine is called and the amount of time spent therein, the number of times each variable is referenced or changed. Some will even monitor the value of a variable and report if an attempt is made to set the variable to a value outside a specified range. This class of tool operates on the compiled code rather than the text and inserts probes and traps at appropriate points in the program being monitored. Again, such systems can be very useful for debugging as well as testing.

The use of testing tools is slowly spreading as their number and quality increases. Some are available commercially whilst others are closely guarded secrets of organizations involved in the manufacture of software. There is little doubt that the use of such tools can contribute greatly to the reliability of the final product.

3. PROVING

Currently, an active area of research in computer science is the development of techniques for proving the correctness of programs. It is sometimes referred to as formal verification. It invokes the use of mathematical arguments based on the semantics of the programming languages used to write the program and the characteristics of the environment in which it will operate to demonstrate the equivalence between the program and a formal definition of the specifications. A proof implies that there exists a formal system of axioms and rules of inference. A statement in a proof is then either an axiom or follows from the previous statement by virtue of one of the rules. Thus, if we have a set of input specifications and a set of output specifications defined formally and can demonstrate that executing the statements of the program will transform data corresponding to the input specifications to data corresponding to the output ones, then the program will be deemed to be correct. This simplified view of the proof process avoids certain practical considerations, for example, whether the program terminates prematurely or enters into an infinite loop. Thus one can speak about total correctness which includes proper termination and partial correctness which ignores it.

The process of proving the correctness of a program involves first deriving invariant assertions at various points in the program. These are statements of some condition which must be true at that point. For example, a loop invariant is an expression which is true before a loop is initiated and is still true after the loop has been terminated. One then applies the constructs of the programming language in the form of proof rules and attempts to proceed from one invariant assertion to the next. If all the assertions in a program can be traversed in this manner, then if the input specifications are correct so are the output specifications and the correctness of the program has been verified.

The above process may be seen to be a very laborious one and, if carried out by hand, it is for other than very simple programs. However, mechanical verification systems have been developed which will carry out the process automatically. Such systems contain a parser, a generator for a particular language to produce the conditions to be verified and modules for algebraic manipulation. Some systems contain strategies for developing a proof; others are highly interactive so that the user can direct the progress of the proof. Constructing such systems is extremely difficult and it will be some time before they are generally available.

There is still considerable debate about how useful program proving techniques will be. Some workers feel that program proving is totally impractical and, as languages and methodologies improve, the need for it will diminish. Others believe that there will always be weaknesses in program production technology and that, whenever the effects of errors are likely to be very costly, then there will be a need for verification systems. One suggestion for a possible application of verifiers is for software that will have a long life but which will periodically undergo small modifications. Once the initial version has been proved to be correct, then it would be relatively easy to check that errors have not been introduced by the changes. In the end, the question of whether to prove correctness or not will come down to one of cost. There is a cost for including the information in the program on which the verifier will work and a cost for processing it to carry out the verification. Current verifying systems are inordinately slow and very expensive to operate. If costs can be reduced to acceptable levels, then program verifiers would be a very useful addition to the tools available to software developers.

4. DEBUGGING

Debugging starts with the manifestation of the error and the object is to locate the line or lines of code which are incorrect. Once these have been corrected, then testing may be resumed until the next error occurs. Since debugging involves understanding the program to the extent of being able to modify it, it is normally carried out by the programmer who wrote it, at least, during the development phase. Once it has been placed in service, this may not be the case and someone could be faced with the difficult task of debugging another person's code. Users of shared software may find themselves in this situation more often than others. Alternatively, the originator may have to debug his code from a distance in a different evironment, again, not an easy task. Every possible effort should be made to avoid this situation when writing software to be shared.

Debugging Procedures

The first step is to obtain a clear understanding of the behaviour of the program when it failed and to check that it was not due to an error in the test data. There is nothing more frustrating than to spend hours looking for an error unsuccessfully only to find that the test data had been set up incorrectly. Next, one commences to think about reasons why the observed behaviour occurred with a view to locating some sections of code as candidates for closer inspection. Observations of both experienced programmers and students tend to indicate that people differ widely in their ability to localize the cause of an error. Some seem to be able to home in very quickly whilst others wander around the code almost aimlessly as though hoping that they will stumble across it. If, however, finding possible trouble spots proves difficult, then it may be necessary to devise and run more test cases. A good debugging technique involves choosing the right balance between desk checking and obtaining more information from the computer. Too much time spent reading the code can become frustrating if the error cannot be located; on the other hand, too much information from the machine can become confusing.

Once a possible source of the error has been located, then the code should be studied very carefully, line by line, to see if it could have produced the observed behaviour.

If this is the case, then one of the possible sources of the error has been found. However, there may be others and one should spend a little time trying to determine if there are or if the same mistake has been made elsewhere. If it could not have caused the error, then it may be necessary to run more test cases or use an appropriate debugging aid.

Debugging Tools

These are tools and techniques which enable the programmer to obtain more information about the state of his program at any point up to and including the occurrence of the error. Debugging tools should be designed in such a way that obtaining this information is a relatively straightforward task and does not involve any changes to the program. After obtaining such information, hopefully, the programmer will have a clearer idea of what caused the error. We will now examine the characteristics of some of the debugging tools currently available.

(a) *dumps*: The ubiquitous dump seems to have been with us since programming began. Dumping refers to the process of outputting some or all of the memory image when the program fails. Usually the output appears on the line printer in the form of octal or hexadecimal digits, forcing the programmer to sift through an enormous amount of irrelevant information searching for clues as to why the program failed. To find them, he often has to carry out many conversions from one number system to another.

The main problem with the primitive form of the dump is that it forces the high-level language programmer to become conversant with the characteristics of the underlying machine, a not inconsiderable task in most instances. High-level languages are supposed to protect the programmer from such details and the way to improve the dump is to output the information in a more convenient form. If the system has access to the symbol table and the types of the variables, then it can output the dump in the correct format together with the variable identifiers. It can even indicate where the failure occurred in the original program text without the programmer having to analyze the loader storage map. One such dump system even goes so far as to suggest a possible cause of the error based on an analysis of previous errors in a large number of cases.

There still remains the problem of the voluminous output. There is certainly no need to output the compiled code since this will be of no interest to the high-level language user; simple variables create no problem but arrays and records can. One solution is to allow the program to set and reset the areas to be dumped dynamically at run time. As the execution of the program progresses, the areas of interest if the program fails will possibly change. By providing a standard function which calls the operating system to set the dump parameters, the program can determine what areas should be dumped depending on the position it has reached in the code. This could create a minor problem if the program is moved to another environment where such a facility does not exist but it can readily be handled by introducing a dummy subroutine of the appropriate name.

(b) *diagnostic statements:* A situation which occurs all too frequently in introductory programming courses is one where the student complains that his program has compiled and executed to normal termination, yet has produced no output. This usually means that he has not included any diagnostic print statements in his program to enable him to follow the course of its execution. The idea of including such diagnostic statements originated at an early stage in the development of the art of programming. Wilkes et al (1951) proposed that extra printing statements be included in all new programs when they are first written rather than waiting for the program to be tried and found to fail. Yet even today, programmers seem loath to include extra statements initially to assist with debugging even though it is an extremely useful technique. Such diagnostic code need not necessarily produce output. It could store values away to improve the information that could be gleaned from a dump, or function as guard code to check the validity of various entities in the program, perhaps producing output only if an error is detected. Of course, the problem is what to do with such statements once the program appears to be working. They could simply be removed but this is not necessarily a wise thing to do. The code which produces no output should be left, as it could still be useful in the event of a subsequent failure. Any print statements which produce excessive output or interfere with the desired output format could be turned into comments. This could quite easily be carried out using a sophisticated text editor or macroprocessor. At some later stage, if program failures occur, such statements can easily be reactivated using the same tools. This is certainly the recommended course of action for software to be shared since it may be necessary to obtain information to diagnose a fault which occurs when the program is moved to a new environment.

(c) *traces:* A trace allows the programmer to obtain diagnostic output from his running program without building the statements into the program itself. Tracepoints together with a description of the required information are defined to the trace monitor which then modifies the load module appropriately so that when control reaches one of the specified points, a transfer to the monitor takes place. Diagnostic output is produced, the displaced instructions executed and control returned to the program. Usually care must be taken in selecting a tracepoint so that constant data stored inline are not overwritten. Using such a tracing facility means that the user must be familiar with the loader storage maps and how to interpret machine addresses. Some trace systems are interpretive and hence can slow down execution speed greatly.

Another form of trace is one which maintains information inside the program which might be of value if the program aborts. For example, a trace-back facility might output the calling sequence and actual parameters for nested procedure calls. By using cyclic buffers to record such information, one could obtain details of the last N calls made in the system where N is determined by the capacity of the buffer. Real-time and data base management systems often maintain audit trails which can be used for recovery in the event of a system crash. The information recorded in this way can be of great value to the programmer trying to determine the reason why the failure occurred.

(d) *Program analyzers*: Another class of tools useful as an aid to debugging are those which analyze the text of the program. A common example is the cross-reference generator which creates a list of all the identifiers in the program and indicates from where they are referenced. Variations on this theme enable specific lists to be created for such entities as modules, procedures and files. Other tools display the structure of the program in terms of procedure declarations and calls thereby enabling the programmer to obtain a better understanding about how the various routines in the program interact with each other. Even a simple context editor which can locate all occurrences of a given character string can be a useful debugging aid, particularly if the pattern to be located can be expressed as a regular expression incorporating special symbols which are interpreted to mean such things as any character, any character string, any or not any of a specified set of characters, end of line, beginning of line, etc. By scanning the text with such tools, the programmer can extract information which can be of great value in helping to locate an error.

(e) *dynamic debugging*: Dynamic debugging refers to the process of debugging a program from a time-sharing terminal where the program being debugged is operating under the control of the debugger. It can be an extremely powerful tool particularly if the programmer can communicate with the debugging package in the original programming language whether it be a high-level or low-level one.

As an example of the facilities available in a dynamic debugger, let us consider the debugging package in the UNIX time-sharing system (Ritchie and Thompson, 1978). When a program written in a high-level language is compiled under UNIX and a load module created, the default option is to append the symbol table to the module. When the program is executed and a failure occurs, the memory image is dumped to a file and control returns to the user. Simply by typing its name with the names of the object module and dump files as parameters, the programmer activates the debugger which takes control of the program. The user can now issue commands to the debugging package to manipulate his program. Notice that no prior planning is required providing that the symbol tables are still available. Thus, the facility can be used even for programs which have been previously put into service. There is no overhead except the extra space required to hold the symbol table in the load module file. The commands available to the user can be classified as follows:

(i) examine

The contents of any memory locations can be output on the terminal in a format specified by the user, e.g. octal, decimal, floating point and even assembly code. The address at which the dump starts can be specified via identifiers used in the original program. The contents of registers including the program counter can also be dumped if these are meaningful to the programmer.

(ii) modify

The contents of any memory location or register may be changed to values supplied by the user in a convenient form.

(iii) breakpoint

The user can specify addresses in the program at which control will be returned to the terminal when execution of the program is resumed. Boolean conditions may also be supplied so that execution will only be suspended when the boolean becomes true e.g. when the breakpoint has been passed a given number of times or when a variable changes value.

(iv) trace

Tracepoints can be specified so that when execution is resumed, specified information will be output to the terminal, again under the control of boolean expressions. This enables the programmer to minimize the amount of information generated when the tracepoint is inside a repeatedly executed loop.

(v) execute

The programmer can specify that execution is to be resumed at a particular address and that instructions are to be obeyed one at a time, or sequentially until a breakpoint is encountered or the program terminates. Execution can be restarted from the point where the original failure occurred or from the beginning of the program.

(vi) search

The system can be requested to scan the dump for a particular bit pattern (supplied by the user in a convenient form) and output the address at which it occurs. This is useful if one wishes to determine whether the program has generated a certain value or not.

Other online systems besides UNIX support dynamic debugging packages. Some require that the user specify at compile time that he proposes to use the system; others will only operate at the machine language level. All provide a powerful debugging aid and all suffer from the same disadvantage, namely, that users are tempted to rely on them far too heavily and become a little careless in planning their testing procedures. They should not be used for testing, only for debugging.

(f) *Debugging compilers*: Some high-level language compilers support extra facilities which assist the user in debugging his program, for example, the IBM PL/I check-out compiler. This goes a stage further than the UNIX dynamic debugger by enabling the user to communicate with it in the source language alone. He can set breakpoints, alter variables, initiate traces and obtain dumps by using an extended PL/I. Thus he does not have to learn a debugging language nor have any familiarity whatsoever with the underlying machine. The disadvantages are that it is restricted to one language and the compiler is an interpretive one. Hence execution is slow and another compiler would have to be used before the program was placed in service. This has implications with regard to shared software since a program which executes correctly on the checkout compiler may fail to do so after being compiled on another machine. Many APL systems incorporate powerful facilities to assist in debugging primarily because of the closed nature of the system in which the APL compiler is embedded.

At a less sophisticated level, other compilers will generate redundant code under programmer control which can help in the location of errors. The CDC Pascal compiler can be instructed to insert checks on array references and the limits on variables of subrange type. The generation is controlled by special comments set up at compile time which therefore represent a form of language extension. Unfortunately, all too often, the checks are removed by recompiling the program before it is put into service. Usually this is done on the grounds of efficiency although it does not seem to be a very wise move in these days of falling hardware costs, faster CPU's and increased memory sizes. The amount saved may not be justified by the cost of repairing the damage if the production program were subsequently found to be in error.

5. MODIFICATION AND MAINTENANCE

Once an error has been located and the reason for the failure determined, then the next step is to correct it. This may involve changing the specification, altering the design or simply removing a programming error. Whatever the reason, it will involve making modifications to the existing code and this itself is a fruitful source of error. All too often there is a tendency for programmers to make a quick "fix" without fully thinking through all the ramifications of the change. Thus, while it may remove the current bug, it may also introduce new ones. If the programmer then proceeds with the current tests, satisfies himself that the error has been corrected and proceeds to the next phase, he may never detect the new errors. Thus, it is essential that, before any modification is made, its overall effect must be considered very carefully. Further, after the change, it is necessary to return to earlier tests to satisfy oneself that these are still valid. This highlights the importance of setting up the tests in such a way that they are easily reproducible. Testing in an ad hoc fashion from the terminal is to be avoided at all costs. Another point to note is the importance of maintaining the ability to return to an earlier version of the program if the changes turn out to be unsatisfactory. Either one must document the changes carefully so that they can be reversed or retain a copy of the previous state of the program.

The problems associated with modification are magnified further in large projects involving a team of programmers. The changes made in one module may affect the operation of others and start a chain reaction which causes the whole system to collapse. This highlights the importance of module design with strict adherence to interface standards and the principles of information hiding. The fact that a programmer has changed a local variable in his program should not cause another part of the system to fail just because the value of that variable has been used elsewhere to save a memory location. The programmer who made the change may not be aware of this and hence could not be expected to foresee the consequences of his actions. The monitoring and recording of modifications in a large project is vital so that when a change is made to one module, the writers of other modules which interact with it are notified so that they can take corrective action. Again, fall-back versions of the system must be maintained in the event that the modifications are themselves incorrect. Some software manufacturers have developed programming systems to aid with these processes. One such system is the Source Code Control System on PWB/UNIX (Rochkind, 1975). This provides a small set of commands to give powerful control over changes to modules of text. It keeps a record of every change made to a module and can recreate a module as it existed at any instant of time. It can also manage a number of different versions of the same module which exist concurrently.

Once a software system has been validated and placed into service, it enters the maintenance phase of the software development cycle where it remains for the rest of its useful life. In principle, the reliability of the software should slowly increase during this phase as errors are discovered and corrected. In practice, reliability tends to fluctuate as the correction of existing errors introduces new ones and because maintenance usually involves enhancement, that is, the addition of new facilities and additional errors. All that has been said previously about the tools and techniques to be used in the various phases of development is still applicable. The main differences to be recognized about this phase are the increased difficulty in locating the cause of the errors and the increased cost of correcting them. It is in this phase that documentation becomes of paramount importance; in particular, ready availability of comprehensive and understandable documentation which corresponds closely to the program as it actually exists is essential if maintenance programmers are to carry out their task effectively.

The maintenance of shared software raises special problems. If the software was developed initially in a user-independent project with a view to its being used in a number of different environments, then hopefully the necessary lines of communication will have been established to handle the reporting of errors. However, the developers of the software may not have ready access to the type of environment in which the error is being detected. Thus, testing and debugging at a distance will be required and, as already mentioned, this is a difficult task. If on the other hand, the project was developer-initiated and transporting the system to other environments the responsibility of other users, then the error reporting paths will be at least rather tenuous and error correcting ones even more so. Usually it will fall to the lot of the user to attempt to locate and fix the faults. Once again, the importance of good support documentation and the availability of validation procedures cannot be stressed strongly enough. In their absence, the desire of users to import transferable systems to their home environment and their willingness to use them will be substantially decreased.

6. CONCLUSION

As software costs continue to rise relative to hardware costs, there is no doubt that, in the future, more and more use will be made of shared software. How successful this will be will depend upon the cost of moving the software and the reliability with which it will operate in the new environment. An appreciation of the difficulty of producing reliable software, an understanding of the techniques that can be used to improve reliability, an awareness of the tools available to assist in this process, all have their part to play in achieving this goal. The program validation phase is vitally important to the task of ensuring that more and more software is shared. Whilst it cannot prevent the introduction of errors, it can be used to guarantee that the probability of the existence of residual errors is extremely low. Acceptance by the user community of the principle of sharing and confidence in using shared software are dependent on this criterion being met.

REFERENCES AND READING

Bauer, F.J. (Ed.) (1973), Advanced Course on Software Engineering. Springer-Verlag.

Buxton, J.L., Naur P. and Randell B. (Eds.) (1976), Software Engineering: Concepts and Techniques. Petrocelli/Charter.

Computing Surveys (1976), Special Issues on Reliable Software, vol 8, nos 3 and 4.

Ebert R., Lugger T. and Goecke R. (1980), Practice in Software Adaption and Maintenance, North-Holland.

Fairley R.E. (1978), Static Analysis and Dynamic Testing of Computer Software. Computer, Vol. 11, No. 4, p. 4.

Gerhart S.L. (1979), Program Validation. Computer Systems Reliability. (Ed.) Anderson T., and Randell B., Cambridge University Press, p. 66.

Hetzel W.C. (Ed.) (1972), Program Test Methods. Prentice-Hall.

Huang J.C. (1978), Program Instrumentation and Software Testing. Computer, Vol. 11, No. 4, p. 25.

International Conference on Reliable Software (1975), Los Angeles, Ca.

Jackson M.A. (1975), Principles of Program Design. Academic Press.

Kerninghan, B.W. and Plauger P.J. (1976), Software Tools. Addison-Wesley.

Miller E.F. (1977), Program Testing: Art Meets Theory. Computer, Vol. 10, No. 7, p. 42.

Mills H.D. (1972), On the Statistical Validation of Computer Programs. FSC-72-6015 IBM Federal Systems Division.

Myers G.J. (1975), Reliable Software through Composite Design. Petrocelli/Charter.

Myers G.J. (1976), Software Reliability. Wiley and Sons.

Osterweil L.J. and Fosdick L.D. (1976), DAVE - A Validation and Error Detection and Documentation System for FORTRAN Programs. Software - Practice and Experience, Vol. 6 p. 473.

Panzl D.J. (1978), Automatic Software Test Drivers. Computer, Vol. 11, No. 4, p. 44.

Poole P.C. (1973), Debugging and Testing. Advanced Course on Software Engineering. Spinger-Verlag, p. 278.

Rees, R.L.D. (Ed.) 1977), Infotech State of the Art Report on Software reliability. Infotech International.

Riddle W.E. and Fairley W.E. (1980), Software Development Tools. Springer-Verlag.

Ritchie D.M. and Thompson K. (1978), The UNIX Time-Sharing System. Bell System Technical Journal, Vol. 57, p. 1905.

Rochkind M.J. (1975), The Source Code Control System. IEEE Transactions on Software Engineering, SE-1, p. 364.

Rustin W.C. (Ed.) (1970), Debugging Techniques in Large Systems. Prentice-Hall.

Shooman M.L. (1979), Software Reliability. Computer Systems Reliability. (Ed.) Anderson T. and Randell B., Cambridge University Press, p. 355.

van Tassel D. (1975), Programming Style, Design, Efficiency, Debugging and Testing. Prentice-Hall.

Wilkes M.V., Wheeler D.J. and Gill S. (1951), The Preparation of Programs for an Electronic Digital Computer. Addison-Wesley.

A PROGRAMMING EXAMPLE

Gerhard Goos
University of Karlsruhe
Karlsruhe, Germany

1. DATA-CONTROLLED PROGRAM STRUCTURE (JACKSON'S METHOD)

It very often happens that from the structure of the data we are able to predict the division of a problem into subproblems and therefore the program structure. The data may be the input, the output or an intermediate data structure. In some applications — as in our first example — there does not even exist a data structure as a whole but one element after the other is generated and immediately processed.

The correspondence of data structure and program structure has been known for a long time; M.A. Jackson used it systematically in teaching programming. We first look at a simple example in Jackson (1975). Our second example deals with incompatible data structures.

Sequential Data Structures

We assume that the data under consideration do not form an arbitrary collection of elementary data but that they follow a certain structure. We are interested in the systematics as far as they correspond to schemes for sequentially processing these data. Interesting structures are therefore as follows:

— Sequence. The data set is a sequence of two or more subsets.
— Repetition. The data set consists of a subset, which may be repeated several times (0, 1, 2, ..., n times).
— Alternative. The data set is alternatively one of several sets.
— Element. The data set consists of a single element which is processed as a whole.

Every subset is built according to the same scheme; it is therefore an elementary datum or it consists of subsets itself. The four cases may be depicted as follows:

D. T. Muxworthy (ed.), Programming for Software Sharing, 87–95.
Copyright © 1983 ECSC, EEC, EAEC, Brussels and Luxembourg.

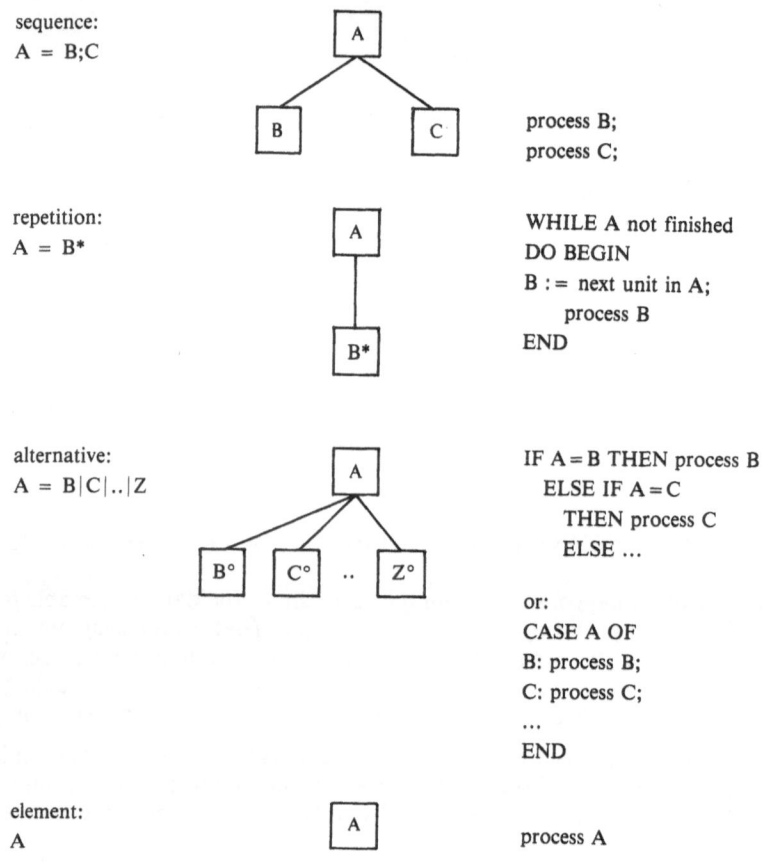

sequence:
A = B;C

B   C

process B;
process C;

repetition:
A = B*

A

B*

WHILE A not finished
DO BEGIN
B : = next unit in A;
      process B
END

alternative:
A = B|C|..|Z

A

B° C° .. Z°

IF A = B THEN process B
  ELSE IF A = C
    THEN process C
    ELSE ...

or:
CASE A OF
B: process B;
C: process C;
...
END

element:
A

A

process A

Mapping to Control Structure

The figure above also shows the conversion of the structuring schemes for data into program elements. Kleene's star operation B* is often used as a mark for repetition. If B must appear at least once we write A = B;B* or A = B +. The corresponding program element is the REPEAT UNTIL loop. The loop invariants of the repetitions usually are "all considered B of A processed". The vertical sign "|" is read as "or". We already know it from the Backus-Naur form.

Example 1: Given a matrix with n rows and columns. We especially consider the infinite matrix A of all positive fractions with $a_{pq} = p/q$. We want to print the first N pairs (p,q) in the sequence of Cantor's diagonalization:

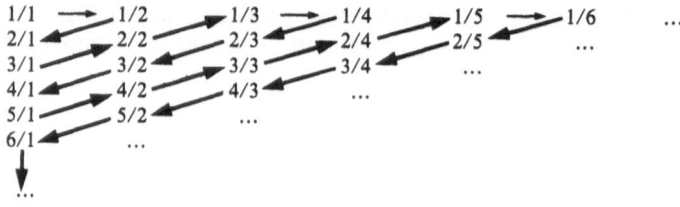

Because we do not work row or column-wise we have little interest in the rectangular properties of the matrix. Instead we think of the matrix as a sequence of zigzag paths. Every zigzag path leads diagonally up and then diagonally down. The set of data is structured as follows:

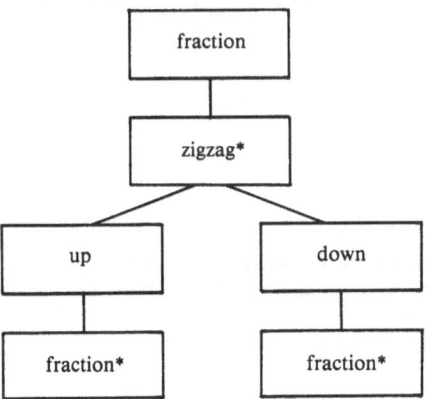

This structure leads to the following program

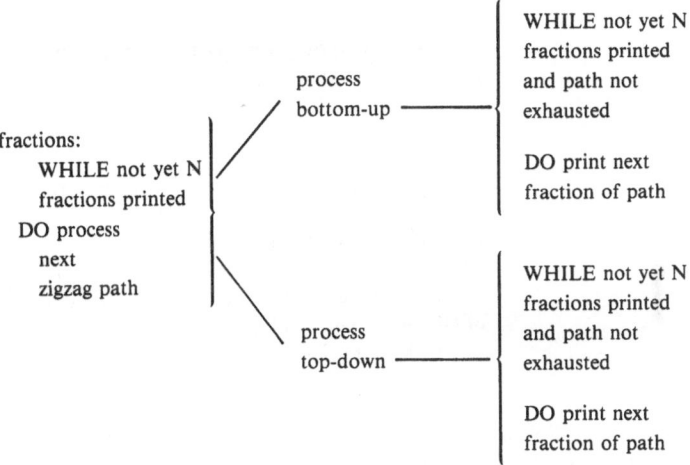

In simple cases we will get the final program by developing the necessary basic operations (assignments, conditions, etc.) and attach them to our program structure. A better method is the subdivision of the given complex operations by stepwise refinement. Special care is needed for the initialization of loops which is still missing in the above figure. The given example does not need to build explicitly a data structure and to store it. It is sufficient if in every place where an element a_{pq} is needed we are able to calculate the two values p and q. To this end we may use the fact that in every diagonal $p + q = const$ holds.

For the program we certainly need a counter k for counting the number of printed fractions. We also need counters for the zigzag paths and the top-down and bottom-up paths. For counting the zigzag paths the sum $c = p + q$ may be used. It is increased for every bottom-up and top-down path by 1, and so for a complete zigzag path by 2. On a bottom-up path the numerator of a fraction is diminished from c-1 to 1, on the top-down path the same holds for the denominator. These ideas lead to the program

```
PROGRAM Cantor's diagonalization (input, output);
VAR c,h,k,N: integer;
BEGIN       read (N);
            k := 0;
            c := 1;
            WHILE k < N
            DO {up to now k fractions are printed,
                all processed zigzag paths have a
                sum ≤ c,
                next zigzag path has the sums
                c + 1 and c + 2}
    BEGIN
            {bottom-up path:}
            h := c;      {h corresponds to the numerator}
            c := c + 1;  {sum for the bottom-up path}
            WHILE (h ≥ 1) AND (k < N)
            DO
                {all fractions (p,q) with p < h,q = c-h are printed}
                BEGIN write (h, '/', c-h);
                      k := k + 1;
                      h := h-1
            END {bottom-up path};
            h := c ;     {h corresponds to the denominator}
            c := c + 1;  {sum for top-down path}
            WHILE (h ≥ 1) AND (k < N)
            DO
                {all fractions (p,q) with p = c-h, q < h are printed}
                BEGIN write (c-h, '/', h);
                      k := k + 1;
                      h := h-1
            END {top-down path}
    END { zigzag path}
END {Cantor's diagonalization}
```

The method to derive the program structure from the structure of the data may also be used if we have several data sets with compatible structure, i.e. which lead to the same program structure. If the structure is essentially the same but there are gaps in one of the data sets then we may completely adjust the structure if we substitute "imaginary" elements for such gaps. The processing of such elements does not involve any action.

Additional problems arise if within an alternative the applicable case cannot immediately be recognized or if there are difficulties in recognizing the last element in a repetition. Such situations sometimes occur in text processing. For example in

Fortran the string "1.E" may be continued by an integer number. We then have a floating point number 1.E1 or 1.E-1. It may also be continued by "Q. ..."giving a logical expression 1 .EQ. x. Which alternative occurs cannot be recognized from the dot although the processing of this character is different for the two cases.

Sometimes we may resolve the problem by delaying the decision between the alternatives. If this is impossible as in the given example we may follow all relevant alternatives simultaneously. This method may be very time-consuming; it is impossible if different alternatives require contradictory processing. In this case we may process the data in two steps: a first step is used only for finding which alternative is to be applied in the second step. The worst possible method would be to arbitrarily choose one of the alternatives and to revise this choice if it appears to be wrong. For such a revision it is necessary to restore the state of processing as it was before the wrong decision was taken. This step is known as backtracking and may turn out to be a very complex undertaking.

2. PROGRAM INVERSION

The case of several data sets with incompatible structure is even more difficult to handle. We call it a *structure clash*.

Example 2: Given a file E of type

        TYPE Erecord = RECORD L:0..N;
                       t:ARRAY [1..N] OF CHAR
                       END;
        Etype = FILE OF Erecord;

In every Erecord only the first L characters are significant. The sequence of significant characters is to be written in file A of type

        Block = ARRAY [1..M] OF CHAR;
        Atype = FILE OF Block;

In A, subsequent Erecords are only separated by "$". (For example if the blocksize is $M = 5$ the output could be as follows

        These| are$| seve|ral$ |Ereco|rds |

The symbol | signals the end of a block. We assume $M > 1$, $N > 1$.

The structure of the files is

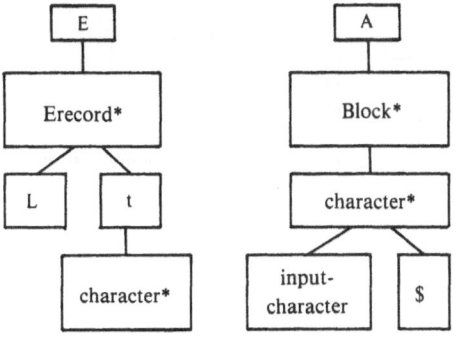

The structures are incompatible because blocks and Erecords do not correspond; we are unable to process a whole Erecord in a loop and at the same time write a whole block.

For solving this problem we should write a separate program for every data structure. These programs are supposed to run simultaneously and communicate with one another. Every communication signals the begin or the end of processing a data element. Possibly the data is communicated itself. This is possible only if the data element is a recognizable unit in both programs. Hence it is advisable to use the largest data element occurring in both programs for communication. In the example this largest unit is a single character (assume the above type declarations, the communication operators are italicized)

input program:

```
VAR E:Etype; s:Erecord; i:integer;
BEGIN
    WHILE NOT eof (E)
    DO BEGIN read (E,s);
    FOR i := 1 TO s.L
    DO transmit (s.t[i]);
    transmit ('$')
    END
END {input program};
```

output program:

```
VAR A:Atype; B:block; j:integer;
BEGIN
    WHILE "input available"
    DO BEGIN
            j := 1;
            WHILE (j ≤M) AND "input available"
            DO BEGIN A↑[j]: = next input character;
                        j := j+1
            END;
            IF j >1 THEN put (A)
    END
END {output program};
```

The interaction of these programs is as follows:

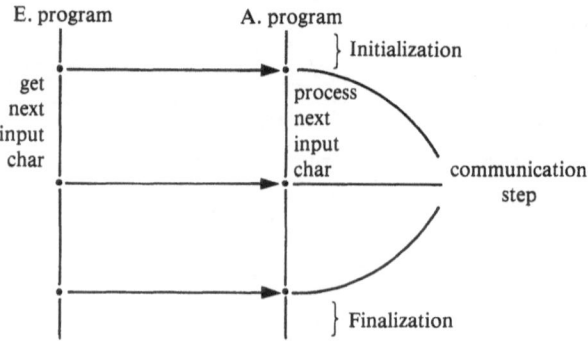

- 92 -

Between two communication steps it is irrelevant whether we first perform the input or the output program. Both parts of the program could run in parallel or merged in time. It is possible to interpret every communication step as an operation of the form:

resume: Interrupt the running program
and enter processing of the second program
at the former interrupt.

In the beginning the starting address of a process is taken as the former point of interrupt.

Communicating programs with this interpretation are called *coroutines*. We may not only consider two coroutines, also arrangements with $n > 2$ coroutines are possible. Coroutine interaction may lead to one of the following control flows:

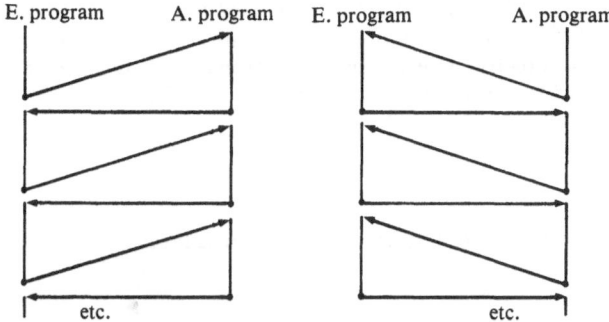

In our example the control flow on the right may also be interpreted as: the operation "transmit" is a process call which initiates the next output step; or the operation "next input character" is a process call which initiates the necessary input step. If we choose the first interpretation we will get the following scheme for putting the input and output programs together:

(1) The initializing phases of both programs are put together in any order.

(2) The output program is cut at the communication step and the statements from one communication step to the next are put together to form a procedure. Thereafter each communication by the input program is transformed into a call of this procedure.

(3) Any final processing of the output program is attached to the final phase of the input program.

M.A. Jackson calls this transformation *(program-) inversion*. The difficulty of the inversion is that we normally cut a loop (in our example even a double loop) into pieces.

In the example the initialization of the output consists of the assignment $j := 1$ and the test "$j \leq M$ AND input available". The cutting of the loops results in a procedure with body

```
A↑[j]: = next input character;
j := j + 1;
{if the condition of the inner loop holds, we are finished; otherwise we continue in the
outer loop}
IF j > M
THEN BEGIN IF j > 1 THEN put (A);
j := 1
END
```

The final processing of the output consists of the statement

if j > 1 THEN put (A)

This is to be executed when the input is exhausted.

If we cut the output program as indicated above we say "the output program has been inverted". The input program then becomes the main program. We could also invert the input program and transform the output program into the main program.

When we invert the output program we delete all tests "input available" because the input program ensures the procedure transmit is called only with available input characters. If we further assume that $M \geq 1$ several more tests can be deleted.

If a coroutine is inverted we may consider the resulting procedures as operations of an abstract data type. This idea is frequently used by experienced programmers to derive the complete program (main program and inverted coroutine) from the statement of work directly. This method is, however, not recommended because it will very often lead to errors in the initialization and finalization.

REFERENCE

Jackson M.A. (1975), Principles of Program Design. Academic Press.

EXERCISES

1. Give a complete solution for example 2 with the input program as main program and the output program inverted.
2. Give a solution for example 2 with the output program as main program and the input program inverted.

Solution to exercise 1

```
PROGRAM input_main (input, output);
CONST M = {some value > 1};
       N = {some value > 1};

TYPE Erecord = RECORD L:0..N;
                      t:ARRAY[1..N] OF CHAR
                      END;
       Etype = FILE OF Erecord;
VAR E:Etype; A:Atype; i,j:integer;
PROCEDURE transmit (c:char);
{inversion of the output loop}
BEGIN  A↑[j]: = c;
       j := j + 1;
       IF j > M THEN BEGIN put (A); j := 1 END
END    {transmit};

BEGIN  {initialization of output:}
       j := 1;
       {input program:}
```

```
                WHILE NOT eof (E);
                DO
                BEGIN get (E);
                FOR i : = 1 TO E↑.L
                DO transmit (E↑.t[i]);
                transmit ('$')
                END;
                {finalization of output:}
                IF j > 1 THEN put (A)
        END;
```

Solution to exercise 2

```
        PROGRAM output_main (input, output);
        CONST M  =  {some value  >  1};
                 N  =  {some value  >  1};

        TYPE Erecord = RECORD L:0..N;
                              t:ARRAY[1..N] OF CHAR
                              END;
                 Etype = FILE OF Erecord;
        VAR E:Etype; A:Atype; i,j:integer;
        available : Boolean;
        PROCEDURE next input (VAR c:char);
        {inversion of the input loop}
        BEGIN   IF available
                THEN IF i ≤ E↑.L
                THEN BEGIN c : = E↑.t[i]; i : = i + 1; END
                ELSE BEGIN c : = '$'; i : = 1;
                        IF eof (E)
                        THEN available : = FALSE
                        ELSE get (E)
                        END
                ELSE {no result if not available!}
        END     {next input};

        BEGIN   {initialization of input:}
                available : = NOT eof (E);
                IF available
                THEN BEGIN get (E);
                ELSE {no input available};
                {main program:}
                WHILE available
                DO BEGIN
                        j := 1;
                        WHILE (j ≤ M) AND available
                        DO BEGIN next input (A↑ [j]);
                        j := j + 1;
                        END;
                        IF j > 1 THEN put (A)
                END;
                {no finalization of input necessary}
        END {main program};
```

MANAGING SOFTWARE DEVELOPMENT

Martyn Dowell
Joint Research Centre,
Ispra, Italy

INTRODUCTION

In this chapter the organizational and managerial aspects of software development are covered. The problems involved and the present set of attempted solutions are considered. Suggestions are made regarding the use of various techniques for software development projects. Such projects may be very diverse in terms of scale, constraints, goals etc.

1. CLASSES OF SOFTWARE DEVELOPMENT PROJECTS

The term "Software development project" encompasses many varied schemes. The following list is designed to show the diversity of projects but is by no means meant to be an exhaustive list.

Time-scale	$\left\{\begin{array}{l}\text{1 man/month} \\ . \\ \text{100 man/years}\end{array}\right.$
Constraints	$\left\{\begin{array}{l}\text{must be finished in 6 months} \\ \text{must be well documented} \\ \text{must run in 100 k bytes}\end{array}\right.$
Resources	$\left\{\begin{array}{l}\left\{\begin{array}{l}\text{1 man research project} \\ . \\ \text{as many people as you need!}\end{array}\right. \\ \left\{\begin{array}{l}\text{complete use of a Cray I} \\ . \\ \text{pocket calculator}\end{array}\right.\end{array}\right.$
Goals	$\left\{\begin{array}{l}\text{must execute test data X} \\ \text{must be free of all errors!} \\ \text{must prove a hypothesis}\end{array}\right.$

D. T. Muxworthy (ed.), Programming for Software Sharing, 97–107.
Copyright © 1983 ECSC, EEC, EAEC, Brussels and Luxembourg.

Some of the particular aspects of scientific research, educational training, commercial and industrial software development can be seen in the above list.

Obviously when talking about "writing programs" or "writing a software package" or "developing a system" or many other loosely related terms, the size, goals, resources and constraints may vary from one end of the spectrum to the other. The set of problems involved in the development may be common to all these types of projects, but the emphasis and importance of individual problems will differ greatly.

When considering the organization and the management of a project, most of the published papers consider the problems in management of large- scale or medium-scale projects. The programs to be developed are large, the staff involved at least a team of five or six persons and sometimes many such teams working together, and manpower required is measured in many man/months or even man/years. In this paper such projects are considered and a review of the various suggested techniques is given. However, consideration is also given to much smaller projects, with typically one or two persons and with programs produced being generally relatively small.

2. CONVENTIONAL ORGANIZATION AND MANAGEMENT OF SOFTWARE DEVELOPMENT

Here the problems involved in organization and management of software development are decomposed into three composite parts:

The *project structure* concerns how the problem is to be solved. That is it involves the methodologies used.

The *personnel organizational structure* concerns how the people who are involved in the project are organized.

The *management* of the project which implies making the project structure and the personnel organizational structure work efficiently.

The Project Structure

Although there is almost universal agreement that it is necessary to define a project structure or project plan, there are some conflicting views as to the type of project structure which should be adopted. The most commonly used structure is the "system life cycle" plan (Rubin, 1970) which sees the development in terms of the stages of: specification, design, implementation, validation and maintenance. Amongst many other possibilities are: an "evolutionary" type of plan or in more specific cases the use of rapid prototyping followed by a conventional life cycle plan. Each of these plans have their protagonists and their opponents. In certain cases one of these plans may be more suitable than another. However, what is important from the standpoint of project structure is that the plan should not be simply regarded as a theoretical decomposition of the problem, but that it should actually be used to manage the project.

In Boehm (1977) a list of reasons for failure of software projects is given as follows:

- plan not used to manage the project
- poor planning
- plan not used to manage the project
- ill-defined contract

- plan not used to manage the project
- poor planning
- plan not used to manage the project
- unstable problem definition
- plan not used to manage the project.

This, although a light-hearted view of the situation, makes very clear the importance given to planning and the use of a project plan.

Boehm takes advice for planning software development much further. He suggests that not only should one use an explicit life-cycle plan, but also that one should have a sequential development approach, completing each step before proceeding to the next. In this way one may attempt to keep iterations in the process between adjacent steps. The tendency, often for seemingly good reasons, to wander from this disciplined planning, may result in belated recognition of problems which in turn may lead to partial or complete software redesign and overruns in schedule and costs.

Personnel Organizational Structure

To some extent the organizational structuring of personnel engaged in large projects should complement the project structure. In Daly (1980) it is suggested that a useful analogy may be made between the concepts employed in organizational decomposition and the concepts employed in software project decomposition.
The analogies are as follows:

1. Software   - each software segment should be small, so that it can easily be understood.

   Organization - each software team should be small so that it can be effectively controlled.

2. Software   - each software segment should be loosely coupled to other software segments.

   Organization - each software team should be assigned a unit of work which allows for minimal coupling of software teams.

3. Software   - each software segment should enjoy high cohesion (perform one function).

   Organization - each software team should be assigned a unit of work which is higly cohesive.

4. Software   - the scope of a software segment should be a subset of the scope of control.

   Organization - software teams should be grouped together under one manager in such a way that these manager groups have minimal effect on the work of other manager groups.

5. Software   - software is decomposed into a hierarchy of segments, higher-level segments performing decision making and lower-level segments doing the actual work.

   Organization - the management hierarchy performs the decision making and the lower organizational levels do the actual work.

| 6. Software | - pathological connections (i.e. ones not following the hierarchical structure) should be avoided or at least fully documented. |
| Organization | - pathological connections should be avoided among programmers or at least fully documented. |

Further discussion is contained in Daly (1980) concerning the appropriate type of organizational structure for software development. Three possible types of structure are considered:

A *project organization* in which individual projects are separated and have individual directors.

A *functional organization* in which one director is in charge of all projects and has at his disposal various groups which are responsible for functional tasks. Examples of the groups might be: the real-time software group, software tools group, mathematical software groups for the appropriate functional tasks in various projects.

A *matrix organization* is a complex organizational structure exhibiting the properties of both previous groups. There is an overall director but also project directors. Simple matrix structures are two-dimensional with a functional and a project dimension. The function director decides how to do the job and provides the resources. The project director decides what to do.

All of these structures may be used effectively in varying circumstances. The type of company involved, the scale of the project or projects being undertaken, the type of directors, all have an impact on which type of organization is most appropriate in any particular case.

Structuring Software Teams

In the previous section large-scale projects with many teams of software developers were considered. In this section the structure of such teams is considered. This applies equally well for the structure of individual teams in large-scale projects and for medium-scale projects which consist of only one such team.

The idea of structuring teams of workers to give individual members specific functions is not a new one, nor is it solely limited to the field of software development. Such structuring is well known, for example, in the building industry. In the context of software development, the best known of many plans and formulae for team structuring is the Chief Programmer Team as described by Baker (1972).

The Chief Programer Team consists of the following:

The *chief programmer* who is the technical manager of the team. All members of the team report directly to the chief programmer. He is, however, not solely a manager but he is also responsible for the coding of the critical segments of the program (or the section of the program for which the team is responsible).

The *back-up programmer* is the second person (along with the chief programmer) who is totally familiar with the overall team project. He is a peer of the chief programmer and participates with him, in making all the important decisions. He, like the chief programmer, participates in the coding of vital parts of the project and often acts as a type of research assistant for the chief programmer.

The *programming secretary* is responsible for recording details of the project in both machine-readable and human-readable form. The programming secretary must make sure that these records are kept up-to-date. This helps to minimize errors due to misunderstandings between members of the programming team of the state of various software modules. An advantage in having a programming secretary is that there is a significant saving in the amount of clerical work necessary for the programmers in the team. It is considered important that the programming secretary is regarded as a full member of the team and not simply an assistant drafted in to take over some clerical rôles.

Typically three or four *programmers* are included in the team, the actual number being decided by the chief programmer. They perform coding tasks as specified by the chief programmer.

The claims are that this type of team structure provides "functional separation, discipline and teamwork" and that such teams substantially improve "the manageability, quality and productivity of programming". Certainly there are good examples showing effective use of such team structure.

Chief Architect Team

The Chief Architect Team structure can be regarded as an extension of the Chief Programmer team. The analogy, which is suggested by the name, is with the building industry. Terms such as "apprentices" and "toolsmiths" are used to described the functional rôles of members of the teams. The important additional to the personnel of the team is the *chief architect* who is reponsible for performing the various levels of abstraction in the design phase of the project.

In the description of the team structure, Lewis (1977) describes the use of the *"blueprint"* specification languages to document the design phase of the project.

As the chief architect may be responsible for many different projects a *job captain* is added who is responsible for administrative affairs and is a general "trouble-shooter".

Other Team Structures

Many other team structures have been suggested most of which are variants of the Chief Programmer Team. However, alternative opinions have suggested that the hierarchical structure of a team is less significant than the functional rôles and the cohesion and "teamwork". A *team of peers* each with a well defined functional responsibility may well produce results as good as a more conventional hierarchical team.

Many of the successful examples of Chief Programmer team efficiency may be attributed to the composition of the teams and the choice of a good chief programmer. A demonstrative negative example of hierarchical team functioning is that of Towster's account of a case study of the use of the Chief Architect Team which is given as an appendix to Lewis (1977). The personnel in the team, although competent programmers etc., did not satisfactorily fit into the assigned rôles. The team interaction system, although excellent in theory, did not work in practice. Consequently the team did not function efficiently.

The moral of this cautionary tale seems to be: *get good people, suitable for the functional responsibility who will work together as a team. If you don't, then you will fail no matter how good your team structure may appear on paper.*

Managing Projects

As already mentioned in the previous sections, the theoretical structuring the projects and the organization of teams may be undermined if the people involved in the work do not fit the job or do not interact well with each other. One of the purposes of project management is to make sure that the set-up of the project in terms of both structure and personnel is performed correctly and also to make sure that it functions well in the course of the project.

Severe problems will be caused by the structure not fitting the personnel or conversely the personnel not fitting the structure. It is certainly not useful to introduce a project structure which does not fit in with the general organization of the company or group. The creation of "team spirit" or "team loyalty" is an obvious important aspect of the well-functioning of the team. The formation of teams in which functional responsibility is well defined seems to be a positive stimulus in this respect.

Tools and Aids for Project Management

In this section we discuss two possible types of sources of assistance in managing software development.

Firstly, *configuration management tools* which can provide an information database about the state of the development cycle.

Secondly, *review techniques* which enable the monitoring and control of the life-cycle and the evaluation of the work at various stages of the cycle.

Configuration Management Tools

For the effective management of software development it is necessary to monitor and record the progess and development of the product (i.e. the program or package). Such monitoring may now be performed by using various computer-based packages or programs. Such aids are often called "software configuration management tools" (Bersoff, Henderson and Siegel, 1979). They provide methods for keeping computer-based information about various versions and variants of the software product, documentation of various segments of the product, a history of testing procedure and many other aids to monitor the various aspects of project development. These types of tools may also provide mechanisms for producing latest object versions of the product from all latest source segments and for directly associating equivalent object and source codes.

Such sophisticated tools are becoming more and more a standard feature of the more modern operating systems of smaller computer systems. They automate the various parts of the management of the development of the project which are normally most susceptible to human error.

Review Techniques

As stated above, one effective way of considering the structure of a project is as an explicit system life-cycle plan with a sequential development approach, completing each step before passing to the next. In order to effectively execute the plan there has to be some evaluation and a decision making mechanism to ascertain whether or not the criteria for the transition from one step to the next in the sequential cycle have been met. This evaluation mechanism may also be used at critical points within the phases. Such *review techniques* must be used in such a way as to effectively control the life-cycle without choking it by controlling it too tightly. It is important to attempt to detect and correct errors in the design and implementation as early as possible. It is clear, for example, that errors in the design of a system will continue into lower levels of abstraction and thus into the finished program.

At later stages errors may by much more difficult and more expensive to repair. The review techniques may be used to review the designer's or the programmer's or the tester's work. Their aim is to eliminate errors at an early stage and also to have a final program which contains many less undetected errors.

The five terms which are commonly used to describe the different types of such review techniques are;

walkthroughs, structured walkthroughs, code inspections, design inspections, and *team debugging.*

The more formal inspection techniques described by Fagan (1976) consist of well defined procedures for inspection of the design, coding, testing phase of the development and also inspections for program documentation (Ascoly, Cafferty, Gruen and Kohli, 1976). This enables a detailed review of the various coded segments giving various checklists depending on the programming language used.

The full inspection series consists of the following:

$$\left.\begin{array}{l} I_0 \\ I_1 \\ I_2 \end{array}\right\} \text{Design inspections} \qquad \left.\begin{array}{l} PI_0 \\ PI_1 \\ PI_2 \end{array}\right\} \begin{array}{l} \text{Publication inspections} \\ \text{(program documentation)} \end{array}$$

$$\left.\begin{array}{l} IT_1 \\ \\ IT_2 \end{array}\right\} \text{Test phase inspections}$$

The inspection team consists of the following personnel:

The *moderator:* the key person in the inspection team. He need not be a technical expert on the program being inspected. In fact it may be advantageous to use a moderator from a totally unrelated project. The job of the moderator is to manage and lead the inspection team. The moderator must schedule the meetings, report inspection results (within one day), and follow-up any rework necessary because of errors found during the inspection.

The *designer:* is the programmer responsible for producing the program design.

The *code/implementor:* the programmer responsible for translating the design into code.

The *tester:* is the programmer responsible for writing and testing the product.

If, however, the coder is also the designer of the code, then he will function as the designer in the inspection team and some other coder from another project will perform the rôle of coder and similarly in the situation where other functions are performed by the same person. Therefore, an inspection team will generally consist of four persons. In a case where the piece of code has external interfaces to other pieces of code it may be necessary to include the others concerned.

In the various articles concerned with review techniques, many cases of considerable saving in manpower and reduction of errors in the finished product have been quoted. Although not significant in a statistical sense, these examples of savings point to the significance of such review techniques.

3. MANAGING SMALL-SCALE PROJECTS

In the first section of this chapter the diversity of the types of projects has been considered. One particular type of project which can be identified could be called the "scientific research and development" project. Amongst the typical attributes of this type of project are:

- very limited manpower is involved in the project (1 or 2 persons usually the same ones for all stages of the project)
- the time taken, although often very short (1-2 months), may also not be as limited and is sometimes of the order of 1 or 2 man years
- the project is performed by persons who are not computer science specialists and may have only limited computer science education.

In terms of "management", there are two important initial points to make regarding these projects. Firstly, the management policies and suggestions described in the previous sections are not always the ideals which are at the top of the priority list of the persons undertaking these projects. The underlying reasons for the general lack of management in these cases are complex in nature. The growth of management methodologies aimed at large medium-scale commercial projects has been caused by the financial necessity of improving the realiability and efficiency of management of projects in this area following many notable project failures. In the scientific research and development field similar failures are not so spectacularly obvious or subject to such exhaustive "post-mortem" investigations.

Scientific research workers have tended to see computer program development as an ancilliary part of their work to be performed with the minimal amount of effort and formality or as an exciting new toy to be played with in a non-systematic way. This attitude has partly arisen because of a lack of education and training in computing aspects (both for the persons undertaking the projects and also their supervisors). There are a number of points to made regarding education of persons concerned with such projects. Many of them have had little or no formal education in the general aspects of computer science. Even less have ever had formal education specifically related to the organization and management of software development (which would normally be found within, for example, a software engineering course). In recent years computer science students have been provided with more formal education in these aspects of the subject. However, students from other disciplines, who receive computer science education as a secondary part of their syllabus, are rarely taught such aspects. It is much more usual to teach them about "programming" as their computer science education. In this way the misguided idea that writing the instructions of the program is the most important part (and perhaps even the only part) of a software development project, is perpetuated. Computer science education of persons from other disciplines should stress strongly the ideas of phased, planned and controlled software development. Further education or re-education of persons, who may have their only formal computer science education more than 20 years ago, is necessary to give them a wider and more modern view of the methodologies associated with software development.

Another reason for the unfortunate attitude towards software development is that projects being undertaken are often conceived as "one-off" or "throw away" with no long-term usefulness. Many times projects are undertaken in the belief that the work is "one-off" and only at a later stage is it decided that the finished product has wider applicability in the organization or could be useful in other organizations. This is usually due to a lack of foresight at the requirements specification stage of the project. Projects conceived as "one-off" not for sharing which are subsequently defined to be of permanent use to be shared with others are usually bad products. A far-seeing management decision at the outset to perform the project with a view to providing a well documented finished product, with thought at every stage to sharing of the software, will not guarantee a good finished product. It will, however, give the project an execellent foundation on which the finished product can be built.

Education will give persons involved in such projects an awareness of the need for method and organization in the execution of projects. It will not, however, present them with an existing overall methodology which is easily applicable to their type of work. For example, one may say that review techniques should be used to check the completeness of the various stages of the development. However, when there is only one person involved in the project the possibility of organizing much a review process often does not seen feasible. So, consideration must be given to adaptation of the various management methodologies to suit such small-scale projects.

The following guidelines can be used:

Project and Personnel Structure

Structuring the execution of the work is very important for this type of project. The few persons involved in the project must be aware of the various functional rôles that they must undertake and must be careful to separate the work involved in each of these functional rôles.

The rôle of the implementor often swamps all of the other rôles in terms of importance, thus, leading to an unsystematic implementation which should be avoided at all costs.

Team structures in such situations of limited personnel are not applicable. Even in this case, the awareness of functional rôles helps to generate an organizational structure, for the performance of the work, which has a positive influence.

Tools for Project Management

When manpower resources are limited, the use of configuration management tools becomes imperative. Such tools can almost be seen as additional members of programmer teams. Much of the burden of the secretarial work can be eased by using such tools. The automation of the management and the enforcement of standards provide a systematic environment for the software developer.

Review Techniques

As previously stated, lack of manpower can make the use of review techniques in small-scale projects very difficult. However, these type of techniques can be particular useful in an environment where there is a tendency towards non-standard approachs to aspects of development due to a lack of professional contact with other member of the project (because perhaps there are no other members of the project). The use of review techniques could help towards a more standard "egoless" approach to the work.

The logistics of arranging and performing review sessions depend on the type of organization in which the work is being performed. There is scope, however, for collaboration between workers on different projects to a "review co-operative" or in a large-scale organization perhaps the computing department could have a specialized "review group" who would provide a service to the user community. It can be seen that specific procedures for management of small-scale scientific research and development projects are not appropriate. However, the following overall guidelines may be given:

- decompose the project into a structured plan. The use of that plan to manage the performance of the project is vital.
- ensure that the persons undertaking the project are always aware of the various different functional rôles (e.g. implementor, designer etc.) they must perform and are aware of the separation of the work involved in each of these rôles.
- use configuration management tools to standardize the project work, assure the quality of the software and add "extra" staff to the project.
- use review techniques to control the various steps of the development plan. (These may have to be organized on a co-operative basis or obtained from some outside agency).
- educate and train project workers to make them aware of modern computer project management techniques.

4. CONCLUSIONS

Managing software development projects is something which is often given either little or no consideration. Only over the last few years, following many notorious examples of the failure of software development projects, has the necessity of having efficient management of software development been recognized.

It is not possible to define the "Laws of Software Development Management" because there is too much diversity in the types of projects involved. Many of the proposed systematic (and rigid) ways of grouping together teams or performing reviews rely heavily, in practice, on the quality of the persons involved and their level of training and education.

For small-scale development projects of the kind which are typically found in a scientific environment, management of projects is also necessary. Many of the ideas which have proved to be successful for large-scale projects may be tailored to suit this type of project.

Education and training of persons involved in all aspects and levels of software development to convince them that a more methodical approach is necessary is by far the most important requirement.

REFERENCES

Ascoly J, Cafferty M.J., Gruen S.J. and Kohli O.R. (1976), "Code Inspection Specification" IBM System Communication Division, Internal Document TR 21.630.

Baker F.T. (1972), "Chief Programmer Team Management of Production Programming" IBM System Journal Vol. 11, n. 1.

Bersoff E.H., Henderson V.D. and Siegel S.G. (1979), "Software Configuration Management: a Tutorial" Computer Vol. 12, n. 1 pp. 6-14 (Jan. 1979)

Boehm B.W. (1977), ''Seven Basic Principles for Software Engineering'' Infotech Report on Software Engineering Techniques.

Daly E.B. (1980), ''Organizational Philosophies Used in Software Development'' Infotech State of the Art Review (1980).

Fagan M.E. (1976), ''Design and Code Inspections to Reduce Errors in Program Development'', IBM System Journal 15, pp. 182-211.

Lewis T.G. (1977), ''Blueprint Languages and the Chief Architect Concept'' Infotech Report on Software Engineering Techiques.

Rubin M.L. (1970), ''Handbook of Data Processing Management Vol. 1, Introduction to the System Life-Cycle'' Princeton, Brandon/System Press.

Flexibility

FLEXIBILITY

William Waite
University of Colorado
Boulder, Colorado USA

The term "flexibility" denotes a property of software which enables one to change it easily to meet a variety of different user and system requirements. This property is important because it increases the useful life of a piece of software and extends its range of application, thereby permitting the development cost to be recovered over a wider market. Reliability is also enhanced, since a new application involves code which has already been proven by extensive use.

1. THE BASIS OF FLEXIBILITY

In general, flexibility is achieved by isolating certain decisions in such a way as to make them easy to change. This is the root of Parnas' (1972) philosophy of modular decomposition: each module embodies one or more related design decisions. Changes in these decisions do not propagate beyond the boundaries of the modules which embody them. The isolation is achieved by providing a fixed module interface whose properties are independent of the design decision(s) involved.

A particular collection of module interface specifications constitutes a set of primitives representing data and operations (Goos 1982b). These primitives may be combined according to given rules into an algorithm which solves a certain problem. The combination of primitives and composition rules is termed a level of abstraction, and may be thought of as a language or as a machine (Tanenbaum 1976). It is important to note that the properties of a level of abstraction are fixed.

There are three kinds of decision which must be made when implementing a module:

— a level of abstraction must be chosen.
— the algorithm must be expressed in terms of the chosen level.
— the primitives of the chosen level must be implemented.

Choice of a level of abstraction occurs early in the process (Goos 1982a), and cannot reasonably be deferred. Flexibility must therefore be achieved by deferring decisions

D. T. Muxworthy (ed.), Programming for Software Sharing, 111–125.
Copyright © 1983 ECSC, EEC, EAEC, Brussels and Luxembourg.

about expression of the algorithm and implementation of the primitives. A module in which the algorithm is easily altered is often termed *adaptable*, while one in which the implementation of the primitives is easily altered is often termed *portable* (Poole and Waite, 1977).

Implementation of the primitives of a level of abstraction requires realization of the interfaces defining the modules which constitute these primitives. Hence such implementation is merely one instance of the general problem of module implementation, and it need not be considered further. A crucial problem, however, lies in the specification of the module interfaces; I shall return to this point later.

Alteration of the algorithm as it appears on a given level of abstraction requires changes in the text of the algorithm. Such textual changes can be made manually or automatically; they are eased if the structure of the algorithm is regular, and its components clearly identified.

As an example of software flexibility, let us consider a package of routines which implement elementary functions (e.g. square root, trigonometric sine, etc.). The level of abstraction chosen to express these algorithms must provide primitives for integer and floating-point arithmetic, decomposition of a floating-point number into exponent and significand, and conditionals based upon integer and floating-point values. There must be provisions for defining constant values (Cody and Waite, 1980).

The assembly language for a particular computer is the usual level of abstraction chosen to express such routines. Some flexibility might be achieved by using macros to define calling sequences, so that the same package could be adapted to the calling conventions of several high-level languages. This would be an instance of automatic textual alteration used to defer a decision on the exact form of the calling sequence.

Further flexibility could be achieved by using a different level of abstraction to express the algorithms. Suppose, for example, that we specify all floating-point primitives in terms of a general model characterized by a set of parameters (Brown and Hall, 1977). The meanings of these parameters, but not their values, are fixed by the model; the values are fixed by a particular implementation. We now make the algorithms dependent upon the parameter values, increasing flexibility by deferring the decision about how the primitives are to be implemented.

2. THE CHARACTERISTICS OF AN ABSTRACTION

As mentioned in the previous section, an abstraction consists of a set of primitives (both operations and data types) and a set of composition rules. Goos (1982a, 1982b) has shown examples of abstractions which are built from modules within the framework of a programming language. The language itself also constitutes an abstraction, one which is crucial to the construction of shareable software. In order to make effective use of the abstraction provided by the language for writing shareable programs, the programmer must be thoroughly familiar with the *official* standard. Particular implementations of the language normally differ from the standard, and hence experience at one or two installations is generally useless when constructing portable programs.

The study of a language standard, or indeed the definition of any abstraction, should be approached systematically. Each has three aspects:

— Syntax.   A specification of all well-formed constructs based upon the abstraction.

— Semantics.   A specification of the meaning of any well-formed construct in terms of the primitives of the abstraction.

— Pragmatics. A description of the meanings of the primitives of the abstraction in terms of concepts lying outside of the abstraction.

For the purposes of this discussion, I shall consider the syntax of an abstraction to include *all* conditions which bear upon the well-formation of a program. Thus I include not only the usual context-free syntax, but also any necessary context conditions. This point of view has been taken in the definition of Algol 68, and shows promise of being carried over into other language definitions as well.

There is reasonable agreement in the literature about formal methods for syntax specification. Context-free grammars have been specified in BNF (Naur 1963) and its variants for many years; more recently, two-level grammars (van Wijngaarden et al., 1975) and attribute grammars (Knuth 1968) have been used to add information about context conditions. Three methods of formally specifying semantics have received considerable attention. They are the so-called operational (Lucas and Walk, 1969), axiomatic (Hoare 1969, Dijkstra 1976) and denotational (Tennent 1976) methods. The last seems to be gaining popularity, but no clear consensus has yet emerged. By its very nature, the pragmatics of an abstraction cannot be specified formally within the abstraction itself. It may be possible to describe the pragmatics of one abstraction formally in terms of another, but such descriptions often lend little insight. (See Liskov and Zilles, 1975, for a summary of definitional techniques applicable to abstractions consisting of collections of modules).

The remainder of this section attemps to provide a taxonomy for abstractions by summarizing the properties of typical programming languages. I shall not attempt to provide details here, but shall merely layout an appropriate framework for studying a language standard. My organization will be "bottom-up", starting with the primitives, but the framework itself is independent of the order in which one chooses to explore it.

Primitives

The starting point for pragmatics is the universe of values described by the language. These values are grouped into classes (called *modes* or *types*) according to the operations applicable to them. Most programming languages provide similar sets of primitive modes, summarized in Figure 1.

Finite modes
> Truth values
> Character values
> Enumerated values

Infinite modes
> Integer values
> Fixed-point values
> Floating-point values

Figure 1
Typical Primitive Modes

The elements of any finite mode can be placed in one-to-one correspondence with a subset of the natural numbers. Finite modes are most often used, however, when a numerical interpretation of the values is meaningless. For this reason, most of the properties induced by such a mapping are irrelevant. One notable exception is the ordering property. It is often useful to know that *some* ordering exists on a finite set, even though the precise details of that ordering are unknown. For example, a binary chop algorithm can be used to look values up in a table if some order exists; the particular order is irrelevant for this task. In most cases a language definition will guarantee that the values of a finite mode are ordered, although it does not specify relationships among specific values.

Only a finite number of elements of a given infinite mode can ever be represented in the computer. Some language definitions do not make this restriction explicitly, but simply rely upon the experience of the reader. Others recognize the limitation but do not characterize it, while still others define some set of "finiteness" parameters which can be used to specify the values existing in a given implementation. Figure 2 gives examples of each of these cases.

ANS X3.9-1978 (Fortran), Section 4.3:

   "An integer datum is always an exact representation of an integer value. It may assume a positive, negative, or zero value."

   a. No specification of finiteness

Algol 60 Revised Report, Section 3.3.6:

   "Numbers ... of type *real* must be interpreted in the sense of numerical analysis, i.e. as entities defined inherently with only finite accuracy."

   b. Specification but no characterization of values

Pascal User Manual and Report, Chapter 2.B:

   "If a and b are integer expressions, the operation a *op* b is guaranteed to be correctly implemented when

   abs (a *op* b) ≤ maxint,
   abs (a)   ≤ maxint, and
   abs (b)   ≤ maxint

   c. Characterization of legal values

Figure 2 Specification of Infinite Modes

Integer operations are exact (provided that no overflow occurs) and are generally implemented in machine hardware or firmware. The allowable range of integers is usually quite small, however, and may be exceeded by many computations. In order to carry out such computations, we employ scaled values consisting of an exponent and a significand of fixed precision. Floating-point values specify both exponent and significand, and are manipulated by hardware, firmware or software operations. The scaling is maintained automatically by the implementation of the floating-point operations. A fixed-point value, on the other hand, specifies only the significand; the programmer must keep track of the scaling explicitly. Fixed-point operations on most computers use the normal integer hardware and hence may be significantly faster than the corresponding floating-point operations. In addition, the fixed-point significand often provides more precision because it occupies the same space as the entire floating-point number.

Languages often define equivalence relations among values of infinite modes, and these form the basis for *transfer functions*. Transfer functions have been classified as "generalizing" when their application does not lead to a loss of information, and "de-generalizing" otherwise. Generalizing transfer functions are sometimes automatically assumed by a language compiler in certain contexts (coercion). The prime example is automatic conversion of an integer into an equivalent real. It should be obvious from our discussion of infinite modes in the previous paragraph, however, that information may be lost in such a conversion. Figure 3 illustrates the evolution of the Algol 68 definition to account for exactly that phenomenon.

Algol 68 Report, Section 2.2.3.1.d:

> "Each integer of a given length number is equivalent to a real number of that length number... These equivalences permit the 'widening' of an integer into a real number..."

> a. No loss of information assumed

Revised Report on Algol 68, Section 2.1.3.1.e:

> "... each integer of a given size is 'widenable to' a real number close to it and of that same size; ..."

> b. Loss of information assumed

Figure 3
Integer-to-Real Conversion

Composite Operators and Operands

The semantics of most programming languages provide similar sets of composition rules. Figure 4 summarizes the typical semantic mechanisms embodied in these rules. The rules are normally defined in terms which reflect the essential relationship of the rule. For example, trees are used to describe both the component relationship in arrays and records and the data flow relationship in expressions. In some cases the semantics of the tree may not coincide with certain properties which we intuitively associate with the construct as it is written. Consider, for example, a two-dimensional array. There are two basic ways of representing such an object as tree:

— Each array element is an immediate component of the composite object.
— Each row (or column) is an immediate component of the composite object, and each element is an immediate component of its row (or column).

Neither representation preserves the intuitive concept of adjacency of elements in two dimensions which we attribute to the original array. This loss of intuition may be particularly serious when the tree is mapped onto the (piecewise) linear memory of a/computer: due to the particular structure of the hardware, advancing to an adjacent element in one dimension may be an order of magnitude more expensive than a similar advance in the other. Some indications of which advance will be cheap can be obtained by studying the tree postulated by the language definition - an implementor will normally use successive storage locations for the immediate descendents of a single node.

Composition of Values and Operations
    Arrays
    Records
    Expressions

Control of Command Execution
    Conditional
    Iteration
    Transfer

State Component Creation and Update
    Variables and Assignment
    Block entry/exit
    Controlled allocation

Abstraction
    Procedures
    Modules

Figure 4 Typical Semantic Mechanisms

Array selectors are computable by the program, whereas record selectors are not. Because we write the definition of a record as a sequence of field definitions, we tend to think of the order as being a property of the record. In many languages it is not. This means that we cannot use records to describe blocks of storage whose structure we know from other information. Some languages do define the order, however; as always one must read the standard carefully.

In some languages, or on some machines, direct comparison of composite objects is not permitted. The reason for this is that alignment constraints imposed by the hardware may preclude compact storage of the object. It will have "holes" - memory locations which are a part of the composite object but not a part of any of its components. Since these locations do not belong to any component, they will never be set when values are assigned to the components. A simple comparison of two records with identical components could therefore yield "unequal" due to differing values of the "holes".

The only constraint on evaluation order imposed by the tree semantics of an expression involves the subexpression property (data flow constraint). A language definition may or may not further constrain the order. Order of evaluation is interesting only when some subexpression has a side effect. If that side effect alters the value of another component of the expression then the value of the entire expression will depend upon the evaluation order. Some languages do not require evaluation of a part of an expression if it will not affect the result. The entire outcome of the program can be affected, however, if the omitted subexpression has a side effect on some other part of the state. The moral is to avoid side effects in expressions if possible. When it is not possible, be very careful to check all pronouncements of the standard regarding order of evaluation constraints or lack thereof.

Language implementors most frequently use partial evaluation rules to perform an optimization known as "short-circuiting" on Boolean expressions. This optimization is very important for expressions involving arithmetic comparisons, particularly when they appear in a context where the result is used only to control the execution sequence. Figure 5 illustrates the concept. The extra cost in figure 5c results from the conversion, retention and testing of the value (I.LT.10). It would still be present, although smaller, if the target machine instruction set provided a comparison operator which left its result in a register rather than the condition code.

Figure 5a *probably* does not conform to ANS X3.9-1978. The key point is the reasoning that led the programmer to include the subexpression (I.LT.10). I would suspect that M has dimension 10 and this expression is supposed to prevent referencing outside the array bounds. If my suspicion is correct then the programmer is assuming that short-circuit evaluation *will* take place, an assumption that is not justified by Section 6.6.7 of the standard.

IF ((I.LT.10) .AND. (M(I + 1) .EQ. 0)) M(I + 1) = M(I)

a.   A Fortran Statement

L	1,I	Register 1 := I
C	1, = 10	Compare to a constant 10
BNL	FALSE	Transfer if I is not smaller
L	2,M (1)	Register 2 := M(I)
SR	3,3	Register 3 := 0
CR	2,3	Compare
BNE	FALSE	Transfer if M(I) is nonzero
L	2,M-1 (1)	Set M (I + 1)
ST	2,M (1)	
FALSE - - -		Continuation

b.   Short-Circuit IBM 360 Code

LA	4,1	Present result = *true*
L	1,I	
C	1, = 10	
BL	NEXT	*if* I < 10 *then* retain preset result
SR	4,4	*else* set result = *false*
NEXT L	2,M (1)	
SR	3,3	
CR	2,3	
BNE	FALSE	
CR	4,3	Check the preset result
BE	FALSE	Transfer if it is false
L	2,M-1 (1)	
ST	2,M (1)	
FALSE - - -		

c.   IBM 360 Code Evaluating Both Subexpressions

Figure 5   Short-Circuit Evaluation

The construct of figure 5a is representative of a very useful class of Boolean expressions that require short-circuit evaluation. In response to this observation, more modern language designs are either defining Boolean expressions to require short-circuiting or providing special short-circuiting constructs. In Ada, for example, Figure 5a could be written "*if* I < 10 *and then* M[I] = 0 *then* M[I + 1]: = M[I] *end if*". I have found it all too easy to fall into the habit of using statements like that of Figure 5a when a particular compiler performs short-circuit optimization; a concious effort must be made to check the appropriate language standard and break the habit!

Sequence Control

Most constructs used to control command sequencing have straightforward semantics. The perennial problem is the *for* loop or its equivalent. Conceptually, this form of iteration corresponds to the universal quantifier ("for all i such that..."). In mathematics, the bound variable of the quantifier has no existence outside the quantified expression. Most programming languages do not regard the *for* as declaring its control variable (although this is becoming more popular), and hence it does exist outside the loop. Unfortunately, the concept of a *for* as the universal quantifier does not imply any reasonable value for the control variable outside the loop. Various languages have therefore defined it in various ways depending upon the historical biases of the language designer.

A second problem with the *for* loop arises from the manner in which it is usually implemented. Common applications of *for* loops include stepping through arrays and performing some operation a given number of times, and an implementor attempts to minimize the overhead of the loop for those applications. A typical implemention schema is shown in Figure 6a. Unfortunately, this schema fails if K is within L of the largest integer value. Suppose that we were running on a PDP11, whose maximum representable integer is 32767. The implementation fails for $J = 0$, $K = 32000$, $L = 1000$ because at statement 10 we attempt to add 1000 to 32000 and produce an overflow.

Figure 6b shows a correct schema for the important case $L = 1$. (Actually, this schema works whenever we can guarantee that I will become equal to K). Since many computers have hardware looping instructions which effectively use this schema, the chances of correct implementation of *for* loops with unit step are somewhat improved. To enhance portability, it is best to avoid large *for* loop bounds. As a rule of thumb, a programmer should probably seek other constructs if the magnitude of either bound exceeds 32766.

```
        I = J
        GOTO 2
1       - - Body of the loop
10      I = I + L
2       IF (I .LE. K) GOTO 1
```

a.   Typical, incorrect schema

```
        I = J
        IF (I .LE. K) GOTO 2
        GOTO 3
1       I = I + 1
2       - - Body of the loop
10      IF (I .NE. K) GOTO 1
3       - - Continuation
```

b.   Correct schema for L = 1

Figure 6   Implementation Schemata for DO 10 I = J,K,L

The Computation State

All of the information available to a computation at a given point in its execution history constitutes the *state* of that computation at that point. In this section we shall be concerned only with the portion of the state comprising the variables (both named and anonymous). The interesting property of these variables is their *lifetime* (or *extent*): the sequence of points in the execution history during which they remain components of the state. Extent is an important property because information can be stored in a variable only so long as it remains a component of the state.

A language definition guarantees some minimum lifetime for each variable. The implementor must provide at least this minimum, but is free to extend it if desirable. Fortran provides a classic example of such an extension. Section 17.3(6) of ANS X3.9-1978 states:

> "The execution of a RETURN statement or an END statement within a subprogram causes all entities within the subprogram to become undefined except for the following:
> (a) Entities in blank common.
> (b) Initially defined entities that have neither been redefined nor become undefined.
> (c) Entities specified by SAVE statements.
> (d) Entities in a named common block that appears in the subprogram and appears in at least one other program unit that is either directly or indirectly referencing the subprogram".

(With the exception of (c), Sections 10.2.4 through 10.2.6 of ANS X3.9-1966 have the same effect). From this definition we can deduce the minimum extents of all variables not mentioned in SAVE statements as:
— Local variables: Execution of the program unit in which they appear.
— Named common: Execution of any program unit in which the named common block appears.
— Blank common: Execution of the main program.

Fortran subprograms cannot be invoked recursively, and hence it is possible to determine the full storage requirements of a Fortran program at the time it is loaded. Most implementations use this fact to allocate the storage statically, thus avoiding the overhead of dynamic storage management. Since the allocation is static, the extent of every variable is the entire execution history of the program. This increased extent is apparent to the programmer in the fact that a value assigned to a local variable prior to exit from a subprogram will still have that value when the subprogram is re-entered. Although the standard does not guarantee the increased extent, many programmers have become so used to it that they believe it to be guaranteed. (Some respected distributors of portable software explicitly state that local variables are assumed to hold their values (Fox et al., 1975)). A somewhat more sophisticated error is to use named common as an implementation of shared storage for a module (Goos 1982b). Unless the common name appears in the main progam, it will not necessarily retain values from one invocation of the module to the next.

There are two situations in which an implementor will adhere more closely to the actual extent properties of Fortran: when overlaying is necessary to fit the program into available memory, and when the hardware of the target machine supports some form of dynamic storage allocation. (Burroughs machines are the most common example of the latter situation.) By studying the difference between overlaid and non-overlaid implementations, we can easily explain the need for rule 17.3(6)b above. Values are "initially defined" by DATA statements. Given the semantics of a DATA statement, a reasonable implementation on most machines is to place the specified value at the point in the load module representing the variable. The loading process thus performs the initialization without any need for initialization code. Suppose now that the program redefines the variable and then exits the program unit in which it appeared. If no overlays are involved, the variable will have the re-defined value when the program is re-entered. If, on the other hand, the program unit is overlaid then the load module will be re-loaded and the variable will revert to its initial value. Since the standard neither requires nor prohibits overlays, it must state that the value of the variable will be undefined. (Note that if no redefinition occurs then the variable will retain the initial value in all cases, and the wording of 17.3(6)b reflects this fact.)

Extent information may appear in a language definition in many guises. As we learn more about the fundamental concepts of programming languages, definitions will become more explicit about such things. Until that time, however, we must deduce important properties from statements about their effects, as in the case of Fortran.

Procedure Interaction

Procedures interact with one another via global variables and parameters. Interaction via global variables is quite straightforward; parameter mechanisms may be more difficult to understand. Figure 7 summarizes the five common parameter mechanisms. (In some cases the value mechanism is further constrained to prohibit assignments to the parameter.) Unfortunately, very few language definitions are explicit about the parameter mechanism(s) which they employ; this fact must be deduced from the effects.

Value:	The parameter is a local variable which is initialized to the argument value prior to procedure entry.
Result:	The parameter is a local variable which is not initialized. Its value is assigned to the argument subsequent to the procedure exit.
Value/result:	The parameter is a local variable which is initialized to the argument value prior to procedure entry. Its value is assigned to the argument subsequent to procedure exit.
Reference:	The parameter is the name represented by the argument prior to procedure entry.
Name:	The parameter is the name represented by the argument at the point of parameter access.

Figure 7 Typical Parameter Mechanisms

As an example of the process of determining the parameter mechanism, consider Fortran as defined by ANS X3.9-1978. Section 15.9.3 states that "at the execution of a function or subroutine reference, an association is established between the corresponding dummy and actual arguments." According to Section 2.14, "association of entities exists if the same datum may be identified ... by the same name or a different name in different program units of the same executable program." Taken together, these definitions eliminate value and result as possible mechanisms. (Since the parameter and argument are names for the same datum, the parameter has an initial value and any changes made in the subroutine will affect the caller.) Section 15.9.3 continues with "If an actual argument is an array element name, its subscript is evaluated just before the association takes place. Note that the subscript value remains constant as long as that association of arguments persists, even if the subscript contains variables that are redefined during the association." This statement eliminates the name mechanism, since if the subscript values change the parameter is no longer the name represented by the argument.

The definition of "association" seems to indicate that the reference mechanism must be used. A deeper analysis shows, however, that either of the two mechanisms not eliminated by the previous paragraph is possible. Let us first consider the difference between them. When value/result is used, the argument value can be changed only upon return from the subprogram. If an assignment is made to a reference parameter, however, the change in argument value occurs immediately. This difference is only apparent when there are several associations for the argument. In Figure 8, for example, the common variable M is associated with both J and K. If the value/result mechanism is used then the assignment to J does not affect the value of K immediately, and the value assigned to N is 4; the effect is immediate with the reference mechanism, and N is assigned 6. Section 15.9.3.6 explicitly prohibits assignment to a variable with multiple associations, however, and thus makes it impossible for a standard-conforming program to distinguish between the two mechanisms. (ANS X3.9-1966 has similar properties - the analysis is left as an exercise to the reader.)

```
FUNCTION I (J)
COMMON K
J = J + 1
K = K + 1
I = J + K
RETURN
END

COMMON M
M = 1
N = I (M)
:
```

Figure 8 A Non-Standard Fortran Program

Most implementations of Fortran use the reference mechanism. Some (such as that for the IBM 360/370) use value/result for simple variables and reference for arrays. The writer of a shareable program must therefore carefully adhere to the restrictions in the standard which guarantee that the behavior of a conforming program will be invariant under changes of the parameter mechanism.

3. THE MECHANICS OF FLEXIBILITY

The basic technology necessary to support flexible software has been available for over twenty years (Mock et al., 1958, McIlroy 1960). Automatic modification of text is used routinely in operating system generation, and entire line of computers has been based upon deferred implementation of a level of abstraction. In spite of this experience, most software is not flexible. The primary reasons seem to be political and economic rather than technical and I shall discuss those in the next section.

A computer manufacturer normally must support a variety of configurations of one machine to meet individual user needs. The cost of writing a distinct operating system for each such configuration would be prohibitive, and hence flexibility is an important consideration. In such a case the level of abstraction is fixed by the machine architecture, and it is necessary to vary the algorithm depending upon certain parameters derived from the configuration. The system is usually written in assembly language, and the variation accomplished by assembly-time operations (variables, conditionals, macros, etc.).

Many assembly languages provide a wide range of assembly-time operation, but PL/I is the only high-level language in wide use which admits similar facilities (Nicholls 1969, Brown 1974). As McIlroy (1960) pointed out, anything possible at execution time should also be possible at translation time. We might take the following list as representative of "things possible at execution time":
— Assignment and access to variables
— Evaluation of expressions
— Conditionals
— Iterations
— Procedure Invocations
— Input/output.
By McIlroy's dictum, a language should allow a compile time version of each.

The first three facilities are closely approximated by any compiler which provides constant folding and propagation (Waite 1974). Iteration is supported by a compile-time GOTO in PL/I, and a macro call is the analog of a run-time procedure invocation. Several compilers permit some form of INCLUDE statement which performs compile-time input from a specified file, and some allow for certain kinds of output (primarily environment information to be used in separate compilation of nested blocks in Algol-like languages).

There are certain technical problems involved in integrating compile-time facilities with a high-level language. No general solutions to these problems exist, and this is one reason why compile-time facilities are not more widely available. The major difficulty lies in the structure of a high-level language. Most assembly languages have a very simple structure: a linear sequence of distinct statements. Assembly-time operations also occur in sequence, interspersed with the normal assembly language statements. These assembly-time operations may generate or delete arbitrary subsequences of statements. A program in a high-level language, however, usually exhibits a more complex tree-like structure. It is unnatural for compile-time operations to view the text as a simple sequence of lines, ignoring the program's structure. On the other hand, if such operations are compelled to follow the program's structure then certain necessary manipulations (such as altering declarations conditionally) cannot be performed (Brown 1974).

The IBM 360 and 370 series employ a common "machine language". In fact, this is not a machine language at all, but an intermediate level of abstraction implemented by microcode interpreters (Tanenbaum 1976). As far as hardware architecture is concerned, the various models have very little in common. Thus we see that flexibility has been achieved (a given program can run on a variety of machines) by deferring decisions about implementation of primitives. A similar technique, using a level of abstraction implemented by software, was employed successfully by Digitek in building a flexible compiler for Fortran. (To my knowledge, this system has not been described in the literature; the best reference I have been able to obtain is the Program Logic Manual for G-level Fortran on the IBM 360 (IBM 1967).)

Users can achieve flexibility in an analogous manner by dividing the translation process into two steps. A *preprocessor* converts the user's language into an intermediate language (usually Fortran), which is then submitted to a conventional compiler. The user's language is designed to permit parameterization of algorithms, but otherwise to minimize the problem of translating to intermediate form. Thus a good measure of flexibility is obtained at little cost; most of the burden of translation falls upon the conventional compiler used in the second step of the process.

RATFOR (Kernighan 1975) is one of the earliest of these preprocessors. The stated purpose of its designers was to provide "decent control flow statements and some 'syntactic sugar'", and it is some of the latter that is most important for improving flexibility. In particular, the user is allowed to define an identifier to be any string of characters. When this identifier is seen again, it is replaced by the string. This simple facility satisfies a large fraction of the parameterization requirement, but McIlroy's dictum (quoted above) should be given strong consideration in any newly-designed preprocessor. This dictum leads to the concept of providing several evaluation mechanisms for a parameter. (For example, instead of being copied it might be evaluated as an integer expression. The "parameter conversions" of STAGE2 (Waite 1973) represent a reasonably complete set of such evaluations).

4. THE ECONOMICS OF FLEXIBILITY

Flexibility is only one property of software. The emphasis placed upon this property during the design and implementation should be determined by rational consideration of alternatives. Seldom can we identify any property which can be maximized without degradation of other properties, and flexibility is no exception. Tradeoffs must be made, in particular, between flexibility and cost.

Increasing flexibility generally increases the cost of producing the program. Consider first the attainment of flexibility of deferral of decisions about the algorithm. Effectively, this involves designing several algorithms and merging them. Care must be taken that the algorithms interact properly, and that the data structures match the associated operations. The merged algorithm must be tested carefully with as many of the valid parameter combinations as possible. Unfortunately, it may be inconvenient or impossible to test certain combinations, and these will almost invariably contain errors. Such errors usually show up when the software is being brought up at a distant installation, far from the immediate supervision of its implementors.

Attainment of flexibility by deferring implementation of primitives has similar weak points. It is important that the originator provide test programs for the primitives which are independent of the flexible software itself. This enables the recipient to validate his implementation without understanding the inner workings of the flexible program. As discussed above, such test programs are made more difficult by the possibility of unforeseen interactions between primitives, induced by the particular implementation strategy. The definitions of the primitives themselves also cause problems because they must neither over- nor under-specify. They must convey the properties essential to correct operation of the software, but they may not constrain the implementor unnecessarily.

Each of the problems mentioned above not only increases the development cost of the software, but may also result in algorithms which are suboptimal in one sense or another. For example, a program capable of running on a variety of Fortran implementations might be forced to use double precision arithmetic in certain places although single precision would be adequate on the current computer. Thus the program would be larger and run slower than necessary on the current machine. (This problem could be avoided by parameterization if compile-time textual manipulation were available in Fortran or if a preprocessor were used.) A more serious suboptimality probably occurs because the program is written in Fortran rather than assembly code.

In some cases, the decision to pursue flexibility is quite clear. The manufacturer who is supplying an operating system for a variety of configurations has already been mentioned. In others, the decision *not* to pursue flexibility is equally clear: a basic interrupt handler for a particular machine is one of the prime examples of a nonflexible routine (although even here one might wish to vary the number or priority of interrupt levels in some way). For most programs, however, the nature of the tradeoffs is much less obvious. I have come to believe that the more experience programmers have, the more they tend to trade in the direction of flexibility. Perhaps they are no longer naive enough to believe that specifications are immutable, or perhaps they have seen enough different machines or languages to realize that there are several ways to do any task. Whatever it is, it seems highly personal and not amenable to standardization.

When we move from an individual programmer to a larger organization, we see that users form the only group with an unqualified desire for flexibility. Manufacturers develop software to sell machines, and have no interest in software which is sufficiently flexible to run on foreign hardware. Many software houses derive a large amount of their "bread-and-butter" business from the conversion of programs, and will hence keep any mechanisms for increasing flexibility for their own work.

Unfortunately, development of systematic procedures and tools for increasing program flexibility is an expensive task. If a user elects to devote resources to this task, he will wish to recover at least a part of his investment from any other user who wishes to take advantage of the results. (For example, the PFORT Verifier (Ryder 1974) is now being marketed by Bell Laboratories.) Any such tool must itself be flexible; this brings up the question of legal protection for flexible software (Harris 1982). Bell Laboratories requires that recipient of one of their packages sign a statement that he will not distribute the package further, but how can this be enforced?

The problem of software protection is not local to flexible software, but flexibility certainly increases its potential seriousness. It also introduces a new element - what might be termed "OEM software". Consider the package of basic mathematical functions discussed in Section 1. These functions could be used in the runtime library of either a Fortran system or a Pascal system. An implementor of a flexible Fortran system might therefore wish to purchase them as a component. Such a transaction would probably be based upon some sort of royalty agreement, but how could the security of the component be guaranteed by the original vendor?

REFERENCES

Brown P.J. (1974), Macro processors and Techiques for Portable Software. London: John Wiley & Son.

Brown P.J. (1977), Software Portability. Cambridge: Cambridge University Press.

Brown W.S. and Hall A.D. (1977), FORTRAN Portability via Models and Tools, In Cowell, W.D. (Ed.) Portability of Numerical Software. Heidelberg: Springer-Verlag.

Cody W.J. and Waite W.M. (1980), Software Manual for the Elementary Functions. Englewood Cliffs: Prentice-Hall.

Dijkstra E.W. (1976), A Discipline of Programming. Englewood Cliffs: Prentice-Hall.

Fox P.A., Hall A.D. and Schryer N.L. (1975), Basic Utilities for Portable FORTRAN Libraries. Computer Science Tech. Rept. #37, Bell Laboratories.

Goos G. (1982a), Design of Programs. (This book).

Goos G. (1982b), Program Structure. (This book).

Harris B. (1982), The Legal Protection of Computer Software. (This book).

Hoare C.A.R. (1969), An Axiomatic Basis for Computer Programming. Comm. ACM Vol. 12 pp. 576-581.

IBM (1967), System/360 Operating System FORTRAN IV (G) Compiler Program Logic Manual. New York: IBM.

Kernighan B.W. (1975), RATFOR - A Preprocessor for Rational Fortran. Software - Practice and experience Vol. 5, pp. 395-406.

Knuth D.E. (1968), Semantics of Context-Free Languages. Math Syst. Theory Vol. 2, pp. 127-145.

Liskov B.H. and Zilles S.N. (1975), Specification Techniques for Data Abstractions. IEEE Trans. on Software Engineering Vol. 1, pp. 7-19.

Lucas P. and Walk K. (1969), On the Formal Description of PL/1. Ann. Rev. in Automatic Programming Vol. 6, pp. 105-182.

McIlroy M.D. (1960), Macro Instruction Extensions of Compiler Languages. Comm. ACM Vol. 3, pp. 214-220.

Mock O., Olsztyn T., Strong J., Steel T.B., Tritter A. and Wegstein J. (1958), The Problem of Programming Communication with Changing Machines: A Proposed Solution. Comm. ACM Vol. 1, No. 8, pp. 12-18, No. 9, pp. 9-15.

Naur P. (1963), Revised Report on the Algorithmic Language ALGOL 60. Comm. ACM Vol. 6, pp. 1-17.

Nicholls J. (1969), PL/1 Compile Time Extensibility. SIGPLAN Notices Vol. 4, No. 8, pp. 40-44.

Parnas D.L. (1972), A Technique for Software Module Specification with Examples. Comm. ACM Vol. 15, pp. 330-336.

Poole, P.C. and Waite, W.M. (1977), Portability and Adaptability. In Bauer F.L. (Ed.) Software Engineering. Heidelberg: Springer-Verlag pp. 183-277.

Ryder B.G. (1974), The PFORT Verifier. Software - Practice and Experience Vol. 4, pp. 359-377.

Tanenbaum A.S. (1976), Structured Computer Organization. Englewood Cliffs: Prentice-Hall.

Tennent R.D. (1976), The Denotational Semantics of Programming Languages. Comm. ACM Vol 19, pp. 437-453.

van Wijngaarden A., Mailloux B.J., Peck J.E.L., Koster C.H.A., Sintzoff M., Lindsey C.H., Meertens L.G.L.T. and Fisker R.G. (1975), Revised Report in the Algorithmic Language Algol 68. Acta Informatica Vol. 5, pp. 1-236.

Waite W.M. (1973), Implementing Software for Non-Numeric Applications. Englewood Cliffs: Prentice Hall pp. 383-389.

Waite W.M. (1974), Optimization. In Bauer F.L. and Eickel J. (Eds.) Compiler Construction. Heidelberg: Springer-Verlag pp. 549-602.

OPERATING SYSTEM INTERFACES

William Waite
University of Colorado
Boulder, Colorado USA

We emphasized in the chapter on Flexibility the fact that the meaning of a program depends ultimately upon the meanings of the primitives from which it is constructed. These primitives are provided by the environment in which the program executes, and it has been pointed out that different environments generally provide different sets of primitives. One of the most difficult tasks facing the designer of a shareable program is that of selecting an appropriate set of primitives for the task at hand. Our discussion of flexibility dealt with most of the usual computational primitives; this chapter is concerned with primitives which normally require operating system action.

Unlike computational primitives, there is no widely-accepted abstraction for such tasks as input/output and storage management. Each language has its own conventions, and some (e.g. Algol 60) leave their definition entirely to the implementor. Exception handling, although not a task in the usual sense, is a necessary adjunct to any program. This necessity is only now being realized, however, and our understanding of the problems involved is far from complete. For this reason there is an even wider diversity of exception handling primitives than there is of other operating system actions.

In this chapter I shall focus on the basic issues involved in interaction with the operating system, and show how those issues appear in the three areas mentioned above. My intent is to provide a framework for understanding a variety of existing primitives, and a basis for defining interfaces which can be used in building shareable software.

1. GENERAL SYSTEM INTERACTIONS

I shall only be concerned with interactions between the user and system in which information transfer occurs. This excludes such phenomena as processor sharing, in which a running program may be suspended for some period of time without

D. T. Muxworthy (ed.), Programming for Software Sharing, 127–137.

altering its state. (Such interactions may be used to transmit information (Lampson 1973), but these uses are outside the scope of this book.) The interactions may be *scheduled* (occur at a point determined by the program) or *unscheduled* (occur at an arbitrary point).

In general, the information transmitted may be classified as *control information* or *data*. Control information is interpreted by the operating system, while data is not. For example, a request to read from a file involves both control information and data; control information flows in both directions, while data flows from the operating system to the program in this case.

Some interactions may involve considerable elapsed time, and hence the user may wish to *overlap* their execution with other processing. There are basically two ways to accomplish such overlap by dividing the expensive interaction into several cheap ones. In each case, an *initiation* primitive serves to begin the expensive interaction. Completion of the expensive interaction may be signalled by an unscheduled interaction which places status information into the user's memory, or the user may be required to request status via a second scheduled interaction. In either case, the expensive interaction is composite rather than primitive.

Because of the variety of primitives provided by existing operating systems, a programmer interested in shareable software cannot assume that a particular primitive will be directly available everywhere. He must therefore define primitives suited to his application, and specify these by means of interfaces. In general, an interface gives the name of an action and some specification of the operands of that action. It is often implemented as a procedure call, although other mechanisms are available (Haddon 1979). Reimplementation of the operating system interfaces is required when the software is moved to a new environment.

Use of procedures to implement operating system primitives is viable for shared software only if the overhead associated with making a request is never a critical economic factor. This is an important assumption, and it influences the choice of primitives which the designer makes. There are two possible ways of satisfying this assumption:
1. The request is made only infrequently.
2. Processing of the request by the operating system is expensive.
In the former case the overhead is not a critical economic factor because it is seldom incurred; in the latter case it is not critical because it is masked by the cost of satisfying the request.

To see how the assumption is used in selecting appropriate primitives, consider the problem of obtaining input text for a batch-oriented page formatting program. A primitive which obtained a single character from the operating system would almost certainly violate the assumption since it satisfies neither of the conditions given above. On the other hand, use of a character input primitive for the control stream of an interactive text editor might be quite reasonable because it satisfies the second condition. (The operating system must obtain the character from a very slow peripheral - the human user.)

A second example concerns the composite interactions discussed above. If completion is signalled by an unscheduled interaction, then the program may be forced to enter a "busy wait": it must loop on a test of the memory which will be set by the operating system. Abstractly, busy waiting is not harmful since the program has nothing else to do anyway. In practice, however, the shared software may be operating in an environment where the processor could be usefully employed on other tasks. Hence busy waiting should never be performed within a shareable program. The correct interface for composite interactions involves a primitive which will test for completion, returning only if completion has occurred. This interface may, in fact, be implemented by busy waiting in a particular environment, but busy waiting is *not* a necessary phenomenon in all environments.

Control information is generally passed in both directions during an interaction. Transmission from the operating system to the user can be implemented explicitly in one of two ways: one or more of the parameters of the request can be variables set by the system, or they may be procedures which the system may invoke. The first method is usually used when the probabilities of several possible responses are roughly equal. When there is one response with high probability and one or more with low probability then the second method is more appropriate.

Consider, for example, the problem of requesting input of information from a large file. The probability of encountering the end of the file is much lower than that of a successfully completed read. Suppose that one of the parameters of the request is a Boolean variable, EOF, set by the operating system to *true* if and only if the end of the file has been reached. The user must test the value of this parameter after each request, even though the probability is very high that its value will be *false*. Suppose, on the other hand, that the parameter was a procedure instead of a Boolean variable. The operating system invokes this procedure if and only if the end of the file has been reached. No test is required after each request, since the low-probability case is handled by the procedure.

Regardless of the precise mechanism used to obtain the operating system's reponse, our concern with it has been *at the site of the interaction*. In some cases it can be argued that the response is of no concern at the site of the interaction, but represents some phenomenon of more global importance. An example is the occurrence of arithmetic overflow within a library procedure - it is not important that a particular operation produced an erroneous result, but rather that the input information did not permit the desired calculation to be carried out. Hence the overflow represents failure of the entire library procedure. This is the distinguishing property of an exception. Unfortunately, it is difficult to make any precise distinction between exceptions and more local responses; this is one of the difficulties which the designer of shareable software faces when dealing with operating system interfaces!

2. INPUT/OUTPUT

In almost all cases, physical transmission of information between a program and the computer's peripheral devices is perfomed by the operating system. This section will concern itself with primitives used to accomplish such *physical transput*.

Many languages merge the notion of "formatting" (conversion between internal and character representation) with that of physical transput. I regard formatting as a completely separate issue; one which is not the province of the operating system, but of a normal library routine. I shall therefore ignore formatting for the remainder of this section, except where a particular language specification forces mention of it.

Physical transput involves the internal store of the program and an external data set normally called a file. Files reside upon physical *devices* and have certain logical properties. Many of these properties are historic, and have been induced by the physical properties of the devices which have become available from time to time. Unfortunately, no agreed-upon taxonomy for the properties of files exists. Since some classification is necessary for a systematic discussion of input/output interfaces, let me propose two orthogonal properties which appear to be fundamental in our selection of primitives.

The first property of a file is its *element* - the basic units from which it is constructed. In practice, only two elements are important: characters and memory units. A character file is generally intended for intercommunication between two programs written in different languages, two computers, or a computer and a human. Memory unit files are generally intended for temporary storage or for transfer to other programs written in the same language. In some broad sense, character files are "universal" while memory unit files are "specific". Because of this "universality", character files generally undergo some translation on input and output while memory unit files do not. (Translation in this context does not refer to formatting, but to changes in encoding necessitated by hardware design.)

The second property of a file is its *access*. Three types of access (*sequential, random* and *interactive*) are currently important. Magnetic or paper tape is the physical prototype of the sequential file. It can be positioned to a particular piece of information only by passing sequentially from the current position to the desired one. The physical prototype of the random file is a disc or drum, which can be positioned to a particular piece of information without sequentially passing the intermediate information. Interactive files, whose physical prototype is a human at a terminal cannot be positioned at all. They represent a more dynamic situation in which synchronization of operations becomes critical.

Each program is written to manipulate a certain fixed set of data. These data are named within the program. When the program is run, the internal data names must be associated with external files in order for the program to carry out its task of manipulating its environment. In general we must regard these associations as dynamic during the execution of the program: it must be able to establish and dissolve them arbitrarily.

To make things concrete, let us consider the file structure of Pascal (Jensen and Wirth, 1975). A Pascal file is a "structure consisting of a sequence of components which are all of the same type. The number of components, called the *length* of the file, is not fixed by the file definition". Pascal provides only sequential access to files. The primitive operations are "put" (write a component), "get" (read a component), "reset" and "rewrite" (set the file position to the beginning), and "eof" (test for the end). Static associations between internal and external file names are established by mentioning the internal file names to be associated in the program heading. The precise manner of association is unspecified.

Dynamic association between internal data names and external file names is provided by an extension of Pascal defined at the University of California (San Diego): "reset" and "rewrite" are each given a second parameter that specifies the external file name. The problem, of course, is what constitutes an external file name. UCSD Pascal assumes that it is a string. This is a reasonable assumption in general, although the format of the string varies with the operating system.

Pascal recognizes a distinction between character files (called *textfiles*) and memory unit files, and provides a set of rudimentary formatting-plus-transput operations for the former. It also notes that textfiles "are a special case insofar as the component range of values must be considered as extended by a marker denoting the end of a line. This allows textfiles to be substructured into lines". The presence of additional marks is a general phenomenon in sequential files, as pointed out by Dunn (1974): "The *ability* to place such marks among the items is dependent upon both the device and the operating system... the *placement* of the marks is at the discretion of the program which initially creates the information... Any [sequential file] has at least one mark, defined by the end of information recorded on the device... There may be a capability to insert more than one type of mark, in which case the marks form a hierarchy of divisions".

Each file is provided with a "window" called a *buffer variable,* which holds the current element of the file. The relationship between the buffer variable, the "put" operation and the "eof" predicate is instructive:

> "put (f)   appends the value of the buffer variable f↑ to the file f. The effect is defined only if prior to execution the predicate eof (f) is true. eof (f) remains true, and the value of f↑ becomes undefined".

The second sentence embodies the common restriction which operating systems place upon sequential files: information can be written only at the end. If the file is positioned at the end prior to the write operation, then it will be positioned at the new end subsequent to the write and eof (f) will remain true. Undefinition of f↑ reflects the buffering strategy which passes pointers to buffers rather than copying information from one buffer to another (Mock and Swift, 1959). When this strategy is used, the "put" operation causes f↑ to refer to an entirely different area of storage, thus making the previous information inaccessible.

As I noted earlier, Pascal has two operations which position to the beginning of a file. The distinction is necessary because of the differing conditions required for reading and writting:

> "reset (f)   resets the current file position to its beginning and assigns to the buffer variable f↑ the value of the first element of f. eof (f) becomes false if f is not empty; otherwise f↑ is not defined, and eof (f) remains true".

> "rewrite (f)   discards the current value of f such that a new file may be generated. eof (f) becomes true".

This distinction also reflects common practice in operating systems, where the form of an initiation primitive depends upon whether the file is to be read or written. Most operating systems combine the task of associating an external file name with an internal data name and that of initiating file processing into a single "open" primitive. Both Fortran (ANSI 1978) and Cobol (ANSI 1974) provide OPEN statements which may carry this additional information. There is an interesting difference, however, between the two languages: Fortran does not indicate whether the file is to be read or written, whereas Cobol does. In other words, the Fortran OPEN (which is not required) is merely serving as a source of information; it is not intended actually to initiate file processing. In some operating systems the association and initiation tasks are handled by separate primitives, and I have argued elsewhere (Waite 1977) that for this reason they should be kept separate at the language level. Shapiro (1977) presents a different argument. His claim is that, since the Cobol Standard defines a required mass storage control system which "nearly every manufacturer" will provide, Fortran "should conform to this real environment, not necessarily to Fortran designers' personal tastes".

Random file operations are generally similar to those on sequential files, except that read and write must specify a particular position. There is no restriction on where a write can take place, but generally it is illegal to read an item which had never been written. Marks cannot be placed in a random file; additional structure is provided by one or more *indexes* which may or may not be integral parts of the file. It makes no sense to have an "eof" predicate, but in some cases it is possible to ask which item was accessed last.

ANS X3.9-1978 introduced random files into Fortran. These files are what Cobol (ANSI 1974) terms "relative files": Individual records are addressed by integer values greater than 0. Some files may be accessible both randomly and sequentially. In that case the integer record addresses specify the sequence. The OPEN statement for such a file must nominate a particular access mode. If the access mode is to be changed, the file must be closed and re-opened with the desired mode.

In many respects, interactive files are similar to sequential files. The sequence in this case is the time sequence of interactions between the computer and the outside world. Only the problems of synchronization distinguish this type of access. As an example, consider the interaction between a program and a terminal user. Let us initially represent the terminal as a single file which can be both read and written. The program might begin the interaction by writing a prompt and then reading the user's reply. Although such a sequence seems reasonable in the given context, it is certainly not possible if the file obeyed the semantics laid down by Pascal!

If the terminal were represented by *two* files, a keyboard and a printer, then there would be no problem with read after write, but we would need to guarantee that the prompt actually appeared on the device. Again looking at the semantics of Pascal, it is difficult to see how such a guarantee could be made. If the device were half duplex, then the guarantee would need to be even tighter: the prompt must appear on the terminal *before* the response was read. Dunn (1974) proposed that it be possible to "synchronize" an arbitrary number of files so that an operation on any one would require completion of the operations on all of the others. Unfortunately, I know of no language which incorporates this facility either!

Since we have no accepted model of an interactive file, any shareable software which requires such files must provide them itself. This means that a module must be designed with appropriate semantics and re-implemented on each new operating system. My co-workers and I have devised a general form for such I/O modules (Waite 1977) which could be used to support any of the files which I have discussed. It is often useful to employ a single module for all transput, rather than to use explicit transput operations directly in the program. The reason is that use of a single module makes it easier to replace expensive general language primitives by more efficient ones tailored to the particular semantics required. This is particularly true with character transput in Fortran, where speed improvement of a factor of 5 is quite common.

3. STORAGE MANAGEMENT

There are several strategies which can be used for dynamic storage allocation (Waite 1973). All rest ultimately upon allocation of one or more contiguous blocks of memory, a task which many operating systems will perform. Because of the need to manage the fundamental resources in an efficient and general way, operating system allocation primitives tend to be expensive to use. We therefore wish to minimize the number of operating system requests. This can be done by using what amounts to a wholesale/retail scheme (Ross 1967), in which large amounts of storage are requested from the operating system and then further subdivided by routines belonging to a local free storage package. The interface seen by the program is the same whether the storage is actually obtained from the operating system at execution time or is allocated from memory assigned to the job step at load time. In addition, the considerations used in the interface design are interesting in themselves because they can be used to design other operating system interfaces for use by shareable programs.

The major problem for the interface designer in this case is to provide the necessary flexibility for the user. Not only are there several basic storage management strategies, but each has many subtle variations, some of them highly dependent upon the precise characteristics of the data to be stored in the allocated area. Fortunately, the basic strategies deal with normal allocation and the variations with the response to a "space exhausted" condition. In other words, the variations are invoked only for exception conditions. Exceptions will be discussed more fully in the next section, but we have already noted that one mechanism which can be used to handle them is to pass an exception handling procedure to the primitive which may generate the exception. In abstract terms, each strategy is embodied in a module (Goos 1982) and any desired variations are supplied as procedures which can be passed to that module. The following discussion of the details of these modules and procedures is based upon the AED Free Storage Package (Ross 1967).

The blocks of storage obtained from the operating system are called zones. Associated with each zone is a strategy and possible variation. For the sake of concreteness, I shall assume that two strategies are available: SPEC allocates blocks of one length, and REG allocates blocks of the length requested by the call. The length of blocks allocated by SPEC is given when the zone is established, and may vary from zone to zone; thus the only difference between SPEC and REG is the point at which the length of a block is bound. Each module would therefore provide the same set of operations, although these operations would have one additional parameter in the case of the REG strategy module.

Let us further assume that the only variations which we shall permit are those involving exhaustion of the storage in a zone. Regardless of the strategy, it may be possible to reclaim some of the zone's storage if one has a knowledge of the use to which it has been put. In the case of REG strategy zones it may also happen that free storage is available, but it has been fragmented into blocks too small to satisfy the request. Adjacent free blocks may then be combined into larger ones which may prove satisfactory. Even after this step has been taken, however, there may be no single free block large enough although the total free space is sufficient. If enough is known about the data, it is sometimes possible to rearrange the blocks in use so that they form a compact group at one end of the zone, leaving all of the free space as a single block (Haddon and Waite, 1967). When none of these suffices, one could request another block of storage from the operating system or abort the job.

To support these variations, both strategy modules must incorporate the concept of *extension*, and the REG strategy module must provide an operation which allows coalescing of adjacent free blocks. (Automatic coalescing represents another basic strategy, which Ross calls the GARB strategy.) A zone with extensions is no longer a single block of contiguous storage. The initial storage for the zone is contiguous, and each distinct extension is internally contiguous, but the extensions are independent of the initial storage and of each other.

When an instance of either module is created, it is supplied with three parameters: the amount of storage to be allocated to the zone initially, the amount by which the zone is to be extended, and the exception-handling procedure. One additional parameter, the block size, is needed to create an instance of a SPEC strategy module. The operations provided by each module are:

— ALLOCATE Deliver a block.
— FREE Accept the return of a block.
— FRESH Re-initialize the allocation mechanism of the zone.
— FLUSH Return all extensions of the zone to the operating system and re-initialize the allocation mechanism in the initial storage area.
— COALESCE (REG strategy only) merge adjacent free blocks into a single free block.

(The COALESCE operation might consider all free blocks, or it might terminate after creating a free block of the desired size.)

The exception handling procedure is invoked when a request cannot be satisfied. It is given parameters describing the request, and possibly additional information about the allocation process (as, for example, the number of free words remaining). Since it is a user-supplied procedure, it executes in the user's environment and has access to any data available there. When it has completed its task, it must return information to the allocation module describing what it has done. Ross suggests that this information take the form of a command which tells the allocation module how to proceed. He proposes the following specific continuations:

— Return the given block to the user; it will satisfy his request.
— Restart the processing of the request.
— Extend the zone and restart the processing of the request.
— Abort the job, reporting the given error code.

The first continuation implies that the exception handler has effectively modified the request in some way, while the second implies that it has modified the state of the zone. The last two continuations are normal escapes which depend only slightly upon the program which uses the storage module.

As Goos (1982) has pointed out, there are many ways to realize program modules. Any of the standard techniques can be applied to the specifications discussed above. There is, however, one aspect of storage allocation which causes problems for certain languages: a storage allocation module deals with the basic storage units of the machine rather than typed data objects of the language. This is necessarily so, because the storage allocator will be allocating storage to objects of different types at different times. (If it did not do this, all storage could be allocated statically by the compiler.) Hence it is impossible to write a storage allocation module in a strongly-typed language. Escapes from the type mechanism, in the form of references to "storage units" are absolutely essential. Since the solution to the problem varies from one language to the next, I shall not attempt to discuss it here.

4. EXCEPTION HANDLING

The general topic of exception handling involves study of a variety of mechanisms and the effect of these mechanisms upon the syntax and semantics of the programming language in which they are embedded (Brown 1965, Goodenough 1975, Levin 1977). A complete treatment is beyond the scope of this book; our interest will be only with exceptions which affect the operating system interfaces of shareable software. I shall only consider two general issues of exception handling: association of handlers with invocations of operations, and how the control flow of the invoker and invokee interact.

As we have seen in the case of the storage management interface discussed in the previous section, the purpose of exceptions is to generalize an operation. Situations arise during execution of the operation which must be handled in various ways depending upon the context in which the operation was invoked. We can generalize the operation by providing exceptions which allow the invoker to deal with these situations in an appropriate manner. Goodenough (1975) distinguishes three situations in which exceptions could be used:

— To permit dealing with an operation's impeding or actual failure.
— To indicate the significance of a valid result, or the circumstances under which it was obtained.
— To permit the invoker to monitor the operation.

Each of these situations may arise in an operating system interface.

Suppose that a transput call specifies an invalid operation for a particular file. This situation is an example of what Goodenough calls a "domain failure" - the operation's inputs fail to pass some test of acceptability. If the operation were, say, a read, and could not be carried out because end-of-file was reached, then a "range failure" (inability to satisfy an output assertion) would have occurred. Each of these situations represents an actual failure of the operation, while the "lack of space" condition in a storage manager represents an impending failure.

When performing transput on magnetic tape, it may be necessary for the system to retry a read or erase over a bad spot on write. If the data are very important, we wish to know when an increasing number of retries indicates impending failure of the tape. This is an example of a situation where it is useful to indicate the circumstances (number of retries exceeded threshold) under which a valid result (the input data) was obtained. A very slight change in this example moves it to the last category: if a tape error cannot be recovered by the usual method, we may wish to be informed of that fact and be given the option of attempting some extraordinary technique. In effect, we are monitoring the progress of the operation and supplying additional information at critical points. (Note that this example could also be categorized as "impending failure".)

We have already seen examples of association of handlers with specific calls on an interface (use of status code, passing of a procedure) and with an interface module (passing a procedure to the module creator). The choice depends upon whether the exception is logically a property of a particular invocation or of the object which the module embodies. I cannot give any general rule for making this choice. I should point out, however, that these two examples represent opposite ends of spectrum: one should consider it possible to attach an exception handler to any syntactic construct of a program. For a complete discussion of the possibilities, see Levin (1977).

Upon completion, an exception handler might return to the module raising exception, return to the code following the invocation which caused the exception, or transfer to some arbitrary point. Goodenough argues that the choice is dependent upon both the handler and the module causing the exception. He proposes that the latter be able to specify ESCAPE (the handler may not return), NOTIFY (the handler must return) or SIGNAL (the handler may return, but is not required to do so). Levin, on the other hand, strongly advocates the position that the handler *must* return in all cases. Let us briefly consider the reasoning involved: ESCAPE is identical to SIGNAL followed by some construct which causes termination of the module causing the exception. It would thus be advantageous only if the language provided no constructs which could cause termination. NOTIFY is necessary because a general module may be in an inconsistent state at the time an exception is raised. (Such a state may be required in order to provide certain responses to the exception.) If a handler is activated by SIGNAL, and chooses not to return, then it must transfer control to some point. The reason for doing this is to abandon a useless computation. Unfortunately, useless computations may also be involved when the handler is activated by NOTIFY. Hence some mechanism should be provided for specifying a resumption point in this case as well. But if such a mechanism is provided, SIGNAL is identical to NOTIFY.

Since our application precludes language modification, the options for associating handlers with invocations and controlling flow relationships are limited. Hill (1971) discusses techniques for Fortran and Algol 60 functions, and most of his treatment is relevant. The one special property of operating system interfaces which is different from those assumed by Hill is the way in which they are written. He assumes that a function returns its primary result as its value, and that it may appear embedded in a complex expression. Thus he rejects as unnatural the possibility of having the function return a status code, and deliver its primary result as a side effect. This usage seems quite natural, however, for an operating system interface procedure. Use of a status code is safe in most languages (if functions are not allowed to have side effects, the status code is provided as an extra parameter to the procedure). It associates a handler with each invocation of a primitive, and activates the handler only after execution of the primitive has terminated. For a detailed example of an interface built on status codes see Waite (1977).

Status codes are inconvenient when a handler is to be associated with an object, and cannot be used when resumption of the signalling module is required. Language restrictions aside, we could use a procedure parameter in each of these cases. If we are willing to associate the handler with an invocation, then a Fortran implementation is straightforward. Association of a handler with an object, however, requires that the procedure be stored in the object's representation. ANS

3.9-1966 and ANS X3.9-1978 both prohibit this by their definition of assignment, and consequently any such interface could not be written in Fortran. Since an external procedure can be passed as an argument, however, the interface could be Fortran-callable even though its internal coding involved either non-standard Fortran or some other language.

REFERENCES

ANSI (1966) FORTRAN. ANS X3.9-1966. New York: American National Standards Institute.

ANSI (1974) COBOL. ANS X3.23-1974. New York: American National Standards Institute.

ANSI (1978) FORTRAN. ANS X3.9-1978. New York: American National Standards Institute.

Brown W.S. (1965), An Operating Environment for Dynamic Recursive Computer Programming Systems. Comm. ACM Vol. 8, pp. 371-377.

Dunn R.C. (1974), Design of a Higher-Level Language Transput system. Ph.D. Thesis, University of Colorado.

Goodenough J.B. (1975), Exception Handling: Issues and a Proposed Notation. Comm. ACM Vol. 18, pp. 683-696.

Goos G. (1982), Program Structure. (This book).

Haddon B.K. and Waite W.M. (1967), A Compaction Procedure for Variable Length Storage Elements. Computer J. Vol. 10, pp. 162-165.

Haddon B.K. (1979), Machine-Independent Real-Time Operating System Interfaces. Ph.D. Thesis, University of Colorado.

Hill I.D. (1971), Faults in Functions, in ALGOL and FORTRAN. Computer J. Vol. 14, pp. 315-316.

Jensen K. and Wirth N. (1975), Pascal User Manual and Report. Heidelberg: Springer-Verlag.

Lampson B.W. (1973), A Note on the Confinement Problem. Comm. ACM Vol. 16, pp. 613-615.

Levin R. (1977), Program Structures for Exception Handling. Ph.D. Thesis, Carnegie-Mellon University.

Mock O. and Swift C.J. (1959), The SHARE 709 System: Programmed Input-Output Buffering. J ACM Vol. 6, pp. 145-151.

Ross D.T. (1967), The AED Free Storage Package. Comm. ACM Vol. 10, pp. 481-492.

Shapiro M.D. (1977), FORTRAN 77 Input-Output Seems Out of Touch. SIGPLAN Notices Vol. 12 Number 10, pp. 65-69.

Waite W.M. (1973), Implementing Software for Non-Numeric Applications, Prentice-Hall, Englewood Cliffs, New Jersey.

Waite W.M. (1977), System Interface. In Brown P.J. (Ed.) Software Portability. Cambridge: Cambridge University Press, pp. 127-135.

LANGUAGE STANDARDS

David Muxworthy
University of Edinburgh
Edinburgh, UK.

1. INTRODUCTION

Standards in General

Most industrialized countries have an organization which is recognized as the body for the preparation and promulgation of national standards in all fields. Historically the standards institutes came into being through a desire for standards in manufacturing industry. As an example the British Standards Institution originated in 1901 as the Engineering Standards Committee and was set up by the Institution of Civil Engineers and other professional bodies. The present name was adopted in 1931. The objects of BSI include:

a) to co-ordinate the efforts of producers and users for the improvement, standardization and simplification of engineering and industrial materials so as to simplify production and distribution, and to eliminate the national waste of time and material involved in the production of an unnecessary variety of patterns and sizes of articles for one and the same purpose.

b) to set up standards of quality and dimensions, and to prepare and promote the general adoption of British Standard specifications and schedules in connection therewith and from time to time to revise, alter and amend such specifications and schedules as experience and circumstances may require.

The BSI also certify quality control and inspection schemes and products passed through such schemes carry a special symbol, the kitemark, which is well known in the U.K. There is also a special safety mark, provided to show that goods have been produced according to standards with a legal safety requirement. Standards have thus come to be associated not only with uniformity but with quality, safety and reliability.

Corresponding to BSI in the U.K. there are organizations such as Association Française de Normalisation (AFNOR) in France, Deutsches Institut fuer Normung

D. T. Muxworthy (ed.), Programming for Software Sharing, 139–147.
Copyright © 1983 ECSC, EEC, EAEC, Brussels and Luxembourg.

(DIN) in Germany, and American National Standards Institute (ANSI) in the U.S.A. It would be a nonsense if each country had different standards for similar products and in fact they collaborate through the International Organization for Standardization (ISO) and through a number of more specialized international bodies such as the International Electrotechnical Commission. The International Organization for Standardization was founded in 1926 and has its headquarters in Geneva. It develops standards for international use and helps coordinate standards activities in the various national member bodies.

A series of formal procedures are laid down for the processes which lead to an ISO standard being adopted. They cover such matters as the format of the standards, the publication of drafts for public comment, processing comments received, voting rules for adoption, rules for revision or deletion and so on. Although these procedures are occasionally considered by some as unnecessarily slow and over-pedantic there is no doubt that they are democratic and thorough and allow anyone interested to voice an opinion on proposed standards.

Computing standards

The standards to be discussed in this chapter are those concerning programming languages. There are other standards which are closely related to programming, such as those for character codes (ISO 646, more widely known in its U.S. insubstantiation, ASCII), flowchart symbols, magnetic tape labels and program documentation. Within ISO the technical committee for data processing is known as TC97. Detailed work is divided amongst various subcommittees and it is a subcommittee known as SC5 which is wholly responsible for standards for the common general purpose programming languages. In turn SC5 may appoint working groups for individual standards, so that for example WG1 is responsible for industrial processing ("real-time") languages. The full abbreviation for this working group is thus ISO/TC97/SC5/WG1 and its papers may be marked as such with possible further subdivisions.

In broad terms the national standards bodies are similarly structured but there is no uniformity since the sizes of the committees and the particular interests in the various countries differ widely.

Standardization procedures

There is a substantial flow of programs between countries and it is recognized that in general there should be a single world standard for each language. It is agreed informally that a national standardization body should take the responsibility of producing a draft standard, in consultation with experts from other countries, on behalf of the international community. This happens for example with the U.S. for Cobol and Fortran and with the U.K. for Pascal.

The formal procedure is rather more complicated. Any member body, or ISO itself or some other interested body may propose that an international standard is needed in a particular area. At this stage it may be only that the need for a standard is perceived, or it could be that considerable work on a proposal has already been done, privately as it were, and there is a desire to have this adopted more widely. The decision on whether an international standard is needed and whether it should lie within the ambit of SC5 is taken by the parent committee, TC97, on which all full

("P" or "participating") members of ISO have one vote. If it is formally considered to be needed, it is said to become a "work item" for SC5.

Rules are then laid down for the procedures. These state that the "responsible body", generally the initiator, should develop a standard according to its own national rules, keeping other members of SC5 informed by distribution of papers. An international meeting of experts may be called under the auspisces of SC5. The responsible body should circulate its draft for public comment both nationally and internationally and SC5 members may both vote on the draft and may comment on it. SC5 members also have the responsibility of informing members of the public in their country of the existence of the draft and of the opportunity for public comment.

The responsible body should review comments and votes and should then either recommend that the draft go forward, possibly with minor amendments, as a final standard, or if major amendments are needed, should revise the draft and reissue it for another round of comment and SC5 voting.

The final processing of a draft standard is as follows. A proposed standard must first be approved by a "substantial majority" of TC97, where each "P" member has one vote, whence it proceeds to the Draft International Standard stage. The DIS must be approved by three-quarter of all ISO members which vote. Even then it may not be accepted if negative vote is accompanied by reasoned comment. The draft becomes an International Standard only when all objections have been removed. In some countries approval by a member body at this stage automatically means that the International Standard becomes also the national standard.

ISO and several other bodies have rules that standards should be revised, reaffirmed without change or withdrawn after five years. This period is not apposite in the case of programming languages and this problem is still to be formally resolved. In practice notice of intention to revise has been thought sufficient to prolong the life of a standard.

2. PARTICULAR LANGUAGE STANDARDS

This section has brief summaries of the status of standards for individual programming languages, as at July 1982. Fortran and Cobol were the first two languages to be standardized and are considered first. Thereafter languages and other subjects within the SC5 area are taken alphabetically.

Fortran

It was in about 1960-61 that it became possible to run programs in high-level languages without change on computers from different manufacturers. The languages concerned were Cobol and Fortran. The number of Fortran compilers increased rapidly and there were stated to be 43 different ones in 1964. Already before this the differences between the language specifications for the eight distinct Fortran compilers on IBM systems had caused IBM to issue a manual highlighting features common to the processors.

In 1962 it was decided by an American Standards Association (ASA, later ANSI) committee that a standard was needed for Fortran for the purpose of "promoting a high degree of interchangeability of (Fortran) programs for use on a variety of automatic data processing systems''. It was decided to base the standard on the then emerging Fortran IV, with a subset language known as Basic Fortran being defined to have approximately the power of Fortran II. The draft proposed standards were published in 1964. These were the first standards for programming languages and were on a scale quite new to the standards organization so it was not until 1966 that they were formally approved as American standards. Meanwhile the European Computer Manufacturers Association (ECMA) had defined a subset language intermediate between the two American languages. The three levels were subsequently published as an ISO Recommendation in 1972.

Because standardization work began when many processors were already in use, to a large extent the committee defined standard Fortran to be the common subset of what existed. Where different processors had different actions, for example the value, if any, which was put in a DO-index on completion of a DO-loop varied, the standard declared such a value or action to be undefined. Entities such as the precision of arithmetic, number of characters per storage unit and limits on the sizes of programs which varied widely were not included in the standard. To avoid making all existing processors non-standard it was decided that to be standard-conforming a processor must implement the standard language but may add other features. Thus the standard was at the same time a lower limit for an implementor and an upper limit for the writer of a standard-conforming program.

In particular it is not true, as some seem to believe, that a program written using a standard-conforming processor is necessarily a standard-conforming program. Because the arithmetic is undefined, but the concept of overflow is recognized and prohibited, it is even possible for a program to be standard-conforming on one processor and non-standard on another. Dahlstrand (1980) gives the example:

```
      K = 5000000
      L = K*K
      WRITE (6,100) L
100   FORMAT (1X,I15)
      STOP
      END
```

On four different systems this program gave the results

(I)   compile time error - constant too large
(II) run time error - integer overflow
(III) wrong result without warning - integer overflow
(IV) correct result

Nevertheless the Fortran standard fulfils an indispensible function: all manufacturers implement (or attempt to implement) the standard so that Fortran is the most portable language, but it is not easy for the average programmer to find out whether or not a program is standard-conforming (see the chapter on Software Tools).

Under the rules of ANSI the 1966 Fortran Standard was due for renewal, revision or withdrawal in 1971. It was decided that revision was most appropriate and the work started in 1970. For various reasons, including that possibly excessive weight was put on being compatible with the earlier standard, the draft revised standard was not published until 1976, the resulting editing was finished in 1977 and revision was formally approved as an ANSI standard in 1978 and as an ISO standard in 1980. The revision included many features commonly available in existing processors and some new facilities, notably the IF-THEN-ELSE construct and the character data type, in a form different from any existing implementation. A subset language was also included; this was intended to have approximately the power of the earlier standard. The revised language is known as Fortran 77 and the earlier standard has become known retrospectively as Fortran 66; this is no longer formally a standard.

Learning from experience, the ANSI Fortran committee immediately considered whether further revision of Fortran 77 would be necessary and decided, on the basis of the large number of outstanding requests from the public for changes to Fortran, that it would. The revision work started in 1978 and a revised standard is expected to be approved in the period 1986 to 1988. The committee function has changed from 1962-66, when it standardized existing practice, and it now acts as both a language development and standardization committee.

Cobol

In the case of Cobol the functions of development and standardization are distinct. Codasyl (the Committee on Data Systems Languages) was formed in 1959 and decided to design a machine-independent Common Business-Oriented Language, Cobol. The first version of Cobol appeared before the end of 1959 and Codasyl has continued to develop the language.

A continually evolving language cannot be common to all machines as the language implemented varies with the date the processor definition was written. To combat this problem an ANSI standard for Cobol was published in 1968, based on Codasyl's version of January 1967. Following the five-year rules of ANSI, a revised standard, based on Codasyl Cobol of December 1971, was approved in 1974 as an American Standard; the same document was adopted as an ISO Standard in 1978. The fact that the language was designed to be machine-independent, and the procurement policy of the U.S. Government have ensured that the standards have been closely observed. A proposed revision of this standard has been circulated to both the U.S. and the international community for comment and at the time of writing the comments are being considered by the ANSI Cobol committee. This proposal has attracted more public attention than most standards because of alleged incompatibilities with the previous standard.

Although adherence to the standards has been good and many of the problems of differences of arithmetic precision and differing environments have been avoided, when compared with Fortran, the portability of Cobol programs is poor. Apart from additions to the language, allowed in Cobol as in Fortran, the 1974 standard provides for a basic nucleus and for eleven modules, each of which may have two or three levels of implementation. There are in fact 104,976 possible versions of Standard Cobol.

Ada

On the initiative of the U.S. Department of Defense its real-time language Ada has been adopted for processing as a potential international standard. This has been accepted by the various ISO member bodies largely as a possible means of influencing development of the language. However serious incompatibilities between the DoD's perception of a standard language and that of the member bodies of ISO remain to be overcome. For example the name "Ada" is registered as a trademark, or application has been lodged for registration, in thirteen countries. This is contrary to ISO conventions. One country is understood to have refused the application. The DoD plans to insist that only officially certificated language processors may use the term "Ada". This too is contrary to ISO conventions. There is concern also at the pressure to adopt Ada as a standard before working compilers exist, as experience shows that clarifications and corrections will be required in the language definition, and it is not clear that the democratic but slow ISO methods of amending standards will be suitable at this stage in the language's development.

An SC5 Expert Group on Ada was established in October 1981 to investigate these and other problems. Ada is considered here and not under real-time languages below because SC5 makes the same distinction and because it seems likely that Ada will be used as a general purpose language.

Algol 60

Algol 60 has never achieved formal standardization at international level. The language began in the form of a report by a committee without reference to any particular computer. Some attempts were made to implement this language, known as Algol 58, but they were overtaken by a new report describing an improved language, Algol 60. Difficulties and ambiguties in the report led to a Revised Report in 1962, whereafter a working group of IFIP assumed responsibility for the language.

It was suggested that the Revised Report go forward for processing as a possible ISO standard, but since that omitted any definition for input-output or for subsets which were considered to be necessary, there was some delay while an ISO working group added these. Finally in 1967 the draft proposal was ready for adoption as an ISO Recommendation, it having been decided that this was a more suitable form than a Standard. For reasons which are obscure the printed version did not appear until 1972 and was so full of errors as to render it useless. It was withdrawn in 1976.

Further maintenance on the language by an IFIP working group resulted in a Modified Report in 1976. Recent attempts to have the Modified Report with addenda processed as a draft ISO standard have met delay because the Modified Report does not conform to ISO rules. Meanwhile the Modified Report remains the de facto, but not the official, international standard.

Algol 68

Algol 68 was designed by the same IFIP working group which is concerned with Algol 60. The original defining report appeared in 1968 and a revised Report in 1974. This is considered by the IFIP group as the final definition of the language. At the time of writing Algol 68 is under consideration for adoption as a work item for SC5.

APL

APL was invented by K. Iverson in the late 1950's. It has become widely used and there are significant differences between implementations which inhibits movement of both programs and users. There was a need for standardization and in 1979

AFNOR took the initiative to have APL adopted as an SC5 work item. An SC5 working group, on whch most participants are from Canada, France, UK or USA, is actively developing a proposed standard.

Basic

Basic (Beginners All-pupose Symbolic Instruction Code) was invented in 1963-64 and was the first language explicitly intended for interactive use. It has become very widely implemented, on all sizes of computers, and a need for a standard was perceived in the early 1970's. ANSI and ECMA committees for Basic were set up in 1974 and, working collaboratively (cf PL/I) published in 1978 standards for Minimal Basic, that is for a minimal subset of the language. Even this proved to have contentious features and it has so far proceded only to the Draft International Standard stage. Meanwhile ANSI, ECMA and EWICS (European Workshop on Industrial Control Systems) are working on a more complete proposal for the language.

Computer Languages for the Processing of Text (CLPT)

A need for some standardization in the field of text editing and formatting utilities was seen and a formal ANSI committee was set up in 1978. Subsequently the work was taken up in ISO and was allocated to SC5 which established an Experts Group. At the time of writing the group has issued a first report.

Data Base Management Systems

Data base management systems are not programming languages but specifying their organization and structure has been considered similar to using a programming language and DBMS have been allocated to SC5 for standardization. There are no standard DBMS, although a number of them, e.g. Adabas, IDMS, IMS, System 2000, Total, are very widely used. ANSI has committees working on data base facilities for Cobol and Fortran and on a data description language. An SC5 working group for DBMS facilities was formed on the initiative of AFNOR and it is working on a technical report on "Concepts and Terminology for Conceptual Schema". In 1981 a second SC5 working group on "Data Definition Language for Network Structured Data Bases" was established. Its initial task was to review the field and to recommend items for possible standardization.

Graphics

In a similar manner to DBMS, graphics has been allocated to SC5 for standardization. There were originally proposals to standardize on one of the existing packages (e.g. DISSPLA, Ghost, GINO and GPGS are all widely used) but eventually a system defined within an SC5 working group and known as the Graphical Kernel System or GKS has come to be processed as an ISO Draft Proposal.

Operating System Command and Response Languages (OSCRL)

Another area in which a need for standardization has recently been suggested is that of operating system command and response languages, known variously as job control languages, system control languages etc. IFIP has organized a number of conferences in this area and SC5 has begun an investigation to see if there is need for formal standards.

Pascal

Pascal was designed by N. Wirth in 1968-71 as a simple, small language partly as a reaction to some of the baroque complexities of Algol 68. It proliferated particularly on microcomputers in the mid - 1970's and two independent projects were begun to devise a standard. The BSI formally established a project in 1977 with the objective of producing a British, and potentially international, standard and on a British initiative Pascal was approved as an SC5 work item in 1978. Meanwhile in 1978 the IEEE Computer Society formed a committee to produce an IEEE standard. A third activity was begun by ANSI to produce an American National Standard Pascal when it was heard that work had started in Europe. The relations between these committees are described in Addyman (1980). Eventually the British activity spawned an ISO activity which produced a document which has been approved as a British Standard (BS 6192) and which is being processed as a Draft International Standard.

PL/I

PL/I was designed to be the first high-level general purpose language and in the late 1960's it was thought that it might supersede both Cobol and Fortran. ECMA began to consider the possibility of a standard in 1965 and ANSI did the same the following year. This led to the establishment of a joint ECMA/ANSI project on standardization in 1969. A draft was produced which was circulated to ISO member countries for comment. Eventually the document was approved as separate ANSI and ECMA standards in 1976 and as an ISO standard in 1979. Joint ECMA/ANSI work has continued in order to define a general purpose subset language which is being processed as a Draft International Standard.

Real-time Languages

One of the working groups of SC5 has as its title "Programing Languages for the control of Industrial Processes", known informally as PLIP. It covers what are generally known as real-time languages, or real-time extensions to general purpose languages, primarily used for process control in a real-time environment. A set of Fortran subroutine specifications to control real-time processes, known as IRTF (Industrial Real-Time Fortran) and developed by EWICS (European Workshop on Industrial Control Systems) based on work by the Instruments Society of America, is being processed as an ISO draft proposal.

There is no real-time language per se which is an ISO standard but some languages have been standardized at the national level, e.g. Pearl (Germany) and Coral and RTL/2 (UK). See also Ada above.

Simula

Simula, or Simula 67, developed from an earlier language known retrospectively as Simula I. It was designed at the Norwegian Computing Centre as an extension of Algol 60, with a few minor changes and omissions, to allow for the description and simulation of discrete proceses. Thus it can be, and is, used as a general purpose language. It is implemented on a wide range of machines but is not so widely used as its elegance and technical merits would suggest, possibly because of all the languages discussed in this chapter (other than Ada) it is the only one for which its originators retain a large measure of proprietorial control. At the time of writing Simula is under consideation for adoption as a work item for SC5.

3. CONCLUSION

The standards for programming languages are as a group different in scale and type from most of the other standards with which the ISO member bodies are concerned. Consider for example the standard for a programming language and a standard for a lifejacket. Not only is one much easier to specify, it is possible to test rigourously whether a lifejacket conforms to a standard or not and to lay down complete test procedures. Even within the group of language standards there are major variations in size, scope and style of language specification. SC5 has therefore set up a group to consider the aim, format and content of such standards and to consider the procedures for their construction and subsequent maintenance or revision. For example different techniques are used to describe the languages: Fortran is described in English with supplementary "railroad diagrams", Cobol uses a distinct metalanguage. As one step to addressing this problem the BSI recently produced a British Standard Syntactic Metalanguage (BS 6154).

Finally the Book by Hill and Meek (1980) is recommended reading for anyone concerned with language standards. It contains full references and further information on all the standards mentioned above. Alternatively information is obtainable through member bodies of ISO.

REFERENCES

Addyman A.M. (1980), Pascal, in Hill & Meek (1980) pp. 81-91.

Dahlstrand I. (1980), Discussion Contribution, in Hill & Meek (1980) p. 189.

Hill I.D. and Meek B.L. (1980), Programming language Standardisation. Chichester: Ellis Horwood.

SOFTWARE TOOLS FOR SOFTWARE SHARING

David Muxworthy
University of Edinburgh
Edinburgh, UK

1. INTRODUCTION

Scope

In this chapter we consider software tools which help in the process of implementing a program at a site other than the originator's. We are concerned not with the installation of basic operating system software amongst machines of the same type but with the transference of "applications" programs written in a high level language on the same or different hardware. Such an implementation typically requires adaptation of a program and it is this adaptation which is the central point. The work may be the responsibility of the supplier or the recipient of the program. The extent of the amendment which is required will be very different according as the program was originally written with the intent of being used on only one computer system, or if it was intended to be as machine-independent as possible.

Software tools are taken to be programs, typically single-purpose programs callable at the operating system command level, which help in this process. We are not concerned with the mechanics of distributing software, which have been well described by Waite (1975) and Day (1978) and are further outlined by Ford in this volume, nor with the problems of converting programs at machine code level, which is usually practicable only in very specialized circumstances, nor necessarily with the problems of using software over a network. Rather we are concerned with the practical problems of installing high-level language programs from one installation at another one.

Portability problems are often thought of in terms of differing machine characteristics. However it is worth remarking that problems may occur not only in moving from one machine range to another, or from one model in a machine range to another, but also between different operating systems on a single computer or even between language processors within a single system.

D. T. Muxworthy (ed.), Programming for Software Sharing, 149–174.

Environmental Change

When the source code of a "foreign" high-level language program has been satisfactorily copied to a computer, that is when any mechanical problems of card codes, character codes, record lengths, tape formats, etc, have been overcome, it may appear so obvious as to be hardly worth stating that the program has suffered a change of environment. But the whole problem of the aspects of portability covered here is to do with adapting a program to its new environment and it is useful to classify the possible changes of environment.

Clearly the changes could be classified as those due to software and those due to hardware but it is more helpful to divide them into those related to the language processor and its immediate runtime system, and those related to the wider aspects of the operating system facilities and the underlying hardware; it is however not always possible to make a clear distinction. Almost invariably the language processor will have been written to a different language specification from that on which the program was developed. It may reject some aspects of the language used by the program. Worse, it may accept the syntax of the statements in the program but interpret them quite differently. Almost certainly it will cause different default actions to be taken if a rule of the language is broken. A common example of this is the treatment of integer overflow and real underflow. Some algorithms depend on one or both of these not being detected at run time; the default action of various processors is different and may not even be stated in user documentation.

The other main class of environmental change is the change of hardware and the supporting operating system software. The hardware changes involve word length, basic numeric precision, the different types of real and integer variable, the form of arithmetic, the number of characters per word etc etc. The pure software changes relate to procedures callable direct from a program which are system - or site-dependent. A trivial but common example is a procedure to find the date and time of day. Many environmental differences may be ascribed to a mixture of hardware and software, for example the number, type and size of files available, the size of fast store available, whether virtual memory is used etc etc.

Software Tools Available

In recent years there has been increase of interest in and use of software tools in software development. Houghton and Oakley (1980) give summaries of about 300 tools and Appendix 1 notes the different functions performed by these tools. This recent growth of interest has thrived, directly or indirectly, on work based on the UNIX system at Bell Laboratories, Lawrence Berkeley Laboratory and other places and more generally on the realization over the past ten years that the cost of program provision was becoming a major expense at most computing centres. Nevertheless software tools are not new: high-level language translators appeared in the early 1960's. Today there is a wider choice available but as yet no consensus of what is desirable or sensible to use in the field of software sharing. A major project to produce a new set of tools, Toolpack, is under way (see Appendix 2). The areas to be covered here are:

> editors
> translators
> syntax checkers

> analyzers and documentors
> debugging systems
> master source systems
> macro-processors and preprocessors
> portable compilers and operating systems

We attempt to give an outline of the uses of these programs; it is of course not possible to mention every type of tool.

A good context editor is nowadays almost indispensable and in order to define this term and set the standard for other tools we describe below editors which are generally considered to have good user facilities.

2. EDITORS

Context Editors

A context editor is the most basic tool for creating and amending program source code as well as data and program documentation. The quality of the editor is important and it is not unknown for programmers to choose between available systems purely on the criterion of the ease of use and power of the editor. For software sharing, where slight modifications of the same text may be required for different systems, the editor takes on added importance. As Kernighan and Plauger (1976) write, "All interactive computing systems... have some form of editing facility, but it is often primitive. The reason most users don't complain is that they don't know what they're missing."

The program described by Kernighan and Plauger is outlined below. Various implementations of this editor have been made which may differ in details. Although the editor is normally run interactively it is not necessary that it be so run.

The basic unit handled by the editor is a line of text. Lines are referenced by their relative position from the start of the file after each command and do not themselves contain sequence numbers. For example if the first eight lines are deleted by a command, what was previously ninth line becomes the first line for the following command. Commands are typed one at time, one per line and cannot be grouped. Unlike some other editors there are no separate "input" and "edit" modes; that is, any command may be given at any time after completion of the previous one. There is a concept of a "current line" after each command; this is amplified below. There is no concept of a current position within a line as the line is the basic unit with which the editor works.

Let us consider some basic commands. The command

> 1,5p

will print the first five lines of the file. The command

> 7p

will print the seventh line. After each of these operations the "current line" is set to the last line printed. As well as line numbers relative to the start of the file it is possible to use symbols to denote the current line (dot) and to denote the last line of the file (dollar) thus

    1,$p

prints the entire file. It is possible to use simple arithmetic expressions as line numbers so that for example

    .—5,. + 5p

prints in all eleven lines around the current line, and

    $—4,$p

prints the last five lines in the file.

The command to delete a line is "d" and is used analogously to "p", except that "d" may be followed by "p" in which case the line following the last one deleted is printed.

The most critical commands in an editor are those for finding and changing text. In this editor the command

    / <text> / ,e.g. / SUBROUTINE MATINV /

means scan forward, starting at the line after the current line, until the specified text is found. If it is not found by the end of the file, the scan continues at line one and goes on either until the text is found or until the complete file has been scanned unsuccessfully, in which case an error is noted. If the text is found, the line is printed and the current line is set to the line containing the text.

The command \ <text> \ is similar but the search is backwards from the current line and there is wrap-round from the first line to the last.

In addition / <text> / and \ <text> \ may be used in place of line numbers in commands, to mean the lines which would be found by their operation, so that

    \ SUBROUTINE \ , / END / p

could, under appropriate conditions, be used to print the Fortran subroutine containing the current line.

The substitution command

    s / <text1> / <text2> /

substitutes the first occurrence of <text1> on the current line by <text2>, which may be null. If the command is followed by a g (global) then all occurrences of <text1> on the line are substituted. For example if the current line is:

    favourite colour

the command

    s / our / or / g

would change it to

    favorite color.

Further, the substitution command may be preceded by one or two line numbers, as for d and p, to extend the range of lines to which it applies. In this case the current line is left pointing at the last line changed.

A common requirement is to move to a line to be defined by its content, not its location, and to change something in that line, e.g.

/ seperate / s / seperate / separate /

In this case the second occurrence of the text which is to be found may be omitted; thus the command be equivalently written as

/ seperate / s / / separate /

The s command will not cause a changed line to be printed unless a p is appended, e.g.

/ seperate / s / / separate / p

Consistent mis-spelling may be corrected by following this by a series of identical commands of the form:

/ / s / / separate / p
/ / s / / separate / p

to step through a file and print each corrected line. The alternative

1,$s / seperate / separate / g p

will print only the last line changed.

The start and end of a line have special symbols, % and $ respectively. Thus

/ Once /

will find the next occurrence of "Once", but

/ %Once /

will find the next occurrence of "Once" as the first four characters in a line. Similarly

/ END$ /

will find "END" only at the end of a line and will not find for example "ENDFILE" or "ENDIF".

The command

/ %begin$ /

will find a line containing only "begin", and

/ %$ /

will find an empty line.

The ampersand character may be used to denote "ditto" in substitution, where the implied copying is from the last text found. For example

s / separate / &d /

is equivalent to

s / separate / separated /

Any symbol may used to delimit the text in the s command. This is particularly useful if it is required to find " / " as part of the text, e.g.

s. / .div.

Alternatively " / " may be preceded in the text by the "escape character"@, so that

@/ is regarded as the symbol / and not as the delimiter, e.g.

s /@/ / div /

The @ character may also be used with %, $, @ itself and other characters to be introduced below.

A major feature of this editor is its ability to match patterns. The symbol "?" is normally treated as a wild character so that for example

/ t?me /

would match "tame", "time", "tome" or any other four-character string with t, m, and e in the first, third and fourth positions. The ? character may be "escaped" if it is required to represent the question mark.

There are in addition character classes, denoted by square brackets. The class

[aA]

will match either "a" or "A". The class

[A-Z]

will match any upper case letter,

[a-zA-Z]

will match any letter, and

[0-9]

will match any digit. Classes may be negated, using the not sign, so that

[¬ a]

will match any character other than "a". Any text pattern matching a single character may be followed by an asterisk to mean zero or more occurrences of that character. Thus

x*

means zero or more x's,

xx*

means one or more x's,

[a-z]*

will match any string of lower case letters,

[A-Z] [A-Z0-9]*

will match a Fortran identifier, including ones that are too long, and certain other strings as well. As further examples,

"?*"

will match anything between quotation marks,

% *$

will match lines of blanks, and

??*

will match any line of one or more characters.

Any command other than "a", "c", "i" or "q" (considered below) may be preceded by

> / <pattern> /

in which case it is taken to apply to the next line on which <pattern> is found, or by

> g / <pattern> /

where g again means global and the command then applies to every line on which the pattern is found, or by

> x / <pattern> /

which is the opposite of "g" and the command applies to every line on which the pattern is not found. Each of these commands may be further refined by preceding them by a pair of line numbers. The default values are 1 and $.

Let us consider further commands. The command to allow insertion of complete lines of text is "a". In an initial, empty, file, the command "a" on a line by itself is followed by lines of text up to, and excluding, a line containing a "." on a line by itself; this is used to terminate the text input. When a file has been established the command "a" followed by text will cause the text to be inserted after the current line. The command "0a" may be used to insert at the beginning of the file and "$a" at the end of the file. In general <n>a causes the input to follow line <n>.

The command "i" is similar, but the next text is inserted before the current line, or in general the nominated line. The command

> <m>, <n>c

causes deletion of lines <m> to <n> inclusive and their replacement by text which follows the command in the style of "a" and "i".

The command "m" is used to move a block of text from one place in the file to another. For example

> 3,17 m 29

will move lines 3 to 17 inclusive to follow line 29.

The command " = " will cause the current line number to be printed and a carriage return by itself will print the next line, and advance the current line, so that giving a series of carriage returns will step through the file printing a line at a time.

There remain only the commands related to entering and leaving the editor and writing files. The entry command is

> edit

in which case one must careful to specify the file to be written in the w command, below, or

> edit <filename>

where the file may or may not exist before entry. If it does exist, and file is being edited rather than simply scanned, as a results file from a program may be, the w command is used to specify the name of the output file. This should be different from the input file to guard against system crashes during the writing of the file. The form of the "w" command is simply

    w <filename>

which writes the entire file to the file specified. The command to quit the editor, "q", does only that so that if editing is to be saved "w" must be issued before "q".

An alternative form of w allows writing a portion of the file to another file, for example

    \ SUBROUTINE \ , / END / w matinv

could be used to write a copy of a subroutine to file "matinv". The lines written remain also in the file being edited.

Correspondingly there is a command

    r <filename>

to copy the content of an external file to follow the current line or the line nominated in the "r" command. The command "f" prints the name of the current file.

As mentioned above the Kernighan and Plauger editor has the concept of finding the first occurrence of a text on a line, and possibly of changing it, and of changing all occurrences of a text on a line. It deliberately does not have the concept of a current position within a line and does not have the ability to perform such functions as moving characters defined by position, not by content, to another place in a record. A common task is the requirement to split a line which has become too long after editing into two lines or conversely to make two lines into one; this function could easily be added to the editor.

We consider briefly some features of another widely implemented editor, ECCE (Dewar, 1981), which has the concept of a current location within a line, and give some examples of its use. The command

    f / <text> /

will find the next occurrence of text, starting from the current pointer position, while

    f <n> / <text> /

will examine the next n lines only. The command

    f / <text> / <n>

will find the n'th occurrence of the text. In all of these cases if the text is not found before the end of the file the command fails. After finding the text the pointer is positioned immediately to the left of the text and a subsequent s command may be used to substitute new text, e.g.

    f / <text1> / s / <text2> /

Unlike the Kernighan and Plauger editor the substitution needs two commands and any number of commands may be typed on one line. Sets of commands may be repeated by enclosing them in parentheses and following them with a repeat count, e.g.

    (f / seperate / s / separate /)*

An asterisk is used to denote an indefinite repeat. The commands "l" and "r" mean move the pointer one character left and right, respectively, on the current line, "e" means delete the next character to the right and "e-" means delete the next character to the left. As examples

    f / begin / r*e-2

means find the next occurrence of "begin", go to the end of the line and delete the previous two characters, i.e. the last two characters on the line.

A distinguishing feature of this editor is the ability to have "programmed commands" including conditional execution. Each command has an associated condition in which the command is said to fail and the pointer is not moved. For example "r" will fail if the pointer is already at the end of a line; "m", which moves the pointer to the next line, will fail if the pointer is at the end of the file. The failure conditions are used to control sequences of commands. A "compound command" is defined to be a set of basic commands enclosed in parentheses and a compound command fails when any constituent command fails. Thus the compound command

    (mr)*

will find the next null line after the current line. There is a command

    v / <text> /

which verifies that "text" appears immediately to the right of the pointer; it does not move the pointer but may give a failure condition. Thus the sequence

    r*(lv / / e)*

will remove all trailing spaces from the current line.

Another facility made possible by failure conditions is the ability to have alternative command sequences, wherein a set of commands is given and each is attempted until one is successful, whereafter the remainder of the set is ignored. Given that "¬" negates the failure condition of the preceding command and that "k" deletes (kills) the current line, the sequence

    r¬

will fail if a right move of one position can be made, and succeed otherwise. Thus the effect of the alternative sequence

    r¬k,m

is as follows. If the line contains one or more characters the first part fails so the second (move to next line) is attempted. If the line contains no characters, "r¬" succeeds so the "k" is executed and the "m" is not attempted. The "k" command causes the pointer to move to the next line so the total effect is to delete the current line if it is empty and to ignore it otherwise. Similarly the sequence

    (v / C / k,m)*

will delete all lines beginning with "C". The sequence

    f1 / begin / ,f1 / end / ,m

will find either "begin" or "end" on the current line, or if neither occurs will move the pointer to the next line. Long sequences may be stored as "macro commands" and reissued by typing only two characters. This editor, ECCE contains other features but the main differences in concepts from the Kernighan and Plauger editor are those which are described above.

Language-intelligent editors

A disadvantage of context editors in some circumstances is that the text they handle is quite general and the meaning of the text is ignored. If for example it is desired to examine all uses of a particular variable a section of code, this is only possible if the variable name is sufficiently long and idiosyncratic. If it is a name such as "N" the editor will not only find all uses of N but also all other variable names containing N in the name and all reserved words, for example ASSIGN, CONTINUE, DIMENSION, END, ENDIF, etc in Fortran. A language-intelligent editor is able to identify particular variable names, as distinct from simple text, and is also able to recognize that character sequences, equivalent apart from spacing within and between lines are indeed the same.

A language-intelligent editor for Fortran is part of the Toolpack project (Appendix 2).

3. LANGUAGE TRANSLATORS

Language and Dialect Translators

If it is wished to implement a program written in a language for which no processor exists on the target system, an obvious but not necessarily optimal recourse is to translate it to a language which is available. Except in the case of very small programs or where the number of target installations is large it is not usually economic to do this by hand and the first tool to be considered is the translator. Apart from the cost the main problem of rewriting programs by hand is that most programmers find an irresistible urge to "improve" them at the same time, possibly introducing new errors as they do so. A cardinal rule in all the work discussed in this chapter is that if a sequence of code works satisfactorily it should not be changed unless the savings are likely to be significant. This means that the total cost of making the change should be less than the probable subsequent savings in computer time. Even in this case the conversion effort should be kept distinct from the improvement.

Translators for high-level languages are almost as old as high-level languages themselves. It was in about 1960-61 that it became possible to run programs without change on machines from different manufacturers (Sammett, 1969), the languages concerned being Cobol and Fortran. The incompatibilities between Fortran II and Fortran IV a year or two later, many of them trivial in nature and easily identifiable mechanically, led to the introduction of translators amongst which perhaps the best known was SIFT - the SHARE Internal Fortran Translator (Allan et al, 1963). These programs established the pattern for future translators: they converted the majority of statements from one language or dialect to another and drew attention to the remainder which needed human intervention. In general it is not possible to guarantee total conversion of a program by a translator because it is unusual for every single concept in a language to be matched in another. To take simple examples a language which supports random-access file statements cannot be translated directly to a language which does not, other than by replacing the statements with references to external procedures; this is usually beyond the scope of a translator. Again, a language which allows arbitrary subscript expressions may contain statements which require non-trivial conversion to a language with restricted expressions, such as ANSI Standard Fortran of 1966. Consider

WRITE (U) (X(L(I)), I = 1, N)

which writes a single record of elements of array X specified by elements of array L. If it were not possible to use this form of subscript, it could be necessary to take a copy of the X elements before the WRITE statement, with costs for both time and space. As a final example, a program in a language which supports item-orientated input-output (e.g. Pascal, some implementations of Algol 60) is not trivially converted to one which supports record-orientated input-output (e.g. Fortran, some implementations of Algol 60).

Translators are often provided by computer manufacturers to aid the conversion of software of new customers and many are available from software houses. They are usually intended to convert between different dialects but a number of interlanguage ones exist, for example Fortran to Algol 60, Fortran to PL/I, RPG to Cobol, Algol 60 to PL/I. Translators have tended to be somewhat expensive to acquire and they are not usually available for the type of occasional use envisaged in this context. Program libraries may well have them available but with advances in micro-code and portable compilers it may be that computer manufacturers will use the high-level translation route less in future. Even so it is surprising that Houghton and Oakley list only one translator, a Cobol dialect converter.

Translator Generators

Besides purpose-built programs there are a number of more general software tools which may be used for translation. Text manipulation languages such as SNOBOL, SPITBOL or ICON allow much of the mechanical work of translation to done more easily and even a context editor, given a fixed set of commands in the form of a script file, could perform a significant proportion of the conversion work.

A tool designed specifically for generating language and dialect translators is described by Wolberg and Rafal (1978); the tool is itself written in PL/I and could also be used as a general text manipulation language.

4. STANDARDS AND SYNTAX CHECKERS

Introduction

A better approach than translation to having programs portable between systems is to write the program initially so that it will, so far as is possible run on more than one system. This means adhering to the subset of a language common to the systems in question, or, better, adhering to the international standard for that language.

The international standard for a language may be a formal ISO standard, a national standard, a draft standard, a report or simply be defined by common usage but for almost all languages such a thing exists. For the major languages a difficulty arises in informing the programmer whether or not a program conforms to the standard. Not all manuals and fewer language processors give indications of when a statement is non-standard syntactically and for all the limitations of a standard to be checked at execution time is quite unusual. In Fortran even such an apparently harmless statement as

A = B + C

is non-standard if the addition causes overflow and the critical value will of course be different on different systems. It is for this reason that few non-trivial programs in the common languages can be guaranteed to be 100% portable without qualifying statements about their data and environment.

Nevertheless a syntax checker which compares a program with a standard is one of the most useful single tools available, both for the originator and recipient of a program. One of the more commonly used is the PFORT Verifier (Ryder, 1974) which relates to the ANSI 1966 Fortran Standard. Although the PFORT Verifier is necessarily language-dependent, its concepts could be applied to any language and because of its importance its facilities and use are described in the following paragraph.

PFORT

Following the usage of its author, PFORT is a portable subset of the ANSI Standard Fortran of 1966 and it is the PFORT Verifier which checks a Fortran program for adherence to PFORT. In common usage, the verifier itself is called PFORT. A program which has been found error-free by the verifier is highly likely to be compilable immediately on all systems offering a standard Fortran 66 compiler. This does not of course imply that the program is free of logic errors but the verifier also provides facilities useful for error detection. Many Fortran programs which contain non-standard statements may easily be changed to use standard statement only and as bonus it is not unusual for analysis by PFORT to lead to a more efficient program.

The verifier checks each Fortran program unit in much the same way as a compiler, but while most compilers (deliberately) consider each program unit independently, the verifier also checks inter-program unit communication, that is it tests for consistency of subprogram arguments between calling and called routines, draws attention to "unsafe" argument association and tests for consistency in common block usage. Apart from warnings of deviation from the PFORT language and warnings about unsafe practices the program prints tables of usage of variables, common blocks and inter-progam unit references. A trivial example in figures 1, 2 and 3 illustrates some of these but cannot show the full power of the program.

In the example the only error detected by a normal service compiler was the mistyping of "U" in the DO statement. Some of the restrictions of Fortran 66 and hence PFORT concerning mixed- mode expressions now seem old fashioned, for example (FI-1) should have been (FI-1.), but the verifier immediately makes obvious one error, that MEAN was not declared to be real, so that all assignments to MEAN would be truncated and the results of the program would be totally incorrect. The verifier also makes obvious implicit type conversions which may be expensive if they are executed within nests of DO-loops.

The list of variables and labels shows the following information. The type column is self-explanatory except that "E" means explicitly typed; Hollerith is considered to be a distinct type. The use column indicates if a name is a variable, function, subroutine, intrinsic function, statement function, etc. Note that SQRT did not have a legal argument and so was not classified as an internal function. The attributes column consists of five different attributes, showing respectively whether the name was in common, whether it was equivalenced, whether it was a dummy argument, whether a value was set in this program unit and whether it was a scalar or array. In the latter case the number of dimensions is also given. Finally there is a list of line numbers in which the names and labels were referenced.

By examining this table it is clear that variable MEAN is considered to be an integer, that there is something wrong with variables I and U since they are local and used without being defined, and that label 10 is redundant. The verifier output for a driver program is shown in figure 2 and the inter-program checks, which are very simple in this case, are in figure 3. In the argument attributes the four codes for each argument show (1) whether the argument is typed explicitly or is a procedure or is neither of these, (2) the type, (3) whether a value is set within the called program and (4) whether it is a scalar or array. In the common block table the columns give the name, whether the block is initialized in BLOCK DATA, the number of double word entries and the number of single word entries.

The PFORT Language is essentially the same as the ANSI Fortran 66 standard except for a few restrictions, notably that Hollerith text may be stored only in integer variables and may be stored only one character per word, there is no extended range of a DO-statement and there are minor restrictions on the statement ordering. The verifier explicitly does not check rules which typically could only be tested at execution time, and does not check certain other rules, e.g. whether a storage unit is initialized in more than one DATA statement.

The PFORT Verifier is used as standard practice in a number of organizations which produce software for multiple target systems. It can also be used to check an established program before installation on a foreign system. There is a disadvantage in this in that PFORT may consider as a fatal error a statement which would prove acceptable to the new host Fortran processor and there would be a natural reluctance to change this only for PFORT. This is particularly true for DATA statements where PFORT requires an array in the variable list to be written out element by element; it is quite common to comment out such statements before using PFORT. Nevertheless if there is a requirement to understand the structure of the program PFORT can be an aid and has played its part in the unravelling of several unnecessarily complicated programs. This leads to the wider area of analyzers discussed below.

PFORT VERIFIER 3/10/78 VERSION

```
    1                    SUBROUTINE MSD (X, N, MEAN, SD)
             C           THIS ROUTINE ATTEMPTS TO COMPUTE THE MEAN AND
             C           STANDARD DEVIATION OF X(1).. X(N) BY THE
             C           RUNNING MEANS METHOD
    2                    DIMENSION X(N)
    3                    COMMON /CMN/ ERROR
    4        10          MEAN = X(1)
    5                    SD = 0.0
    6                    IF (N .LE. 0) GO TO 40
    7                    DO 20 U = 2,N
*** CONTROL VARIABLE NOT INTEGER SCALAR

    8                    FI = FLOAT(I)
```

```
     9              D = (X(I) - MEAN)/FI
*** ILLEGAL COMBINATION OF DATA TYPES

    10              SD = SD + FI*(FI-1)*D**2
*** ILLEGAL COMBINATION OF DATA TYPES

    11      20      MEAN = MEAN + D
*** ILLEGAL COMBINATION OF DATA TYPES

    12              SD = SQRT (SD/(N-1))
*** ILLEGAL COMBINATION OF DATA TYPES

    13      30      RETURN
    14      40      ERROR = 1.0
    15              GO TO 30
    16              END
```

PROGRAM UNIT MSD

ARGUMENTS		X		N	MEAN	SD		
NAME	TYPE	USE	ATTRIBUTES	REFERENCES				
D	R	V	SS	9	11			
ERROR	R	V	C SS	3	14			
FI	R	V	SS	8	10			
FLOAT	ER	IF		8				
I	I	V	S	8	9			
MEAN	I	V	ASS	1	4	9	11	
N	I	V	A S	1	2	6	12	
SD	R	V	ASS	1	5	10	12	
SQRT	R	V	S	12				
U	R	V	S	7				
X	R	V	A A1	1	2	4	9	
10				4				
20				7	11			
30				13	15			
40				6	14			

COMMON BLOCKS

CMN   ERROR

Figure 1

PFORT VERIFIER 3/10/78 VERSION

```
    1              DIMENSION X(100)
    2              REAL ERROR
    3              REAL M
    4              COMMON /CMN/ ERROR
    5      1       READ (5,100,END = 5) N
```

*** WARNING - NON-PORTABLE EOF CONSTRUCT

```
    6      100     FORMAT (I3)
    7              READ (5,200) (X(I),I = 1,N)
    8      200     FORMAT (10F8.4)
    9              ERROR = 0.0
    10             CAL MSD (X,N,M,S)
    11             IF (ERROR .NE. 0,0) GO TO 10
    12             WRITE (6,220) M,S
```

- 162 -

13	220	FORMAT (2F10.3)
14		GO TO 1
15	10	WRITE (6,240)
16	240	FORMAT (1X, 'ILLEGAL N')

*** WARNING - NON-FORTRAN CHARACTER IGNORED

*** ILLEGAL FORMAT ITEM

17		GO TO 1
18	5	STOP
19		END

PROGRAM UNIT   *MAIN

NAME	TYPE	USE	ATTRIBUTES		REFERENCES			
ERROR	ER	V	C	SS	2	4	9	11
I	I	V		SS	7			
M	ER	V		S	3	10	12	
MSD		SN			10			
N	I	V		SS	5	7	10	
S	R	V		S	10	12		
X	R	V		SA1	1	7	10	
1					5	14	17	
10					11	15		
100					5	6		
200					7	8		
220					12	13		
240					15	16		
5					5	18		

COMMON BLOCKS

CMN   ERROR

Figure 2

PFORT VERIFIER 3/10/78 VERSION

*** MISMATCHED TYPE ASSOCIATED WITH
*** PARAMETER NUMBER 3
*** IN REFERENCE TO --MSD
*** AT STMT NO 10 IN PGM UNIT *MAIN

* MAIN

COMMON BLOCKS	CMN	S
CALLS SUBPROGRAMS	MSD	

MSD

ARGUMENT ATTRIBUTES	-R-A		-I-S	-ISS -RSS
COMMON BLOCKS	CMN	S		
CALLED BY SUBPROGRAMS	*MAIN			

COMMON BLOCKS

NAME	SET	DP, COM	INT, RL, LOG
CMN		0	1

Figure 3

Other Syntax Checkers

Another tool which compares a program against the ANSI 1966 Fortran standard is AUDITOR (Softool Corporation, 1977). This program makes similar restrictions on the standard language in the interests of portability for instance that Hollerith text be stored in integer variables and that the order of statements and the use of the EQUIVALENCE statement be restricted. It goes further than PFORT in making some flow checks so as to warn that certain variables may be undefined and it also checks constant subscripts against the corresponding dimension statements. It makes explicit warning statements about variables or labels being declared but not used and computes a portability index, defined as the average number of portability problems per statement.

A verifier for Fortran 77, similar to the PFORT verifier, is part of Toolpack.

5. ANALYZERS

Introduction

In recent years much emphasis has been placed on the benefits for design, implementation and maintenace of using top-down design and structured programming techniques. This has been accompanied by a new awareness of the interaction between a program and its environment and the need for all system dependencies to be clearly identified and described. In real life too few programmers have taken heed of this and many programs need considerable effort before they can be understood. Therefore the matter of changing the dialect, or more drastically the language, of a program is only the first step in obtaining the correct results. Problems of adapting to the new environment, for example with regard to the numerical precision, character codes or files used, have still to be investigated by, and remain the responsibility of, the programmer.

Fortunately in the past five years there has been a great increase in the number of tools which analyse and test programs and which thus aid exploration and assist comprehension not only by a programmer attempting to transport a program but by the original programmer at development time. In the future it is possible that program proving and validation techniques will supersede the need for these tools; with the current state of the art the responsibility for using the available tools intelligently and effectively lies with the programmer.

Before considering program analyzers it is useful to distinguish the concepts of control flow and data flow in a program. Control flow is the movement of code execution from statement to statement and from procedure to procedure. Data flow is the sequence of changes of state of a data structure, from undefined to initialized and then possibly referenced, reassigned and so on. Flow information can be obtained from an examination of the program source (static) and while a program is being executed (dynamic).

Static Analyzers

Static analysers cover a range of functions but broadly are used to detect inconsistences in the structure of programs and to detect certain kinds of errors without execution of the program. One of the better known static analyzers is

DAVE (Osterweil and Fosdick, 1976) which works by deducing data flow between and within modules in Fortran programs. Reporting this is useful to the programmer for efficiency considerations but more important is the fact that inconsistent or erroneous data flows are highlighted.

Like the PFORT Verifier DAVE considers the program as a whole, not program unit by program unit. It checks that the program is syntactically correct, prints a call tree of the program, and makes checks on the consistency of arguments between calling and called programs, again like the PFORT verifier. It prints warnings if for instance a constant argument is assigned a value or if a procedure argument is used as it were a variable. It will warn if a variable is referenced before it is assigned a value on some or all paths through the program and it will print warnings if variables are used when the 1966 Fortran standard says they are undefined, for example DO control variables after completion of the DO-loop and local variables in sub-programs. There are a number of interesting warning messages where the program is not illegal but where there is a possibility that the code is not what was intended. Examples are when a variable is assigned and never used, declared and never used, assigned and then assigned again before being referenced. A more subtle example is when a variable in common is assigned and not used in a subroutine and the calling program does not access the common block in question. All of these messages, where appropriate, distinguish between the situation arising on all, or some, paths through the program. Informative diagnostics include such information as common blocks available to a sub-program which are not actually referenced by it.

Another class of analyzer is that which examines the control flow of a program and may produce indented listings or flowcharts on a line printer or graphical device. Such flowcharts tend to be less useful than hand-drawn ones but are often cheaper to produce. More sophisticated are those which take code and rewrite it as a structured program, for example Favs (Donahoo & Swearinger, 1980) and Structuring Engine (Applied Systems Design Section, 1979) for Fortran and Sow's Ear (Miller) for Cobol. Attention is also drawn to the Fortran-to-Fortran optimizing translator of Schneck and Angel (1973) which rewrites the program in Fortran having performed the type of analysis typically associated with an optimizing compiler, e.g. removing invariant code from loops, identifying common sub-expressions across statements.

A simpler form of static analysis is that of the NBS Fortran 77 Analyzer (NBS, 1979). This calculates the frequencies of use (statically) of the different types of statement in a program. This is of more use in other contexts, e.g. programming teaching, benchmark characterization, than in program development, but the main purpose of this program is dynamic analysis. Similar tools for Algol 60 are described in Wichmann (1973).

Dynamic Analysis

The object of dynamic analysis is to determine the frequency of execution of each statement during an actual run of a program, with a view to obtaining a better understanding of its action and hence leading to an improvement in its design both with respect to accuracy and efficiency. Most dynamic analyzers work in the same way, that is they "instrument" or insert "probes" into the code (in the same high level language) before its execution and then produce a report by executing a post-processor after the execution of the program itself is completed. The post-processor will typically print the required statement frequencies and details of execution of all condition tests in the program. The NBS Fortran 77 analyzer also allows assertions to be made before execution and will check the assertions at run time. It can also accumulate statistics over several independent runs of the program.

This facility, also known as profiling or profile generation, was called for in Knuth's 1971 Fortran study and is now being supplied as an option in some compilers. A number of these analyzers are available for both Cobol and Fortran.

Another technique is dynamic data flow anlysis used in for example the Productivity Library (Softool, 1979a). This tool will report on the changes of state of a data item during execution. The user may declare the expected sequence beforehand and will be informed immediately there is any deviation.

Documentation Aids

Some relatively simple static analyzers can be useful in helping to understand programs. Apart from the flow chart generators mentioned above there are a host of programs to tidy source text and rewrite it in a standard form. A typical such program for Fortran would do some or all of the following:

— remove unused declarations, labels and FORMAT statements
— rewrite all declaration statements in a standard order and with dimensions consistently in either type statements, dimension statements or COMMON declarations
— remove IMPLICIT and generate explicit type statements as necessary
— put all FORMAT statements together, either before or after the executable statements
— renumber statement labels in increasing order
— renumber continuation lines consistently
— reform statements so that all reserved words and operators, etc are delimited by space (i.e. DO10I = 1,5 becomes DO 10 I = 1,5)
— indent DO-loops
— rename entities
— rearrange IF statements to reduce the number of statements.

Such programs often also produce cross-reference listings. They are an exception to the rule that program-generated source programs are illegible to humans.

Lower Level Tools

There are now beginning to appear lower level tools, such as lexical analyzers and parsers from which the programmer can construct his own more specialized tools. Some of these appear in Toolpack; a Fortran statement recognizer was published by Sale in 1971.

These would be useful in connexion with specialized tools such as those to change the precision used in a program for example from double precision to single precision or from single to quadruple.

6. DEBUGGING COMPILERS AND SYSTEMS

Definition

Debugging compilers are usually supplied, or not, as part of the standard systems provision and may not always be considered as software tools, but so far as the tools for software sharing are concerned they form part of the minimal set, along with a good context editor and a checker such as the PFORT verifer.

A debugging compiler may be quite separate from the main service compiler for a language; fewer problems arise if the two are basicly the same with the different functions selected by switches. The requirements for such a processor are that it flags any nonstandard syntax and that, so far as possible it monitors the execution and informs the user if anything untoward happens, in particular it checks that:

> unassigned values are not used for computation
> subscripts are always within bounds
> procedure parameters are of the correct type, dimension, etc
> no mathematical domain errors occur
> in Fortran, none of the myriad possible errors
> relating to formats and input-output operations occurs.

When any of these events do occur it should be possible easily to find the exact location in the source code, the current values of all local variables, and calling sequence back to the start of the program including local values at each level. These should be printed in human terms, rather than as octal or hexadecimal dumps. Other features of debugging compilers are often that it is possible easily to trace the control path between procedures and within procedures, for example by printing sequences of procedure references and line numbers, to display variable values at any point or even to print a complete trace-back to the top level at any point. However those interpretive systems which allow the programmer to change the code during program execution while sitting at the keyboard appear to offer a rich source of new errors.

Use for Portability

It is astonishing how many well-established widely distributed programs will fail when put through a debugging system. Such a system cannot of itself prove that a program will work under all conditions but experience shows that it will draw attention to a considerable number of errors which have escaped detection on the development computer.

A trivial and common example is the following which is the result of poor design and of course absence of use of any or the checking tools under discussion. An array subscript is used in the definition of a variable when the subscript may not be defined. Later, in the case in which the subscript was not defined, the variable is reassigned, i.e.

    A = X(K)
    if K was undefined then A = B

The probability that this sequence may cause an address error on some system is non-zero; therefore it will cause an address error sooner or later with absolute certainty. At least an address error is a clear sign that something is wrong. More insidious are errors, often related with unassigned values, which simply cause incorrect results.

The main reason for using debugging compilers is thus that they provide an easy means of drawing attention to certain types of logical errors and give information useful in locating and correcting them.

7. MASTER SOURCE SYSTEMS

Introduction

When software is written which is intended from the beginning to be portable a new set of tools becomes relevant. Such software is likely to be written with an eye on avoiding system dependencies so far as possible and on documenting them when they are inevitable. The tools mentioned above are available but even so, if a program is to be complete, rather than simply a subroutine, it is unavoidable that assumptions are made about the environment. If these differences are held in a coded form within the program it is possible to take a major step forward in the efficiency of distributing and maintaining programs to run on different systems: this is by use of the master-source concept.

Description

The basic concept of master-source is that code tailored for a number of different systems is held in a single file and that a program to run on a particular system may be selected from this file by a preprocessor or "customizer". This simplifies maintenance and, by holding many versions together, makes easier the identification and elimination of unnecessary differences between versions. This scheme in various forms is in use by many software producers. Some prefer to keep the master file directly processable on one computer and to keep the pre-processor controls and source variations as comments; some use distinct pre-processor control statements. Again, some keep the explicit names of computer systems in the master file; others keep only attributes so that a program for a new system may be selected by specifying its attributes, e.g. REAL 32 BITS, INTEGER 16 BITS, CHARACTERS 8 BIT ISO, I/O UNITS 1 - 24, etc. Examples of this concept in use are described by Richardson and Hague (1977) for a subroutine library and by Buhler (1975) for a complete package program. An extension is to build different historical releases of a program into the same file so that it is possible for the customizer to produce a particular machine version as it was on any specified date.

8. MACROPROCESSORS AND PREPROCESSORS

Macroprocessors

Macroprocessors were originally most used in assembler-level languages but now many exist for high-level languages and they allow the programmer to extend these languages considerably. (See e.g. Cole, 1976; Kernighan and Plauger, 1976). To give a simple example, it is possible to add a new variable type to a language provided the new type can be expressed in terms of the existing language. The user can then write a program in the extended language, gaining ease of expression possibly with some loss of efficiency.

By using a macro processor a program can more easily be written in a form which takes account of the different environments in which it will be run. For example it is possible to parameterize array sizes, virtual storage page sizes and environmental constants should the language not provide the latter as standard facilities. This parameterization appears to be mainly used by the numerical software community although it could be used when any program source is distributed. An example of a package which does use this technique is Facsimile (Chance et al., 1977) for which the source is supplied complete with macro processor so that the implementor may himself set appropriate constants for his installation. In this case the macro processor also inserts updates on a line replacement basis so that the original source file need never be changed.

Preprocessors

Before the advent of Fortran 77 there was widespread interest in preprocessors used especially for allowing structured programming in Fortran; see for example, Croes and Deckers (1975), Kernighan (1975). These programs allow definition of a new language which consists basically of Fortran with additional control structures (and in the case of Croes and Deckers the removal of all forms of GO TO) and which is transformed to Fortran by means of a preprocessor. Croes reported that use of the preprocessor in his company considerably improved programmer productivity and almost eliminated the use of Fortran per se. The next logical step in such a company, which uses many different computers, would be to use the single enhanced Fortran as a standard language and to have different preprocessors converting to possibly different Fortran dialects for the different computers. This would thus be another software tool for software sharing but would probably work satisfactorily only in a closed environment such as that in a single large company.

Other preprocessors exist to allow the user to define data structures natural to the problem, to write the program in terms of those structures and then to have the preprocessor translate to a standard language (e.g. Softool Corporation, 1979a). At a higher level Softool Corporation (1979b) also have a tool to generate preprocessors which implement user-defined control structures.

9. PORTABLE COMPILERS AND OPERATING SYSTEMS

A relatively recent development which may obviate some of the problems of language differences is the portable compiler. Although the concept of a universal intermediate language (UNCOL) was developed in the 1950's it is only recently that portable compilers for the main languages have come into common use. At the University of Edinburgh, for instance, a Fortran compiler is available on three different machine ranges under six different operating systems (Edinburgh RCC, 1976) and Barrington et al (1979) mention that they have compilers for Algol 60, Basic and Fortran running on five different types of computer.

Another, more powerful, development is the concept of the portable program environment. Hall et al (1980) describe their experience in defining a uniform program development environment (text editors, language processors, file systems, system command languages, etc), i.e. virtual operating system, and implementing this on six different underlying operating systems. The problem of moving programs (and programmers) to a new system is then reduced to the problem of implementing the virtual operating system as a real system. In the six cases in question this took between one and five man-months per implementation, given that there was functional equivalence between the virtual and target operating systems; there was no need to alter the vendor-supplied operating system.

10. CONCLUSION

An ad-hoc collection of somewhat hit-or-miss tools has been presented which are typical of what is available at present. The situation is intellectually unsatisfactory; it ought to be possible to bring more method to the process of moving a program from one machine to another, but then it ought to be possible to bring more method to the process of writing a program in the first place. There is for example usually little scientific basis for believing that a program is absolutely correct before the transfer to another system is even begun. The process of transferring a program often detects errors in the original program as well as allowing the possibility of introducing new ones.

To summarize, the best approach now is to adhere to language standards as closely as possible and to document all system dependencies. If it becomes possible not only for a compiler but for the whole environment of a high-level language program to become portable between machines then much of the portability problem will have been solved and some of the tools described above will become redundant. It may be that such a solution will not give the highest possible execution times in all cases but it is likely to be overall the most efficient when human and machine costs are calculated. Parallel with this development, advances in program proving should improve the quality of the original programs and allow any adapted programs to be checked more easily. One cannot imagine however that computer manufacturers will welcome total absolute portability of applications programs and it seems unlikely that such perfection will ever be achieved.

11. ACKNOWLEDGEMENTS

The author would like to thank Wayne Cowell, Stephen Hague, Jeanne Martin, Karen Oakley and Leon Presser for providing further information on some of the tools mentioned.

BIBLIOGRAPHY AND REFERENCES

The literature on portability and tools is large and unfortunately not always of high quality. Roitzsch et al (1980) provide a bibliography of some 900 items in a book (Ebert et al, 1980) most of whose contents are relevant to this subject. Muxworthy (1976) gives about 100 references to Fortran portability, and as mentioned above Houghton and Oakley (1980) give abstracts and references for about 300 tools.

REFERENCES

Allan J.J., Moore D.P. and Rogaway H.P. (1963), SIFT - SHARE internal Fortran translator. Datamation, vol. 9 (March) pp. 43-46.

Applied Systems Design Section, TRW Defence and Space Systems Group (1979), Software Tools: Catalogue and Recommendations. TRW Automated Software Tools Series, January 1979.

Barringer H., Capon P.C. and Phillips R. (1979), The Portable Compiling Systems of MUSS. Software Practice and Experience vol. 9, pp. 645-655.

Buhler R. (1975), P-STAT portability. Proc. Computer Science and Statistics, 8th Annual Symposium on the Interface, UCLA, February 1975.

Chance E.M., Curtis A.R., Jones I.P. and Kirby C.R. (1977), Facsimile - a computer program for flow and chemistry simulation and general initial value probelms. AERE Harwell Report No. AERE - R 8775, December 1977.

Cole A.J. (1976), Macro Processors. Cambridge University Press, Cambridge.

Croes G.A. and Deckers F. (1975), Aspects of structured programming in Fortran. Informatie, vol. 17, pp. 121-131.

Day A.C. (1978), Compatible Fortran. Cambridge University Press, Cambridge.

Dewar H.M. (1981), ECCE - Edinburgh Compatible Context Editor. Edinburgh University Department of Computer Science report no. 84.

Donahoo J.D. and Swearinger D. (1980), A Review of Software Maintenance Technology. General Research Corporation Interim Report RADC-TR-80-13, February 1980.

Ebert R., Lugger J. and Goecke L. (1980), Practice in Software Adaptation and Maintenance. North Holland Publishing Company.

Edinburgh Regional Computing Centre (1976), Edinburgh Fortran Language Manual.

Hall D.E., Scherrer D.K. and Sventek J.S. (1980), A Virtual Operating System. Comm. ACM vol. 23 pp. 495-502.

Houghton R.C. and Oakley K.A. (1980), NBS Software Tools Data Base. National Bureau of Standards, Washington report no. NBSIR 80-2159, October 1980.

Kernighan B.W. (1975), RATFOR: A preprocessor for rational Fortran. Software Practice and Experience, vol. 5, pp. 395-406.

Kernighan B.W. and Plauger P.J. (1976), Software Tools. Addison-Wesley, Reading, Massachusetts.

Knuth D.E. (1971), An empirical study of Fortran programs. Software Practice and Experience, vol. 1, pp. 105-133.

Miller J.C. (undated), Structured Retrofit, in Techniques of Program and Systems Maintenance. Ethnotech, Lincoln, Nebraska.

Muxworthy D.T. (1976), A review of program portability and Fortran conventions. Eurocopi Technical Paper Report No. 1, Ispra, Italy.

NBS (1979), Fortran 77 Analyzer. National Bureau of Standards, Washington report no. NB79SBCA0128, August 1979.

Osterweil L.J. and Fosdick L.D. (1976), DAVE - A Valuation, error detection and documentation system for Fortran programs. Software Practice and Experience, vol. 6, pp. 473-486.

Osterweil L.J., Hague S. and Miller W. (1982), Toolpack Architectual Design: The User's Perspective. University of Colorado. April 1982.

Richardson M.J. and Hague S.J. (1977), The design and implementation of the NAG Library File System. Software Practice and Experience, vol. 7, pp. 127-137.

Roitzsch R., Lügger J. and Goecke L. (1980), Bibliography on Methods and Tools for Software Adaptation and Maintenance, in Ebert et al. (1980).

Ryder B.G. (1974), The PFORT verifier. Software Practice and Experience vol. 4, pp. 359-377.

Sale A.H.J. (1971), The Classification of Fortran Statements. Computer Journal vol. 14 pp. 10-13.

Sammett J. (1969), Programming Languages: History and Fundamentals. Prentice Hall, Englewood Cliffs, New Jersey.

Schneck P.B. and Angel E. (1973), A Fortran to Fortran optimizing compiler. Computer Journal, vol. 16, pp. 322-330.

Softool Corporation (1977), A Comparative Analysis of the Diagnostic Power of Commercial Fortran Compilers. Softool Corporation, Goleta, California Report No. F001-10-77. October 1977.

Softool Corporation (1979a), Productivity Library Product Manual. September 1979.

Softool Corporation (1979b), Structurizer Product Manual. September 1979.

Waite W.M. (1975), Hints on distributing portable software. Software Practices and Experience, vol. 5, pp. 295-308.

Wichmann B.A. (1973), Algol 60: Compilation and Assessment. Academic Press, London.

Wolberg J.R. and Rafal M. (1978), Convert - a language for program and data file conversion. Software Practice and Experience, vol. 8, pp. 187-198.

APPENDIX 1

Software tool facilities

The following list shows the facilities of the software tools in the NBS Data Base (Houghton & Oakley, 1980). The classification used is that of the authors and the figure in parentheses is the number of tools with that facility. Tools are usually counted under several different categories.

Abort diagnosis (2)

Assertion checking (4)

Automated module driver (1)

Automated module simulator (1)

Bit manipulation (1)

Breakpoint control (2)

Code auditing (20)

Code restructuring (7)

Comparison (6)

Compiler generation (2)

Compiler validation (1)

Completeness checking (1)

Complexity measurement (4)

Component testing (1)

Configuration control (4)

Configuration Management (12)

Consistency checking (8)

Conversion (5)

Cost estimation (2)

Coverage analysis (23)

Cross reference (33)

Data auditing (2)

Data base analysis (8)

Data entry (1)

Data flow analysis (12)

Data range analysis (1)

Data structuring (1)

Design analysis (4)

Design language processing (5)

Design simulation (1)

Design specification (2)

Documentation generation (16)

Editing (1)

Environment simulation (2)

Error analysis (3)

Error detection (1)

Execution monitoring (7)

Expression analysis (1)

Expression testing (1)

File layout generation (1)

File maintenance (1)

File management (5)

File structure testing (1)

Financial modelling (1)

Flow chart generation (20)

Global data analysis (1)

Global data management (17)

Graphical representation (2)

Graphing (1)

Hierarchical file structures (1)

HIPO generation (1)

Interface analysis (7)

Label resequencing (10)
Library management (8)
MTBF asnalysis (1)
Modification validation (7)
Online application design (1)
Path constraint generation (5)
Path structure analysis (2)
Preprocessor generation (1)
Program flow analysis (7)
Program generation (1)
Program optimization (1)
Program restructuring (1)
Project management (16)
Real time software design (1)
Relational file structures (1)
Requirements analysis (3)
Requirements language processing (6)
Requirements tracing (5)
Run time analysis (4)
Simulation (3)
Specification refinement (1)
Structured language processing (11)
Test case generation (7)
Test effectiveness measurement (23)
Timing analysis (8)
Trace (8)
Translation (1)
Type analysis (3)
Version control (7)

Language structuring (1)
Macro expansion (4)
Memory management (1)
Module ordering (1)
Online application development (1)
Path constraint solution (4)
Performance measurement (13)
Profile generation (10)
Program formatting (12)
Program maintenance (3)
Program reformatting (1)
Program structure checking (5)
Proof correctness (1)
Reference analysis (2)
Report generation (15)
Requirements simulation (1)
Requirements specification (2)
Resource monitoring (8)
Screen layout design (1)
Software quality evaluation (2)
Standards enforcement (5)
Symbolic evaluation (5)
Test data management (9)
Test harness (2)
Top-down design (1)
Translate (1)
Tuning (3)
Units analysis (1)

APPENDIX 2

Toolpack

Toolpack is a project "to provide strong, comprehensive tool support to programmers who are writing, testing, transporting or analyzing mathematical software" (Osterweil et al., 1982). It is a collaborative effort supported by the U.S. National Science Foundation and Department of Energy and has the following participating organizations: Argonne National Laboratory, Bell Laboratories, Jet Propulsion Laboratory, IMSL Inc, NAG Ltd, Purdue University, University of California Santa Barbara, University of Colorado Boulder.

The user will be provided with an overall command language and most of the following tool facilities, all assuming Fortran 77 as the programming language.

> language-intelligent editor
> source formatter
> control flow structurer
> macro processor
> extended Fortran translator

structure and programming convention checker
dialect verifier
static data flow analysers
dynamic control flow analyser
data generator
precision type changers
low level tools (lexers, parsers, symbol table manipulators, etc).

PROGRAM DOCUMENTATION

Giancarlo Gaggero
Schlumberger W.S., Austin, Texas, USA
(formerly Joint Research Centre, Ispra, Italy).

It is now widely accepted that there has been and there still is an enormous waste of programming effort in the production of software. This wasted effort is due to many causes, including the lack of adequate documentation. A well-documented program must have both internal and external documentation suitably interfaced in order to provide a coherent software package. A survey of existing documentation standards and guidelines is presented. An attempt is made to extract common basic concepts and to present them in the form of a consistent set of practical conventions and guidelines for internal and external documentation of scientific and engineering programs.

1. INTRODUCTION

Among the problems involved in the sharing and transfer of software, the availability of adequate documentation is certainly not the least important. It is widely accepted that there has been and there still is an enormous waste of programming effort in the production of software and that one of the causes is the general lack of adequate program documentation. At the same time the documentation is the only link between the author and the user.

"Good documentation promotes understanding, reduces duplication of effort, eases conversion to different computer environments and aids modification for extended applications. Good documentation is essential for implementation and effective use of programs obtained from other installations" (American Nuclear Society, 1974).

In spite of its recognized value, documentation has been the least coordinated of the program development activities. A comprehensive study concerning the utilization and utility of application software performed by CEPA (1975) identifies three basic factors responsible for this unsatisfactory situation:

D. T. Muxworthy (ed.), Programming for Software Sharing, 175–188.

— no generally applicable and accepted standards exist for software documentation;

— the process of documentation is "anathema to programmers (who would rather get on with the next project)";

— the cost of documentation is high.

The first two factors are strictly related. In fact, documentation standards are not only useful to the user of a program to find the information he needs to apply the program, but "they also serve as a motivation and tool to the program developer to adequately describe his product and communicate its functions to the intended user" (Wolfangel, 1978b).

The fact that documentation is anathema to programmers is, in our opinion, due to the combined effect of the lack of internationally accepted standards of program documentation and the scant attention paid to teaching programmers how to write proper documentation. As for the cost of documentation, it can certainly be reduced by a more professional approach to its production process and it is certainly worthwhile if the present waste of resources (manpower, computing power, means and funds) associated with the duplication of software can be reduced. It is natural to expect that standards for documentation are useful to determine the types and level of documentation to be produced for different types of programs and different categories of users, thus avoiding unnecessary or unproductive work.

In fact, the level of adequacy of documentation varies significantly with the type (size, complexity) and duration of utilization of the program. A small program essentially used by its author for a short period of time requires a minimum of formal documentation, while a program used over a long time period and/or by several individuals requires comprehensive formal documentation. On the other hand, different users have different information requirements and thus need different types of documents. The potential user looking for a program capable of solving his specific problem needs a program short description; an individual concerned with the actual use of a program needs a user reference manual and possibly a theoretical manual; a programmer concerned with the installation, maintenance and adaptation of a program requires system and programming documentation. From a more general point of view one should not forget that the object to be documented, i.e. a program, is itself a document which can carry information not only for a computer but also for an individual reading it.

This fact suggests the opportunity that a well-documented program have both internal and external documentation. Internal and external documentation should be interfaced in a suitable way in order to provide a coherent software package, (Jubenville et al., 1976).

This chapter does not pretend to cover all the aspects of and to provide solutions for all the problems associated with the documentation of computer programs, but it is aimed at providing information and practical suggestions which may hopefully be of value for those concerned with program documentation. A survey of existing program documentation standards and guidelines is first presented. Then an attempt is made to extract common basic concepts and to present them in the form of a consistent set of practical conventions and guidelines for internal and external documentation of scientific and engineering programs.

2. EXISTING STANDARDS AND GUIDELINES

In several countries the need for standardized software documentation led to the elaboration of proposals for a standardized documentation. These proposals were developed not only by the competent standards bodies of the individual countries, but also by industrial and scientific associations.

In the United States, a standard entitled "Guidelines for the Documentation of Digital Computer Programs" was published by the American Nuclear Society in 1974 as report ANSI-N413-1974. More recently, in 1976, the National Bureau of Standards published a more detailed and comprehensive standard entitled "Guidelines for Documentaton of Computer Programs and Automated Data Systems" (NBS, 1976).

So far, in Europe, four papers have become known and have been presented to ISO bodies, namely a Swedish paper (ISO, 1979), a British one (BSI, 1976), and two German papers (DIN, 1976 and 1977). An ISO standard titled "Symbols and Conventions for Program and Data Flowcharts, Configuration Charts and Program Network Charts" was also published in 1976 (ISO, 1976). A useful survey of program documentation standards as well as of related manuals and instruction books is presented in a report and a paper by P. Wolfangel (1978a, 1978b).

It is our aim here to illustrate some aspects of program documentation standards which emerge from the above mentioned documents. These documents differ considerably in the interpretation of the concept of "program documentation" and also in the suggested structural organization of the documentation itself. Some standards consider the program documentation to consist of all papers produced during the development of the program and, in a certain sense, they also standardize the methodology of software development. Other standards make a distinction between program development documentation (which is usually left out of the standard) and the "final" documentation which is an integral part of the program package and is supposed to provide adequate support to distribution, application, maintenance, and user training activities.

The various standards show also two distinct approaches with respect to the structural organization of the program documentation, namely:

— the role-oriented approach, and
— the function-oriented approach.

In the role-oriented approach, the various document types are defined in relation with different intended users or document audiences. "The audience may be an individual or a group of individuals who are expected to use the documents to perform a function, e.g. application, maintenance, programming. The information should be presented using terminology and level of detail appropriate to the audience" (NBS, 1976). Consequently the documentation is divided into such items as:

— Program Short Description or Abstract;
— Users Manual;
— Theoretical Manual;
— Operations Manual;
— Program Maintenance Manual;

each of which is subject to a content-oriented as well as a formal standardization.

The second approach structures the documentation according to functional aspects. The standard contains a list of all data required for documenting a program in such a way that completeness and comparability of any important data are ensured. This list is organized according to functional logic aspects. Individual documents do not have to be established according to this order and their form is not standardized. However, function-oriented standards often suggest for practical purposes some headings for role-oriented documents.

There are advantages and disadvantages in both approaches. However, while the function-oriented standards provide a useful check-list of all the information items which are necessary for complete program documentation, the role-oriented ones are more likely to provide a direct guide to the documentation author.

We must remember here that, in addition to the official proposals of documentation standards, several compilations of suggested guidelines have been published, and numerous authors have made contributions in the form of a chapter here or a section there, e.g. Gray and Landon (1970), Harper (1973), Lomax (1976), Walsh (1969), Banks et al. (1972), Kreitzberg and Shneiderman (1972), McCracken and Weinberg (1972), NASA (1971), Tausworthe (1976) and Tanenbaum et al. (1978). Many of the published suggestions are redundant and some are not appropriate for the documentation of scientific and engineering programs.

A lot of effort has still to be made before usable internationally agreed standards for program documentation are available and actually used in practice. We are, on the other hand, convinced that there is an urgent need for them and that in the meantime sound practical guidelines can be useful in educating and helping programmers.

3. GUIDELINES FOR PROGRAM DOCUMENTATION

Suggesting conventions and guidelines is always a difficult task, as in one way or another they introduce constraints and limit the freedom of other persons. Even when they are, and they always should be, based on rational elements and they have proved to be useful in practice, guidelines often remain somewhat subjective and a matter of personal taste.

We hope that everybody can agree on the following general guidelines (Kreitzberg and Shneiderman, 1972):

— Always provide more documentation than you think you need.
— Document as much of the program within the code as possible.
— Document unto others as you would be documented to.
— Be neat.

They are certainly valuable, but too general to be of real help in practice. For this reason, we tried to supplement them with more specific guidelines extracted from the available literature on the subject.

The result of this effort is presented in the two following paragraphs dealing with external and internal documentation respectively.

External Documentation

The following structure, established according to the needs of different persons/functions associated with computer programs, is suggested for the external program documentation:

A - Introductory Documentation
    A.1 - Publicity Information
    A.2 - Program Short Description or Abstract

B - User Documentation
    B.1 - User Reference Manual
    B.2 - Theoretical Manual
    B.3 - User Training Manual
    B.4 - Operation Manual
    B.5 - Installation Manual

C - Maintenance Documentation
    C.1 - System and Programming Manual
    C.2 - Testing Manual
    C.3 - Program History File

Not all documents listed above are appropriate in all circumstances. The degree of conformance (formality, extent and level of detail) is a matter of judgement for each individual situation. In general, as the program complexity, size, expected life and use increase so does the need for more complete documentation. Each document may range from a few to several hundred pages in length. It may also be necessary to combine several document types under one cover, e.g. the User Reference and Theoretical Manuals or the Operation and Installation Manuals. When this is done, the substance of the contents covered by each document type should be preserved.

Document Purpose and Contents

The purpose and contents of each document is defined in the following.

A - *Introductory Documentation.* This is directed to the potential user of the program.

A.1 - *Publicity Information.* It should contain a general functional description, a brief technical description, including software/hardware environment, a description of available material and user support services, and relevant marketing information.

A.2 - *Program Short Description.* This is directed to program libraries, software information centers, and potential end-users. It should be concise, but convey sufficient information to permit the reader to assess the applicability of the program to his needs, the effort required to make it operational, and the availability. A formal standardization of this document is highly desirable as completeness and comparability of information is essential in the process of selecting the program which best fits the user needs. To this purpose, the Program Short Description Form developed by EASIT, (European Association for Software Access and Information Transfer), and shown in Appendix 1 is recommended for use.

B - *User Documentation.* This is directed to the individuals who are concerned with the operation and application of the program.

B.1 - *User Reference Manual.* The purpose of this document is to describe sufficiently the functions performed by the program in non-EDP terminology, so that the user can determine its applicability. It should serve as a reference document for preparation of input data and interpretation of results. It should also provide information on the type and amount of resources needed to run the program. A possible layout of this document is shown in Appendix 2.

B.2 - *Theoretical Manual.* The purpose of this document is to provide a thorough understanding of the theoretical and mathematical foundations, referencing the open literature where appropriate. It should define the problems solved by the program, describe the mathematical model employed, and document the computational algorithms and numerical techniques implemented in the program. Mathematical equations should be presented in conventional terminology avoiding awkward programming language syntax. It should also reference or include validation of the program by comparison of the results, with analytical results, with bench-mark experiments or with numerical solutions.

B.3 - *User Training Manual.* The purpose of this document is to help the new user to become familiar with the program. A tutorial approach is recommended together with ample use of simple but meaningful sample problems. Reference to documents B.1 and B.2 should be made whenever appropriate.

B.4 - *Operation Manual.* The purpose of this manual is to provide computer operation personnel with a description of the program and of the operational environment so that the program can be run. It should explain, as necessary, the system control commands required to execute the program including operator commands and messages. It should specify the names, usage and medium of each data file and give data file retention and allocation requirements. Restart, recovery, and successive case capabilities should also be discussed.

B.5 - *Installation Manual.* This is directed to the individual responsible for implementing the program on his computer. It should describe the organization and contents of the transport medium and indicate the operations and utilities required to install the program. It should specify hardware and software requirements (machine configuration, main memory storage requirements, amount and type of auxiliary storage, operating system, language processors, and associated subroutine libraries invoked by the program). It should provide computer oriented details of temporary and external data files. It should describe the functions performed by machine-dependent subprograms and other installation-dependent software that may be necessary.

C - *Maintenance Documentation.* This is directed to the individuals responsible for maintaining, modifying or extending the program to meet local needs, or converting it to a different computer environment.

C.1 - *System and Programming Manual.* It should describe the overall program structure and logic, and provide all the necessary technical details on the program and its data files. It should provide the following information concerning program and subprograms: role and function of each subprogram, argument list and their use; a cross-reference dictionary of subroutine names and entry points; relationship between the problem variables and the program mnemonics; shared storage assignments. It should describe internal data structure and allocation, and specify structure, mode and data elements of each external data file. Hardware and software support facilities required by the program should also be described.

C.2 - *Testing Manual*. The purpose of this document is to provide a set of sample problems to test the program. Sample problems should be chosen in such a way to exercise the largest possible portion of the available programmed options, while requiring only a reasonable amount of computer time. Edited output for each of the test problems should be provided.

C.3 - *Program History File*. This does not need to be a formal document, but a file recording all relevant information concerning the life of the program such as known errors and error fixes, program modifications and extensions.

Internal Documentation

Internal documentation consists of all information contained in the program listing which describes the program and its evolution.

"Internal documentation should be developed to optimize the following software attributes: maintainability, adaptability, portability" (Jubenville et al., 1976).

There are various elements which contribute to making a program readable and understandable and, thus, self-documented. However, some of these elements, like a clear modular structure, avoiding the use of GOTO, clear and standard code are more related to programming methodology and standards than to documentation standards. For this reason we will confine ourselves to present some guidelines for the composition of code and the use of comments. Specific reference is made in the following to programs written in Fortran.

Code Composition

The following guidelines are suggested:

A - Assign meaningful variable names. Variable names should be chosen in a way to convey as much information as possible and to avoid confusion regarding their mode.
   VEL = DIST/TIME   is clearer than   A = B/C
   Apply the same rule to subroutine and function names.

B - Parenthesize to avoid ambiguity. Use parentheses whenever they clarify the meaning of a statement.
   IF ((A + B).GT.0.5) GOTO 15 is better than
   IF (A + B.GT.0.5) GOTO 15

C - Begin every statement in column 7 unless you are within a DO loop, in which case indent two columns for every DO level.

```
      DO 30 I = 1,N
        DO 20 J = 1,N
        SUM = 0.0
          DO 10 K = 1,N
          SUM = SUM + A(I,K)*B(K,J)
10        CONTINUE
        C(I,J) = SUM
20      CONTINUE
30    CONTINUE
```

   The use of the CONTINUE statement to close the loop is also recommended.

D - Assign statement labels systematically. Arrange labels in ascending order and reserve specific ranges for executable statement labels (e.g. 1 to 999) and

FORMAT statement labels (e.g. 1000 and above).

E - Do not break a variable name or constant between two records and when you continue onto a new record, indent the continuation so that similar parts line up.
Example:

```
    ALPHA = U(1)*V(1) + U(2)*V(2) +
   1                U(3)*V(3)
```

The same rule is recommended for FORMAT statements and for declaration statements. For COMMON statements it may be useful to line up individual variables.
Example:

```
    COMMON    ALPHA , RAD , A    , BETA ,
   1               B      , CIRC
```

Use of Comments

''The most important concept to remember when planning comments is that the commenting structure should parallel the program structure'' (Jubenville et al., 1976).

For this purpose it is useful to make use of:

A - heading comments for the main program and each subroutine to provide the reader with an overall information about the program structure and logic, and with a concise description of the function of each component;

B - current comments strategically placed within the program to identify logical divisions or blocks, to clarify program statements, and to point out deviations from the standard programming language, if any.

The following guidelines are suggested in relation with the above two categories of comments:

A.1 - Include a program heading on top of the main program. The Program heading should contain the following elements:
1. Program name, version, and date
2. Program author
3. Short description
4. References
5. Subroutine directory
6. Common Block directory
7. External files directory
8. Programming language
9. Maintenance record

A.2 - Include a subroutine heading at the beginning of each subroutine. The Subroutine Heading should contain the following elements:
1. Subroutine name, version, and date
2. Subroutine author
3. Short description
4. Calling sequence description
5. Return codes
6. Called subroutines directory
7. Notes

B.1 - Do not comment bad code, rewrite it. Good code is more easily understandable and, thus, requires fewer comments.

B.2 - Comments and code should agree, but comments should not simply echo the code. The programmer should comment to reinforce the code and to explain the meaning of the statement in the context of the program, not tell the reader what is obvious from the statement syntax.

B.3 - Do not begin comments in different columns each time, but select a rule that suits you and then stick to it.

B.4 - Utilize space to separate major blocks of code.

B.5 - Utilize special symbols such as the asterisk, equal sign, or period to set off groups of code or to distinguish different types of comments.

An application of the guidelines given here for internal program documentation is shown in Appendix 3.

4. CONCLUSION

The development of quality external and internal documentation can assist in the development of adaptable, portable, and easily maintained (i.e. shareable) programs. It is not essential that you follow these guidelines, if you do not agree with them, but is important that you follow some guidelines when you document your programs.

REFERENCES

American Nuclear Society (1974), American National Standard Guidelines for the Documentation of Digital Computer Programs. ANSI-N413, 1974.

Banks D., Percival I.C. and Wilson J.M. (1972), Stirling FORDOC-01: A Set of Documentation Conventions for FORTRAN Packages and Routines. Computer Physics Communications, Vol. 3, pp. 180-196.

British Standards Institution (1976), Draft British Standard Specification for Decision Tables in Data Processing. Technical Commitee DPS/15, Doc. 76/64270.

CEPA, Civil Engineering Programming Applications, Inc. (1975), A Proposal for a National Institute for Computers in Engineering. Oct. 1975.

DIN Deutsches Institut für Normung (1976), Informationseverarbeitung - Programmdokumentation - Rahmenangaben Fachnormenausschuss Informationsverarbeitung, Norm DIN 66233, Teil 1 Beuth-Verlag, Berlin.

DIN Deutsches Institut für Normung (1977), Informationsverarbeitung - Programmdokumentation - Detaillerung Fachnormenausschuss Informationsverarbeitung, Norm DIN 66233, Teil 2 Beuth-Verlag, Berlin.

Gray M., Landon K. (1970), Documentation Standards Princeton, N.J.: Brandon Systems Press.

Harper W.L. (1973), Data Processing Documentation - Standards, Procedures, and Applications Englewood Cliffs, N.J.: Prentice Hall.

ISO, International Organization for Standardization (1976), Symbols and Conventions for Program and Data Flowcharts, Configuration Charts and Program Network Charts. ISO/TC 97/SC 7/WG 1.

ISO, International Organization for Standardization (1979), Documentation of Computer Based Systems - Code of Practice. ISO/DP 6592 submitted to ISO/TC 97/SC 7 by the Swedish standards body SIS.

Jubenville D.M., Heinze E. and Schiffman R.L. (1976), Software: Internal Maintenance Documentation in Proceedings of the Specialty Conference "Methods of Structural Analysis" Univ. of Wisconsin, Madison, Aug. 22-25, 1976.

Kreitzberg C.B., Shneiderman C. (1972), The Elements of Fortran Style: Techniques for Effective Programming. Harcourt Brace Jovanovich, Inc., N.Y.

Lomax J.D. (1976), Documentation of Software Products - Recommendations for Producers and Users. NCC, National Computing Centre Manchester, U.K.

McCracken D.D. and Weinberg G.M. (1972), How to Write a Readable Fortran Program. Datamation 18, 10, pp. 73-77.

NASA (1971), Computer Program Documentation Guidelines NHB 2411.1, NASA, Washington DC, July 1971.

National Bureau of Standards (1976), Guidelines for Documentation of Computer Programs and Automated Data Systems. FIPS PUB 38, 1976 Feb. 15.

Tanenbaum A.S., Klint P. and Bohm W. (1978), Guidelines for Software Portability. Software-Practice and Experience, Vol. 8, pp. 681-698.

Tausworthe R.C. (1976), Standardized Development of Computer Software. JPL SP 43-29, Jet Propulsion Laboratory, Pasadena, July 1976.

Walsh D. (1969), A Guide for Software Documentation. Advanced Computer Techniques Corporation, N.Y.

Wolfangel P. (1978a), A Survey of Program Documentation Standards and Guidelines. EUROCOPI Technical Papers Series, Report N° 2, Aug. 1978.

Wolfangel P. (1978b), Standards for Program Documentation. Ispra Course on "Program Library and Information Service Techniques". Oct. 17-20, 1978.

APPENDIX 1

Program Short description

1. Program Identification
    1.1   Number
    1.2   Name
    1.3   Author

2. Program Abstract
    2.1   Title
    2.2   Subject Classification
    2.3   Keywords
    2.4   Purpose of the Program and Application Fields
    2.5   Method of Solution
    2.6   Restrictions
    2.7   Versions
    2.8   Auxiliary and Related Programs
    2.9   Input and Output Files
    2.10 References

3. Technical Information
    3.1   Release Information
    3.2   Programming Language(s) and compiler(s)
    3.3   Number of Statements
    3.4   Computer(s), Operating System(s)
    3.5   Minimum Storage Requirements
    3.6   Peripheral Requirements

APPENDIX 2

User Reference Manual

1. *General Information*
    1.1 *Summary.* Summarize the application and function of the program.
    1.2 *References.* List directly-related publications and other reference materials.

2. *Application*
    2.1 *Description.* Describe the nature of the problem solved, define the processing tasks performed, and outline the methods and procedures employed. If useful, schematically display the flow of calculations.
    2.2 *Function.* Discuss the function of each major program option. Indicate restrictions on the range of problems and data.
    2.3 *Operation.* Discuss dependence of data storage requirements on problem input parameters. Discuss any man-machine interactions. Provide information to estimate execution time.
    2.4 *Data Base.* Outline the general contents and organization of each external data file. Relate the usage of data files to the execution of the program.

3. *Input.* Define the requirements of preparing input data and parameters. Provide the layout of the forms for data preparation or describe the grammatical rules and syntax of the input language. Provide sample input.

4. *Output.* Discuss the program output in relation to input options. Provide a layout of each output. Provide sample output.

5. *Error and recovery.* List error codes or conditions generated by the program and corrective action to be taken by user. If appropriate indicate procedures for restart and recovery.

APPENDIX 3

```
00010        SUBROUTINE AXEQB (A,B,N,IER)
00020  C
00030  C     ================================================================
00040  C
00050  C     IDENTIFICATION -  AXEQB, VERSION 1, AUG.22,1979
00060  C
00070  C     AUTHOR -  G.GAGGERO
00080  C
```

```
00090 C     DESCRIPTION -  AXEQB SOLVES THE LINEAR SYSTEM  AX=B OF ORDER
00100 C        N BY CROUT REDUCTION FOLLOWED BY BACK-SUBSTITUTION.
00110 C
00120 C     CALLING SEQUENCE -
00130 C        A     /R,INP/     A DOUBLY SUBSCRIPTED ARRAY CONTAINING
00140 C                          THE MATRIX A
00150 C        B     /R,INP,OUT/ A VECTOR CONTAINING THE RHS ON ENTRY
00160 C                          AND THE SOLUTION ON RETURN
00170 C        N     /I,INP/     THE ORDER OF THE LINEAR SYSTEM
00180 C        IER   /I,OUT/     ERROR CODE
00190 C
00200 C     CALLED SUBROUTINES -  NONE
00210 C
00220 C     RETURN CODES -
00230 C        IER  = 0  IF SOLUTION WAS SUCCESSFUL
00240 C             = 1  IF SEARCH FOR NON ZERO DIAGONAL ELEMENT FAILED
00250 C
00260 C     NOTES -  THIS SUBROUTINE IS A MODIFIED VERSION OF SUBROUTINE
00270 C        SYSSLV DESCRIBED IN CACM ALGORITHM 432.
00280 C        IT SHOULD NOT BE USED FOR LARGE LINEAR SYSTEMS.
00290 C
00300 C     ============================================================
00310 C
00320       DIMENSION A(N,N),B(N)
00330 C
00340       NM1 = N - 1
00350 C     ------------------------------------------------------------
00360 C     COMPUTES THE LU FACTORIZATION OF MATRIX A
00370 C     ------------------------------------------------------------
00380       DO 80 K=1,N
00390         KM1 = K - 1
00400         IF(K .EQ. 1) GO TO 20
00410         DO 10 I=K,N
00420           DO 5 J=1,KM1
00430             A(I,K) = A(I,K) - A(I,J)*A(J,K)
00440     5     CONTINUE
00450    10     CONTINUE
00460    20    IF(K .EQ. N) GO TO 100
00470 C
00480 C        ... SEARCH FOR PIVOT ELEMENT
00490 C
00500          KP1 = K + 1
00510          INTR = K
00520          TMAX = ABS(A(K,K))
00530          DO 30 I=KP1,N
00540            AA = ABS(A(I,K))
00550            IF(AA .LE. TMAX) GO TO 30
00560            TMAX = AA
00570            INTR = I
00580    30    CONTINUE
```

```
00590 C
00600 C      ... TEST TO SEE IF PIVOT IS ZERO
00610 C
00620         IF(TMAX .EQ. 0.0) GO TO 900
00630 C
00640 C      ... PIVOT IS NOT ZERO
00650 C
00660         IF(INTR .EQ. K) GO TO 50
00670 C
00680 C      ... INTERCHANGE K AND INTR ELEMENTS OF VECTOR B
00690 C
00700         BB = B(K)
00710         B(K) = B(INTR)
00720         B(INTR) = BB
00730 C
00740 C      ... INTERCHANGE K AND INTR ROWS OF MATRIX  A
00750 C
00760         DO 40 J=1,N
00770          AA = A(K,J)
00780          A(K,J) = A(INTR,J)
00790          A(INTR,J) = AA
00800    40   CONTINUE
00810 C
00820    50   DO 70 J=KP1,N
00830          IF(K .EQ. 1) GO TO 65
00840           DO 60 I=1,KM1
00850            A(K,J) = A(K,J) - A(K,I)*A(I,J)
00860    60      CONTINUE
00870    65     A(K,J) = A(K,J)/A(K,K)
00880    70   CONTINUE
00890    80 CONTINUE
00900 C      --------------------------------------------------------
00910 C      SOLVE LX=B
00920 C      --------------------------------------------------------
00930   100 B(1) = B(1)/A(1,1)
00940         DO 120 I=2,N
00950          IM1 = I - 1
00960          DO 110 J=1,IM1
00970           B(I) = B(I) - A(I,J)*B(J)
00980   110    CONTINUE
00990          B(I) = B(I)/A(I,I)
01000   120 CONTINUE
01010 C      --------------------------------------------------------
01020 C      SOLVE UX=B
01025 C      --------------------------------------------------------
01030         DO 140 II=1,NM1
01040          I = NM1 - II + 1
01050          IP1 = I + 1
01060          DO 130 J=IP1,N
01070           B(I) = B(I) - A(I,J)*B(J)
```

```
01080    130   CONTINUE
01090    140 CONTINUE
01100 C
01110 C     ... NORMAL EXIT
01120 C
01130         IER = 0
01140    150 RETURN
01150 C    ----------------------------------------------------------
01160 C    FAULT SECTION
01170 C    ----------------------------------------------------------
01180    900 IER = 1
01190         GO TO 150
01200         END
```

Transfer and Sharing

SOFTWARE TRANSFER AND SHARING - AN OVERVIEW

Brian Ford
NAG Central Office
Oxford, UK

1. INTRODUCTION

A substantial effort is being spent each year in the design and development of software application packages. Careful preparation is required to ensure that such packages may readily be transferred to different computing environments and that the means exist for their effective circulation and use. Computing software is a fundamental means of knowledge and technology transfer. Its transfer and sharing permit return to the developer and substantial saving to the user. In the scientific and engineering community the software will generally be written in Fortran. However an applications package must possess a number of characteristics if it is to justify its wider availability.

2. REQUIREMENT FOR TRANSFER

The vast majority of computer users from a science and technology background have a problem from their own technical area which they wish to use the computer to solve. A percentage of these users will wish to write their own programs under all circumstances but even this group of programmers will often be willing to use library routines etc. provided certain conditions are met. However the majority of users have far more interest in answers (preferably solutions!) than in the process by which they are computed. The requirement for transfer of medium-sized and large programs is therefore considerable. There is also great demand for computing abilities and tools not tied to particular scientific and technical areas, e.g. statistical packages; graphical systems; numerical algorithms libraries; language verifiers; tidying programs.

Each technical area has its brand leaders, e.g. XRAY 80 in XRAY crystallography; IBMOL, ATMOL or GAUSS 78 in quantum chemistry; ICES in structural engineering.

D. T. Muxworthy (ed.), Programming for Software Sharing, 191–201.
Copyright © 1983 ECSC, EEC, EAEC, Brussels and Luxembourg.

These packages in general are well tried and understood. Often their weaknesses as well as their strengths are known. Results computed using the package stand a good chance of being accepted by the particular community; a de facto certification of the package has taken place. Primarily by using such packages, and less well-known ones, engineers and scientists can save themselves enormous amounts of time, often man-years, and gain access to an expertise and to knowledge, covering a number of related technical areas, which they simply could not expect to be able to command on their own. The return to the actual brand package developer is the knowledge that perhaps even thousands of individuals solve problems with his or her package every day.

So far we have largely concerned ourselves with the Olympian heights of applications software. A large majority of programs written could be of use to people in addition to their writer and often of greater use to the programmer if certain levels of programming, documentation and support were provided from the inception of the activity. The cost is an increase in the use of the programmer's time.

The fundamental question to be faced by any user is: "is it easier to transfer a program than to write a new program myself?" The primary reasons for transfer are given above. That more programs are *not* transferred underlines the poor standard set and achieved by many programmers, the difficulty of effectively knowing what is available and the technical and legal problems associated with physical and intellectual transfer. One of the great challenges for the computing community is that transfer in its field can be completed whereas using other media, for example books, certain work and ability is essential for the recipient. The problems of copyright, intellectual property and proprietory rights for applications software are only now being generally recognised in the scientific and technical communities.

In general the program will be easiest to use on the configuration (computer family hardware, operating system, compilation system) on which it was developed, directly or by network. Failing that ability, transfer to a similar configuration is the easiest option. This we shall call *installation* of the program. Depending on the size of the program, and on the facilities of the local computing service it employs, a change of compiler, of operating system and of computing family hardware and any combination of these may lead to an increasing degree of work and of understanding of the program by its *implementor. Implementation* of a program can provide many challenges (see the chapter on experience in multi-machine software development); it can often be quite uneventful. Before embarking on the development of a new program its writer should recognise that software projects invariably take substantially longer to complete than anticipated, factors of 5 to 10 being quite common, that their demands on human and computing resources are significant and that this field of technology (algorithm and software development) receives limited recognition in the scientific and technical community. As with a child, once born a program can bring unending responsibility and pain.

Transfer and sharing must be the optimum strategy if the required facility, prepared and supported with due care, exists.

3. ABILITY TO TRANSFER

We have noted already that in the scientific and technical community a program is most likely to be written in Fortran. For that program to be of general use it must become a tested, loadable program on a specific configuration. To achieve that goal it will have passed three conceptually distinct phases of development.

Having specified the computations the programmer wishes to be able to complete, he finds or designs algorithms that will compute the various elements needed for problem solution. In our wish list, "For Easy Transfer and Sharing", the first requirement is therefore for *adaptable algorithms*. An algorithm is adaptable if it can be expressed in such a way that, relative to some specifications, the algorithm performs in an equivalent manner on a wide range of computing evironments.

The second conceptual phase in software development is realisation of the algorithms as source language subprograms. For the package developer this means the careful engineering of *transportable* Fortran subprograms. Notice *transportable,* not *portable*. It is not possible to compile the same source text without change and achieve acceptable performance on every configuration. But it is possible to minimise the changes to mould the software for a particular computing environment and to implement these changes as far as possible by automatic transformations; this is what we mean by *transportable* Fortran subprograms.

Transportable software is the second entry in our wish list.

The third conceptual phase in software development is the testing of the compiled program on a given configuration, and its detailed documentation for that configuration. The third entry to the wish list is a *reliable test program suite*. Prepared with issues of adaptability of algorithms and transportability of software in mind, it tests all phases and aspects of the scientific computation *and* achievement of prescribed levels of efficiency and of accuracy in each computing environment.

"Any software package is only as good as its user documentation". Good documentation, to meet several different needs and requirements, is essential "For Easy Transfer and Sharing". The program text should be well documented internally, and be described in a supporting manual, preferably machine-based. Ideally the internal and external documentation will cover, separately, the distinct requirements of software support and implementation, and those of the applications area. In addition there will often be a need for a user's manual.

The fourth entry in the wish list is *well documented*!

The program should be *well-structured* (entry 5). This volume contains much advice and counsel on how to achieve this objective.

Finally one looks for the program to be maintained (at a centre or centres where the originators or their successor may be contacted to overcome fundamental difficulties), for errors to be notified and where possible corrected, and for version development of the program. Each of these aspects inculcates user confidence. Each requires supporting documentation of a fixed style, format and content. The final entry of the wish list is *maintenance, error correction* and *version development.*

Wish List Summary

For Easy Transfer and Sharing

Adaptable algorithms
Transportable programs
Reliable test program suite
Well documented
Structured Program
Maintenance, error-correction and version development

The potential barriers to software transfer and sharing are numerous. In the context of the present chapter, with its particular emphases, three points are immediately of concern.

The first is Fortran language dialects. Despite the acceptance of the Fortran standards [1966, 1978] and the widespread availability of "standard-conforming" compilers, there are still many purely linguistic obstacles to the transfer of Fortran software. Some compilers do not implement the standards completely or correctly. The standards are not always clear, are self-confessedly incomplete and are permissive. Use of the PFORT subset (Ryder and Hall, 1975) supported by the PFORT verifier will overcome most difficulties whilst generally posing few limitations for scientific and technical computing.

Configuration characteristics, particularly those involving machine word-length and aspects of machine arithmetic, require careful consideration. Many programs simply cannot be transferred to other configurations because of the use of machine-specific heuristics in convergence tests, which are either never satisfied or require such limited precision that the arithmetic power of the new configuration can never be utilised, or function expansions that depend upon a particular base of arithmetic or strategy of rounding or truncation. Algorithms that perform excellently on long word-length machines may quickly lose all figures of accuracy on short word-length machines, which can be particularly important for example in determining step lengths or new search directions.

For many programs the precision of computation is of vital importance. If programs are to be transferred between 60 or 64 bit and 4/8 byte machines (from Cray 1 or CDC 7600 to IBM 370/168) and from 32 or 32/64 bit minis to 60 or 64 bit or 4/8 byte mainframe machines (VAX 11/780 to CDC 7600) an ability to transform the precision of the program from single to double precision representation and vice versa is essential. This was a tortuous operation for a Fortran 66 program and is still a messy activity for a Fortran 77 program. At least one configuration had an automatic precision conversion option for its Fortran 66 standard compiler. It is to be hoped that this facility will be emulated more widely for Fortran 77 compilation systems. However a number of manufacturers see no need for such a facility, and to get the conversion correct in all instances is a significant challenge. Tools for precision conversion are available but to date have been rather limited in their applicability. Toolpack will however include a Fortran 77 program conversion transformer (Hague, 1980). Careful attention during program development to the requirements of precision conversion are invaluable. Whilst the software aids mentioned above can assist with the activity, the investment of planning and thought solves the problem at source.

The third barrier is limitations in machine resources. A program may be too dependent on features of the operating system of a particular configuration. It may require a degree of packing into each machine word or the use of half integer storage which the implementor's machine does not have. The program may be too big (in source text or in object form) to be compiled and loaded on the new system. The required data may be too voluminous for available backing-store. It may be possible to store everything on the machine, but take inordinate resources (human or otherwise) to transfer the information to it, or the machine may simply not have the processor power to complete the computation. All such problems may be overcome, or not be relevant, yet the local computing service may simply be unable or unwilling to support the transferred program ("it requires all our tape decks": "we cannot give you all the machine": "the output would take three months to print"). A realistic assessment of the resources demanded and their availability in the new configuration is essential before the program transfer is attempted. It is also fair to ask if the return to the user justifies the use of the resources! The viability of a transfer is a most important consideration.

4. USER ASSENT TO TRANSFER

The scientist and technologist save themselves substantial time if they agree to use transferred software. The cost comes in installing and maintaining the package, tailoring it to local and individual requirements and using it to solve individual problems. It is a black-box, manufactured elsewhere. User assent to transfer and willingness to use a black-box is often a question of control and confidence. In one sentence: is the package usable and user-friendly?

Control

The control required by the user operates at least at three levels. Does the package have sufficient flexibility through the user interface to permit the user to input all desired information, monitor the proceeding computation and collect all necessary results and information? The concern here is control over the computation.

The second level of control concerns the data. Does the package accept the data the user has available, permit use of facility with incomplete data and offer a variety of services so that all relevant available data can be used? If the program requires the data in a particular form, can the user's data be readily transformed to that form? At the next stage does the package have a facility for intermediate output and input, to monitor the path of the computation and to divert the calculation to another course? Finally can we collect all the numbers we require to complete the research or production activity in hand? Our interest here then is control over the data.

The third level of control relates to the ability to use the package in a given computing service. For larger programs this is particularly important as they will rely heavily on local operating system features and resources. Typical questions are: is the package easy to stop; can its output be readily redirected (and if necessary limited); does it have an efficient stop/restart facility (which does not waste substantial parts of earlier computation)? The sociability of the package when running with the rest of the local jobload can be an important feature in the life of its user. The concern here is control of the program when in use.

Confidence

We mentioned above those aspects which give users confidence in the behaviour of the package and hence encourage them to transfer and use it. Another crucial aspect is package documentation. It is all important both for the scientist, from the application area viewpoint, and for the person who must mount the package, from the software viewpoint. Ideally one seeks documentation in three forms on-line, microform and printed. The chapter on transportable user documentation hopefully covers the points and issues involved.

For user confidence a high level of presentation and preparation of documentation is needed at each instance of communication: in the installation/implementation guide, in the notes accompanying distributed software, in error notification and error correction, in update notices, in the user manuals/information system database and package software support manual. If the documentation is bad, the package will rarely if ever be successful.

Example programs of package use with results and a detailed test program suite (plus data) for installation/implementation are vital to inculcate confidence and to maintain it.

User confidence is like a delicate flower. It brings great pleasure - whilst it lasts. Unfortunately it is easily damaged, or destroyed.

5. MEDIUM OF TRANSFER

The immediate physical stumbling blocks to the transfer of software concern character sets and media. An appreciation of the problems involved in these two topics is essential if one is to understand the activities later and will therefore be discussed in some detail.

Character Set

The choice of character set to be used when writing a program can be critical for its later distribution for use on other configurations in non-Fortran based languages. Even with Fortran programs teasing difficulties may still be met. For the majority of programmers the problem of character sets is solved by using that available on their local machine. That simplistic solution is possibly the greatest technical obstacle (in percentage terms) to software transfer and sharing. Choice of character set does involve a trade-off: a restricted character set requires awkward constructs (but can be generally available) whilst a broad set will be unacceptable to at least one configuration. Exclusion of the package from those configurations may be a serious blow to all concerned.

IBM codes

Since some 70% (by value) of the world computing market buys and employs IBM hardware, the influence of the company regarding decisions on character sets has been most important.

The Hollerith code was the earliest punched card code in general use. It had 48 graphic characters and no control characters. There was almost complete agreement regarding the assignation to 37 of these characters (space, 0-9, A-Z) but the remaining 11 varied. IBM had two sets, the commercial (the "A") and FORTRAN (the "H"). These became the "de facto" standard.

The development of 7-track magnetic decks posed problems of reliability for character reading and necessitated that each tape character be represented by at least two bits. IBM adopted an even-parity representation for each character, which gave a 63-character set. It became known as the binary-coded decimal interchange code (BCDIC), and involved both graphic and control characters. Other computer manufacturers evolved a similar-styled set of characters but unfortunately there was a wide variation in the graphics assigned to characters outside the Hollerith set.

In time the size of BCDIC set proved to be too small, and IBM introduced EBCDIC with the System/360. For the last fifteen years it has been defined by the ubiquitous "green card".

An extension of assignment of graphic characters took place with the introduction of the IBM 370 series of machines. This set was defined by the "yellow card". The contents of the two cards have recently been specified in IBM literature to permit definition of a unique mapping between the ASCII (ISO) and EBCDIC character sets. It is not yet evident whether this laudable objective has been achieved.

ASCII (ISO) and its subsets

ISO has approved a character code which is fundamentally based on the ASCII character set standard (ISO, 1973). However since IBM and other American manufacturers refer to the ASCII code that will be the base for our discussion. (The ISO standard expressly permits "national variants" of specific entries in the ASCII set, for example £ for $ in the United Kingdom.) There are 128 distinct characters in the ASCII set, 95 are graphic characters and 33 control characters.

Within the ASCII graphic character sets there are five recognised subsets containing 63, 64, 66, 89 and 95 characters respectively.

Media

It should be noted at the outset that in many instances it will now be possible to distribute the software by network. The primary limitations of this approach are line-speeds and reliability. The problems of code conversion should have been solved by the designers of the network. For large programs (30000 to 100000 Fortran records), substantial test suites, including results, and large databases, transfer by magnetic tape is often still preferable, but the technology for distribution by network is improving rapidly.

Assuming that the peripherals available permit a choice from several media, other criteria become operative:
Character set
Convenience
Durability
Volume and weight

Character set concerns the size of set permitted by the medium: *convenience* is the effort required to retrieve and record the program: *durability* is the half-life of the medium and of the program recorded upon it; *volume* and *weight* are the cost of shipping the information from producer to installer/implementor/user.

Cards

Punched cards (of 80 columns) are still a reasonable and reliable medium for transmitting programs of up to 6000 records. Hole combinations are defined for all 128 ASCII characters but many card readers cannot read the full set (if a system accepts binary cards then the card reader is capable of reading any hole combination).

Cards are usually convenient to produce and to enter into another machine. Whilst local system conventions at the receiving site may cause difficulties, these can usually be easily overcome, once the problem is recognised.

If packed carefully, cards are relatively durable but dislike high humidity and can be rendered useless by careless handling. A distribution deck should always be numbered serially and accompanied by a full listing.

Many receiving sites will be happy to pay the additional costs of receiving a few boxes of cards because of the comparative ease of handling them.

Paper tape

Paper tape is still widely used within the mini-computer community, although even here the use of networks, hooking-up small machines to the local mainframe specifically for communication of software and data, is increasingly common.

Magnetic tape

Most computing systems include at least one tape deck (although some mini-computers and many micro-systems are increasingly based upon floppy discs for inputting software).

For any software of significant size (greater than 6000 records) magnetic tape comes into its own as a communication medium. The largest regularly used tapes are 2400 feet long, and depending upon the recording density (6250 bits per inch, 1600 b.p.i., 800 b.p.i., 556 b.p.i.) a single reel can hold from around 10K to 100K records.

Information is recorded in either 7 or 9 tracks along the tape, with 9 tracks becoming increasingly common. Standard 9-track representations are defined for all 128 ASCII characters. There is no standard 7-track representation but it is common practice to encode three 8-bit characters as four 6-bit characters on a 7 track tape to allow representation of the full ASCII set. Many systems support a 63 or 64-character subset.

Magnetic tapes are the least convenient of the media discussed so far, as each computer system appears to have its own tape format (i.e. format for recording information). However most general purpose machines permit any tape to be read, provided that 7 and 9 track tape decks are available, with readers of the required speeds and parity checking, and that a good tape reading program is to hand.

For some operating systems a tape label (for example an IBM tape label) is obligatory. Since a system for which a label is irrelevant can skip over it as an extra file, if in any doubt include a label on the tape.

Each record of text on the tape constitutes a logical record and each group of characters on the tape, a block. Logical records may be grouped into blocks provided:

1. No explicit indication of the boundaries between records is required.
2. There shall be an integral number of records per block.
3. Truncated blocks are permitted.

Record length may be fixed (all logical records in the file are of the same length), variable (each record contains its length in the first four character positions) or undefined.

As a tape is a magnetic medium it can be adversely affected by being passed through an electric or magnetic field. Wrapping a tape in tin-foil, and taking particular care to avoid baggage inspection devices at airports appears to avoid these problems. Tapes, even in tape cases, require careful handling and packaging.

Tapes are available in different lengths and are light, so that transportation costs can be minimised. Passage of magnetic tapes through the post is common and comparatively cheap. It can be hazardous, but this is beyond any programmer's or user's control.

Floppy disks

With the advent of the micro computer, the use of floppy disks as a transfer medium has grown though, regrettably, a similar pattern of variation to that in earlier computer developments seems present. Physically, there are two widely used disk sizes; 8 inch and $5^1/_4$ inch, the latter now becoming the more popular. Disk handlers on some systems can accept information recorded on one side only of the disk; others accept double-sided disks. The recording density level may be designated as single, double or (more recently) extended. Before despatching disks with specific recording characteristics it is essential to check that the receiving device is physically capable of handling them.

A further complication is the formatting of information; on some disks, the information is grouped into sectors by hardware, on others this is done by software. Software-sectored disks cannot be read directly by devices which use the hardware-sectored technique, and vice versa. Finally (!) there are variations in the way the information is logically laid-out by the recording software. There are no industry-wide conventions; probably the nearest approximation is the IBM 3740 format (single/double density) for 8 inch disks. One of the most widely available micro computer operating systems is CP/M. Provided that the disks and disk handling devices involved are physically compatible, it is probably straightforward to transfer disks between CP/M systems of different origin though a conversion utility program may be necessary.

Regrettably, the moral for the time being is "do not assume that you can transfer data via floppy disk to another micro computer (or to a mainframe system perhaps) unless someone has successfully tried the transfer already."

6. MECHANISMS FOR SOFTWARE SHARING

How does one learn what programs are available for transfer and sharing, what they can do, under what terms and conditions they are available, from where they may be obtained, who supports them and what other user-experience has been of them? These are just a few of the questions that spring to mind regarding basic information about programs, and hence about the mechanisms that exist for providing information about software for transfer and sharing.

The producer of a program will generally publicise its availability within his technical community, answering the questions given above and many more! Again if the producer is making a package commercially available he will publicise and market it. If the service is a generally required one (on many machine ranges to many different scientific and technical communities) the producer will again be responsible for the information.

Information regarding available programs, packages and databases may be acquired from computer program libraries (e.g. EUROCOPI, Ispra; Program Library Unit, Edinburgh). The contents in such libraries are usually defined according to computer application, geographical area and computer family.

From program library units and independently from libraries in large organisations and institutions one can gain access to program indices compiled by national bodies; professional, scientific and technical associations and specialised publishing companies.

The information systems on computer networks are increasingly structured to provide details of all programs available on the network, or to provide direction as how to acquire such information from each individual installation.

The creation of these centres of information, and of the bodies of information they provide is a time-consuming and painstaking activity, which is a vital service to the computing community. Cooperation and collaboration between voluntary workers are often the key to all these activities.

7. ASPECTS OF SHARED SOFTWARE

Installation and Implementation

The background and requirements for installation/implementation of shared software have been discussed above. Succinctly one looks for contact with the originator, an installation/implementation guide, a test suite of programs and data, and direction as to when installation/implementation is judged to have been successfully completed. For a scientific/technical computer program involving numerical output there are problems of deciding what is an equivalent source text of a program and what is equivalent numerical performance in the new computing configuration.

Modification

It was noted above that user assent to program transfer is often a question of control and confidence. After some experience the user may wish to modify the software he has received, to provide additional features or to satisfy more closely his own requirements. This he may do, of course, only with the originator's agreement.

In general the requirements are contact with the originator, and the external and internal documentation of the program. For a number of reasons this may be insufficient and the proposed modification not possible.

If the modification is completed, an extension of the test program suite and data and of the documentation will be required to describe and to take account of the new features.

Availability

Once software has been made available to other people the originator has a fundamental responsibility to support it in use. This responsibility covers his own self respect, the needs of his program users to whom he is committed and support of the ideal of shared software. In increasing order of demand and time the software may be available to colleagues at his local site, to colleagues in the technical community (invariably geographically dispersed) and via a computer network.

Software Producers

To ensure continued user confidence, producers of software should provide maintenance and advice on the package and its use, an error reporting and correction service and new releases of the package from time to time.

For their own use, producers should maintain a master copy of all releases and implementations of the program (and of the test program suite and data). This is a non-trivial activity eased on some machines by the availability of software maintenance and support program systems (e.g. CDC 6000/7000/Cyber Update system).

8. CONCLUDING REMARKS

This paper has sought to review some of the problems and issues in software transfer and sharing. What emerges is the many aspects of software, computing and (human) organisation that are involved in an increasingly important technical area and activity. Voluntary cooperation and collaboration are the key forces that ensure utilisation of valuable and finite human resources.

REFERENCES

Hague S.J. (1980), "APT-X: Automatic Precision Transformer" Toolpack Memorandum Ref. SJH00430, April 1980 NAG Central Office.

ISO (1973), ISO 646: 7-bit coded character set for information processing interchange.

Ryder G.B. and Hall A.D. (1975), "The PFORT Verifier" Computing Science Technical Report No. 12, 1975. Bell Laboratories, New Jersey, U.S.A.

THE LEGAL PROTECTION OF COMPUTER SOFTWARE

Bryan Harris
Commission of the European Communities
Brussels, Belgium.

During recent years it has become increasingly evident both that computer software, and especially the ideas and skills which go into its preparation, ought as a matter of justice to have legal protection and that there are various problems arising from the protection of computer software under existing laws. The World Intellectual Property Organisation in Geneva has been examining the problems and has proposed some model provisions directed specifically to the protection of computer software (WIPO, 1978). The Organisation justifies the need for legal protection by reference to the volume of investment in computer software, the expected developments in the uses of computer software, the incentive to disclose the technology implicit in computer software, the security required for trade based on the use of computer software and the general vulnerability of computer software, in view of the case with which it may be copied and relayed. The Organisation looks at existing forms of legal protection — that is, by way of patent laws, copyright laws and laws on unfair competition and the protection of trade secrets — and concludes that provisions specially designed for the protection of computer software are justified.

Whether the model provisions prepared by the World Intellectual Property Organisation on the legal protection of computer software should be adopted, and, if so, whether by individual states at their own discretion or collectively by international convention or Community instrument, depends on the interest which individual governments have in such provisions and in the interest of computer software users in the efficacy of that form of protection. The Organisation has addressed enquiries on the present legal position to the governments of interested states, as well as to the Commission of the European Communities; and the Commission has in turn addressed an enquiry to selected firms, known to be users of computer software, to ascertain their views on the practical aspects of the proposals. The greater part of this chapter concerns the results of the Commission's questionnaire.

D. T. Muxworthy (ed.), Programming for Software Sharing, 203–210.
Copyright © 1983 ECSC, EEC, EAEC, Brussels and Luxembourg.

First, however, there are some preliminary points to settle. At the outset, it is useful to have a working definition of computer software. As a rule, national legislation does not use the term; it is therefore useful to refer to the definition proposed in the model provisions, referred to above. According to this definition, computer software means a computer program, a program description and supporting material. The expression, "computer program" is sometimes to be found in national legislation; but this is usually for the purpose of excluding computer programs from patent laws. Moreover, even when mentioned in national legislation, the expression is not usually defined. Once again, the model provisions come to our help. These define a computer program as a set of instructions capable, when incorporated in a machine-readable medium, of causing a machine having information-processing capabilities to indicate a form or achieve a particular function, task or result. A proposed Canadian patent law in 1976 had a similar definition; but it referred to statements in, or capable of conversion to, a machine-readable form, as well as instructions. It spoke of a "computer or data processing apparatus which is adapted to responding to various types of computer programs or series of instructions" instead of to a "machine..." as in the model provisions (a somewhat circular definition) and it adds the words "and includes the algorithm associated therewith" (reflecting the exclusion, in certain patent laws, of mathematical methods and the like).

This reference to the algorithm raises an awkward legal problem, recently discussed by the Court of Customs and Patent Appeals (1980) in the United States, which held that "the mere fact that digital computers operated on a number radix was not conclusive of the existence of a mathematical algorithm, otherwise any computer-related invention must be regarded as mathematical in nature". In other words, a distinction had to be drawn between what the computer did and how it did it. The Court emphasised the need to look at what the computer was doing, whether the process was in mathematical form or not. Some of the actions of the computer had no mathematical significance. Some processes represented the performance of a mathematical algorithm; for example, where it represented the solution to a complex vector equation describing the behaviour of a rocket in flight. But, in some cases, processes combined hardware elements and algorithm. Neither of the first two programs could be protected in law; the third could be protected only to the extent that the algorithm formed part of a larger claim.

So much for the basic definitions. A second preliminary point concerns the role of the Commission, which itself needs some explanation. It is not simply that the Commission was one of the bodies invited to reply to the World Intellectual Property Organisation in its request for information about the state of the law. There was a further reason for the Commission's interest, grounded in a proposal from the Commission in 1979, as a result of which the Council of Ministers reached a formal Decision on the establishment of a five year programme for the Community in the field of data processing. Under the first article, and paragraph 1.3.5 of Annex to the Decision, the objectives of the Community, as regards the legal protection of computer program, were, first, to consult interested bodies and, secondly, to develop appropriate relations between the Commission and national or international bodies dealing with the problem (CEC, 1979).

Much therefore depended on an assessment of the nature of the problem itself. According to the Economist (1979), "the problems are growing. Easily copyable software has become more readily available; for example, standard software packages, recorded on magnetic tape, can be bought on the high street and are little harder to copy than a much less valuable tape recording of somebody's music." Even so, the Economist wondered whether there was really an urgent need to do something. "One claim is that finance for software development is being held back for lack of clear protection. Evidence that this is so is still being sought. Another claim, one that is easier to substantiate, is that computer manufacturers and users often fail to publish their software because of the unclear legal position. Industry as a whole is the loser".

This view appears to be borne out by experience in the United States where there has been far more litigation than in Europe on conflicting claims to rights in computer software. These cases range from criminal actions for the theft of software (even though nothing is physically taken) to actions for infringement of software copyright. An example of the former concerned a man found guilty and fined fifty thousand dollars for copying his former employer's software programs and using them in a competing business which he started. The employee maintained throughout the trial that he had originally developed the programs and that he had re-created rather than copied them once he left his employement. Nevertheless the jury found enough circumstantial evidence to convict him of theft. The fact that the software was intangible did not affect the jury's finding (Computerworld, 1980).

An example of a claim involving infringement of copyright in software has arisen in an action between the two micro-software dealers Molimerx and Kansas City Systems. The latter is selling a domino playing program for the Tandy TRS80, which Molimerx claims is a copy of "Dominoes" marketed by their company. The proceedings began after a discovery made by the author of Dominoes, a computer service engineer, who sold his program to Molimerx, and received from them a royalty on each copy sold. The engineer wished to compare the new version with his own and ran a copy of Kansas City Systems Dominoes game, bought by a friend through a mail order, only to find it almost identical. Furthermore, he found an unerased "watermark" by which Molimerx identifies its products. ("Watermarks" or "exclusive devices" are the names given to certain forms of electronic identification which can be inserted in the computer program.) According to Kansas City Systems, every effort is made to identify where the legal rights in any given program may lie; but this is often more difficult than it seems. Apparently, firms like Kansas City Systems are often sold software on the basis that the vendor owns the legal rights and is assigning the rights, or licensing them, to the purchaser; but, because of the uncertainty of the law over the authorship of computer programmes and the rights of the author, the vendor in these cases is not often justified in claiming the copyright (Computer Weekly, 1980).

It was in the light of this sort of problem that the Commission decided to devise a questionnaire, addressed to software users. The terms of the letter containing the questionnaire are set out in the Annex to this chapter. The letter was sent to selected addressees at the end of December 1980; and replies reached the Commission during the first six months of 1981. The rest of this chapter is devoted to an analysis of these replies.

Some interesting general points were made in response to the first question in the questionnaire. As it happened, only one of the correspondents said that the legal protection of computer software, under existing laws, worked well: this was a correspondent from the Federal Republic of Germany referring to German laws. Correspondents from France and Denmark, on the other hand, said that the protection was either inadequate or altogether non-existent. The inadequacy of the laws was explained by another correspondent in terms which have a ring of truth: legal developments, this correspondent claimed, were simply never in time to keep up with technical developments. No sooner had the law been changed than new technical developments made the law out of date. One of the consequences of this was that the swindler was one jump ahead of the law. One correspondent emphasised that specific cases of swindle and theft, susceptible of proof, were extremely rare; but the qualifying words are vital, since one of the problems of the protection of computer software is the "policing" of the property. On the other hand, another correspondent pointed out forcibly that there were increasing signs of the pirating of computer software packages and that this was in the long run to cause even greater losses to the respective industries than pirating of audio or video cassettes.

Some of the most interesting points made by the correspondents in answer to the first general question were those expressed in terms of the distinction between various kinds of firm, software or objective. One correspondent said that, while the protection of computer software was relatively easy for the larger firms, it presented serious difficulties for small firms. Another correspondent drew a distinction between the different types of program: some were easy to protect in law, others difficult. Yet another correspondent said that the vital distinction was between the form and the content of the software; there was apt to be a confusion between the two; but it was clearly the latter which needed protection. Several correspondents drew a distinction between the protection of computer input and the protection of computer output; several also emphasised the policy distinction which a firm might wish to make between computer software which it explicitly intended to remain secret and computer software which it saw some commercial advantage in publicising. One correspondent saw a fundamental distinction, obvious enough when stated in this way, but nonetheless useful, between the commonplace program and the one which showed real originality: the full weight of the law was not needed to protect the nine out of ten programs which were commonplace, but rather to ensure the exceptional program, in which real originality was displayed. One correspondent made the point, which is implicit in many other correspondents' replies, that there was a distinction between direct and indirect copying of programs: direct copying was rare, but incontrovertible; indirect copying, including imitation and "parallel originality" (especially by former employees), was frequent and hard to prove. Finally, one of the correspondents made the all-embracing point that, while the content of the law might be exactly right, it was enforcement which created the problem: three things appeared to be needed; a revised law, a practice of policing and swift effective judicial procedures.

The answers to questions 2 and 3 in the questionnaire, relating to specific instances of problems and in particular instances resulting in litigation, were somewhat disappointing. Some correspondents referred to the United States litigation, but said that the same problems did not seem to arise in Europe. It was nevertheless helpful to have the notes of cases reported in the UK journal "Practical Computing"; their issue for January 1981 contains details of the British litigation involving Kansas City, together with one or two other cases coming to its attention. Significantly, the journal comments that, following the settlement of the principal case, the legal questions regarding copyright protection had still to be looked at definitively by the Court. An interesting explanation of the relative scarcity of specific cases in Europe was offered by one of the correspondents who attributed it to the prevalence of arbitration. This correspondent knew of cases solely because he himself had acted as arbitrator; but, as arbitration was regarded as confidential in his country, he was neither able to give more specific information about those cases nor able to say for certain whether more cases had been settled by other arbitrators.

The answers to question 4 of the questionnaire, as to what means are most often employed for the protection of computer software, clearly indicate that the most favoured and, in some countries, the only effective form of legal protection is that of confidentiality clause in a contract. This firmly places the protection of computer software within the field of contract and trade secrecy laws; but it has, as correspondents pointed out, the serious disavantage of not binding third parties. As between the licensor and licensee of the protected material, and as between employers and employees, the contractual relationship is satisfactory, provided that the relevant clauses of the contracts in question are well drawn up. It is, however, almost completely ineffective against those who imitate or steal computer software and are not in any way bound by the contract itself. Where there is no contract, most correspondents relied on the law of copyright for their protection; but many correspondents pointed out that national laws on copyright needed to be amended before they were fully applicable and appropriate to the protection of computer software; and some correspondents pointed out that it was by no means clear in their particular countries — France was a case in point — that copyright laws could be successfully invoked. All correspondents agreed that no patent legislation could, as things stood at present, be used for the protection of computer software. One or two correspondents looked with envy at the developing case law in the United States where there has been a slackening of the outright exclusion of computer programs from patent protection.

This leads to the fifth question in the questionnaire, concerning suggestions for possible action to improve legal and technical protection in this area. Broadly, there were three proposals, relating to copyright, patents and the WIPO Model Provisions respectively. So far as copyright is concerned, several correspondents suggested two fairly simple reforms. The first would be to enact specifically that computer software, properly defined, should be the subject of copyright protection. The second is that the period of protection for computer software should be a relatively short period - say 10 - 15 years - unlike the current period of copyright protection for literary and artistic works which runs to fifty or more years after the author's death.

So far as patent law was concerned, opinions ranged from a grudging acceptance of the present exclusion of computer software patentability under the European Patent system to the bold suggestion that the European system should be explicitly amended, and with it national patent systems, to permit the inclusion of computer software. In between these views, there was a suggestion that, while computer software should continue to be excluded from normal patent protection, it might benefit from a special patent protection similar to that once applicable to "petty patents". In other words there should be a special system, tailored for computer software, similar to the patent system and parallel to it.

As for the WIPO proposals, it has to be admitted that most of the correspondents appear not to have fully understood the implications of the system which these proposals envisage. It must be emphasised that the WIPO Model Provisions are essentially based on a copyright law approach and do not require deposit as a condition for special protection. Mandatory deposit would make the system a protection rather more closely similar to patent protection; and, in the light of the discussions which have taken place under the aegis of WIPO, the merits of the systems of optional deposit or optional registration are in some doubt. Those correspondents who recognised that the WIPO Model Provisions comprised essentially an adaptation of the copyright law approach tended to support the proposals: they are not so different from the more modest suggestions for the explicit application of copyright law.

In addition to these legal suggestions, several correspondents came up with practical suggestions, consisting primarily of ideas for coding the software. As one correspondent puts it: "each licensee's name and licence number are coded invisibly into the program: then, if the copyright owner finds software licensed to A in B's hands, he can sue A in contract and prosecute B for illicit possession of copyright material". As the same correspondent points out, hardware devices, essentially locks, are also used to restrict the use of particular software packages to the owners of the devices. To another correspondent the essence of the matter is policing the illegal use of software: there should perhaps, in that correspondent's view, be a Computer and Software Users' Rights Society, presumably on the analogy of the Performing Rights' Society. Finally, one of the other correspondents says that the essence of the matter is a clear internal policy within the firm regarding the security to be given to software, coupled with a conscious choice between the commercial merits of disclosure and of secrecy respectively.

In the light of the replies to the questionnaire, the Commission will have to consider carefully, first, whether there is a sufficient demand for an improvement in the law and, secondly, given a demand, whether it is more appropriately met at national or Community level. The Commission will continue to consult interested parties and to welcome their views on the matter.

REFERENCES

Commission of the European Communities (1979), Decision 79/783/CEE: Official Journal L.231/23 dated 13th September, 1979.

Computer Weekly (1980), 27th November, 1980, p. 12.

Computerworld (1980), 24th November, 1980, p. 18.

Court of Customs and Patent Appeals (1980), Diamond v. Bradley & Franklin; 600 F zd 807 (U.S.).

Economist (1979), 8th December, 1979, p. 84.

World Intellectual Property Organisation (1978), Model Provisions on the Protection of Computer Software.

COMMISSION
OF THE
EUROPEAN COMMUNITIES

———

Directorate-General
for internal market and industrial affairs

———

III/D-4

Brussels, ...
BH/hv

Subject: **Legal Protection of Computer Software**

Dear

1. The question of the adequate and appropriate legal protection of Computer Software is of increasing importance throughout the Community; and the Commission would like to invite industrial and commercial concerns and their professional associations to throw light on their experience of, and satisfaction with, the current position.

2. As I am sure you are aware, it is becoming increasingly possible for customers or for other computer users to obtain or use the system supplier's software without fair and adequate fees, or to use it with other hardware or software to obtain extended benefits without fair and adequate fees; and for competitors (such as system competitors, or software houses or software specialists) without the supplier's consent to obtain or use the system. It looks increasingly doubtful whether existing laws are adequate or suitable for the prevention of these developments.

3. However, the purpose of this inquiry is to benefit from your knowledge of this subject and to discover whether the need for legislation within the EEC is as urgent as it appears elsewhere, and how far you consider that present laws on software protection suffice. The Commission believes that this inquiry is necessary before further discussions can take place which might lead to eventual harmonisation of Member States' laws.

4. With this in mind, you reaction to the following matters in particular will be appreciated:

(i) *general problems encountered in the field of legal protection of software; for example,* is the protection too difficult or expensive to acquire or maintain?

(ii) *specific instances of such problems*; can you, for example, cite any cases within your experience in which protection was impossible or confidential programme material was borrowed, copied, stolen or otherwise unlawfully handled by a third party?

(iii) *any instances which resulted in litigation*; have you been involved in any legal proceeding or are you aware of any such matter affecting third parties, and if so, what was the final outcome of the litigation;

(iv) *whether existing protection is adequate*; what means do you most often employ, for example, patent, copyright, or trade secret protection;

(v) *suggestions for possible action to improve legal and technical protection in this area*; the Commission is studying the WIPO model provisions but is conscious this may not be the only solution to the problem and therefore would welcome any other ideas on the approach to this problem (e.g. economic aspects, nature of software to be protected, etc.).

I look forward to hearing from you. If the information concerned is confidential, you may be assured that it will be treated as such; however, if you are willing for references to be made to what you say (either with or without explicit attribution), this may be useful in our forthcoming report.
It would be extremely helpful if we could hear from tou within one month of dispatch of this letter. Meanwhile, if you have any queries about this request for information, or would like to communicate your reply by telephone, could you please ask for Mr. Harris's Secretariat on extension 1861?

Yours.

F. Braun

EXPERIENCE IN MULTI-MACHINE SOFTWARE DEVELOPMENT: THE NAG LIBRARY - A CASE STUDY

Brian Ford

NAG Central Office
Oxford, UK

1. SUMMARY

If a reliable, high quality numerical algorithms library is to be developed then it is essential that we recognise the need for collaboration between different technical communities in the development of the library. This paper suggests an ultimate design for the library, the stages required for preparation of the library and why separate implementations of the library are necessary.

2. INTRODUCTION

Since its inception the Numerical Algorithms Group (NAG) project has pursued four aims:

1. To create a balanced, general purpose numerical algorithms library in Fortran to meet the mathematical and statistical requirements of computer users.
2. To support the library with documentation giving advice on problem identification and algorithms selection, and on the use of each routine.
3. To provide a test program library for certification of the library.
4. To implement the library as widely as user demand required.

There are at present 178 members of NAG who are involved in the preparation of the NAG Library. Generally each person has a specific interest or function within the library development process. They may be:

— contributors, who contribute library contents and write test programs and documentation. They are academics or government scientists who are selected for their individual ability in an area of numerical mathematics.

— validators, who certify that the work of the relevant contributor is of the required standard. They are of comparable stature to the contributor in their field of numerical mathematics.

D. T. Muxworthy (ed.), Programming for Software Sharing, 211–223.

— translators, who translate the algorithms into other languages, usually Algol 60 or Algol 68.

— implementors, who implement the library on a particular machine range or one of the 28 full-time staff employed either in the Central Office or as machine range coordinators.

The Group appreciated in 1970 that collaboration between different technical communities, whose members would inevitably be geographically dispersed, was necessary if a library was to be produced. The library would be reliable and of high quality if each phase of the activity was performed to defined standards, in a prescribed manner, in pursuit of specified objectives. A Central Office of full-time staff was established to process, monitor and maintain the contents of the library and to coordinate the manpower that created and implemented the software.

Two service organisations, one in Europe (Oxford, England) and the other in North America (Chicago, U.S.A.) finally make a Library Service available to users worldwide.

The disciplined employment of the energy, interest and ability of each individual member of NAG in the creation, development and maintenance of the library is the key to the NAG project. The project is a living flexible organisation - evolving as technical and organisational factors demand.

In this chapter we suggest an ultimate structure for the library, outline the major components of the library activity and review their functions, explain the continuing requirements for separate machine range implementations, underline the operational principles of the activity and finally comment on its performance and continuing technology.

3. LIBRARY DESIGN

We require a library structure designed to satisfy the requirements of all users of the library (Ford and Bentley, 1978). The spectrum of users, in their knowledge of numerical analysis, of programming and of problem formulation and solution, will be very broad.

Types of software

In general, however, we can satisfy the majority of their requirements by three types of library software.

Type	Function	Example
Problem solvers:	one routine to call to solve the problem	solution of set of simultaneous real linear equations
Primary routine:	each routine contains one major algorithm	LU factorisation
Basic module:	basic numerical utility designed by the chapter contributor for his own and his fellow contributor's use	extended precision inner product.

Communication of information

A consistent approach should be employed throughout the library for communication of information to its constituent parts and to the users in particular. Wherever possible, information should be passed through calling sequences. The design of calling sequences, the ordering of parameters within them and the naming of routines and variables should be systematic throughout the library. A common error-mechanism should be used.

At least three operational requirements can be recognised in the design of each calling sequence:
— convenient and correct use by the programmer;
— satisfaction of the needs of the algorithm;
— use of the data structures of the numerical area.

These requirements underlie the preparation of interfaces for the three types of user software.

— problem solvers: minimum calling sequence;
— primary routines: longer calling sequence, if necessary to permit greater flexibility and control;
— basic module: optimized calling sequence reflecting perceived needs of all contributors yet recognising demands of efficiency of use.

The three types of library software could ultimately provide the three tiers of a steady-state library structure. At the present time a number of chapters within the NAG Library do not fit into such a design.

This illustrates a dilemma faced by library designers in general. The state-of-the-art in many branches of numerical software continues to develop, and notions about optimal library design may change also. A library currently in use represents a very significant investment in effort, guided by the state of affairs and of thinking several years ago. The library designer who wishes to keep abreast of developments must not lightly disregard this investment.

Contents of Library

The contents of the library must evolve as research and development permit. Hence we require a library structure which enables the library contents to change with the minimum inconvenience to users.

It is convenient to divide the contents of the library in accordance with areas of numerical mathematics. Further subdivision will be required following the natural substructure within each mathematical area. The number of algorithms included will reflect the user demand for problem solution and the resolution of problem type within each area.

4. NAG LIBRARY PREPARATION

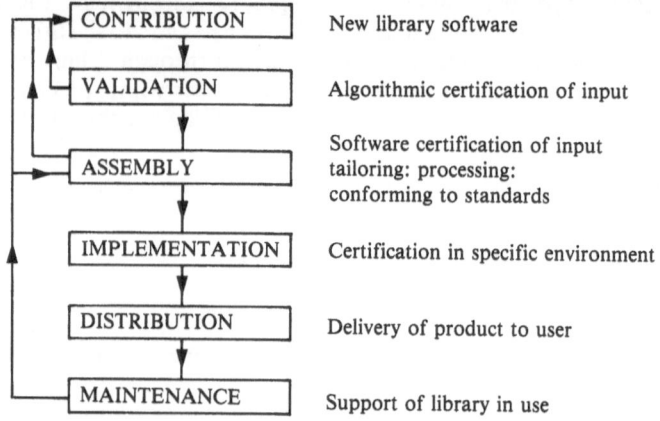

CONTRIBUTION	New library software
VALIDATION	Algorithmic certification of input
ASSEMBLY	Software certification of input tailoring: processing: conforming to standards
IMPLEMENTATION	Certification in specific environment
DISTRIBUTION	Delivery of product to user
MAINTENANCE	Support of library in use

Contribution

The primary function of a contributor is to identify the major types of problems met by users in his area of interest and to provide the "best" algorithm in the library for each type. The algorithms are selected following a stringent performance evaluation of contending methods. The test program and data sets are retained by the contributor.

Ideally we require routines which will run, virtually without change, to prescribed efficiency and accuracy, on all the machines to which we carry the library. We need adaptable algorithms (Ford et al. 1978) which then can be realised as transportable subroutines (Hague & Ford, 1976).

The contributor uses an agreed subset of the language (Ryder, 1974). As has been shown (Bentley & Ford, 1977), this approach can largely overcome the problem of language dialects, yet permit a reliable and robust subroutine (Cody, 1974) to be developed.

The aim of the contributor is to write a single routine, which can be tailored to perform to the required accuracy and efficiency on each machine.

As a basis for the development of all NAG software, a simple model has been developed of features of any computer that are relevant to the software. This conceptual machine is described in terms of a number of parameters (e.g. base of floating point number representation, overflow threshold). Each parameter may be given a specific value to reflect a feature of a particular computer (e.g. SRADIX (Ford, 1977) is 16 for IBM 360 and is 2 for CDC 7600).

Hence the contibutor writes his single routine for the conceptual machine. The routine is then tailored for each distinct configuration by selection of the values of the parameters. In this way the individual demands of accuracy and efficiency for the routine are met for every machine range.

For each routine the contributor provides an implementation test which will be used by implementors to demonstrate the operational efficiency and accuracy of the routine in each environment.

It might be thought that the assembly of new software into the Library should be a straightforward task. But it is not, and a recent case study (Du Croz & Fosdick, 1982) has analysed some of the difficulties. This case study concerned the assembly of a suite of routines and test programs - amounting to 14000 lines of Fortran altogether - for the Mark 7 Fortran Library. Thirty four problems (or types of problem) were encountered, which were classified as follows:

a) Use of non-standard Fortran - 8 problems (5 of which involved run-time features or communication between program units).

b) Undesirable programming style (which could cause difficulties in using or maintaing the software) - 11 problems.

c) Semantic or pragmatic programming errors (which came to light when the software was tested on different machines) - 5 problems.

d) Unsatisfactory design of routines, examples or test programs - 5 problems.

e) Error in the existing NAG Library - 1 problem.

f) Errors in software tools (compounded by human errors in their application) - 4 problems.

Classified from a different point of view 13 problems came to light during the application of software tools; 6 during visual examination of the software; 25 during compilation and execution on three different machines (ICL 1906A, CDC 7600 and IBM 370).

All these problems were of course remedied. They remind us that it is not enough to specify standards and guidelines; we must have adequate (i.e. automatic) means of ensuring that they are adhered to. Increasingly NAG is making software tools such as the PFORT verifier available to contributors, but we cannot expect them to have access to such a wide range of facilities and machine environments as the Central Office.

Many users welcome an example of the use of each routine. The contributor writes this example program and the draft documentation to support his work. Contribution to the library is an onerous but invaluable activity that makes extensive algorithmic, programming and literary demands.

Validation

The task of the validator is to certify the algorithmic and literary work of the relevant contributor. The second stage in the development of the NAG Library seeks to ensure that the problems addressed by the library contents are relevant to user requirements, that each algorithm is selected after due consideration, and that the user documentation is clear and concise. Substandard or ill-conceived material is returned to the contributor for modification and improvement.

As all these activities involve individual assessment rather than incontrovertible fact, discussion and lively debate often ensue between contributor and validator.

Assembly

Once validated, the software and draft documentation are sent to the Central Office, whose staff are responsible for assembling and processing both the code and the documentation ready for general distribution at each new release (Mark) of the library.

As the library is the work of many individuals, there is inevitably inconsistency and confusion in interpretation and in satisfaction of agreed standards. Hence in assembling the codes and documentation provided by contributors, it is essential that we check for compliance with these standards. Wherever possible, these are machine proven, but there are certain standards which need to be checked by hand; for example, we must ensure that the relevant chapter design is being followed and that the user interface chosen for routines satisfies the demands of the general library structure.

Having checked that the draft documentation conforms to content and format standards, the material is added to a documentation data base. The input form is in a type-setting language (TSSD (Hooper, 1976)), to permit preparation of phototypeset masters for printing of the Library Manual, but from which an on-line form of documentation is extracted by program (Hague et al., 1980).

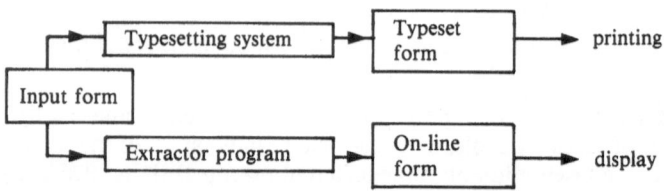

The following diagram indicates the major steps in the Central Office procedure for software processing.

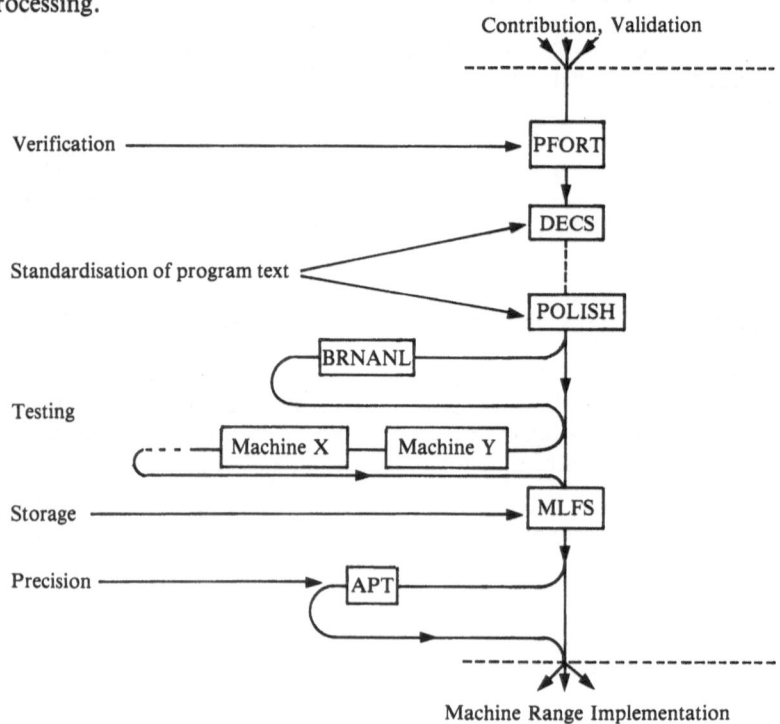

A few explanatory comments may be required:

— the verification stage is primarily linguistic; algorithmic validation has taken place at an earlier stage
— several minor text standardisation processes to introduce NAG conventions may be applied between DECS and POLISH
— in the testing phase, the purpose of the test runs on machines X, Y, ... is to gauge the extent to which test results may differ. This is in anticipation of the formal Library implementation activity later on.

Processing of the contributed software by the Central Office, whether automatic or manual, is designed to achieve the following functions (see Du Croz et al (1977), Hague (1978), Ryder (1975), Dorrenbacher et al. (1974), Fosdick (1974)):

— diagnosing a coding error either of an algorithmic or linguistic nature;
— altering a structural property of the text, e.g. imposing a particular order on non-executable statements in Fortran;
— standardising the appearance of the text;
— standardising nomenclature used, e.g. giving the same name to variables having the same function in different program units;
— conducting dynamic analysis of the text, e.g. by planting tracing calls;
— ensuring adherence to declared language standards or subsets thereof;
— changing an operational property of the text, e.g. changing the mode of arithmetic precision;
— coping with arithmetic, dialect and other differences between computing systems.

As further certification of the efficiency, accuracy and effectiveness of the contributed codes, Central Office staff run routines, together with implementation and example programs, on three different machine systems (ICL 1900 which has a 48 bit floating point word, IBM 370 with 4/8 bytes and CDC 7600 with 60 bit word).

Once certified, the routines are used to prepare an updated version of the "Contributed Library". This new version, known as a new Mark of the Library, is released once a year and consists of the last generally released version of the library, supplemented by the newly-certified routines and any other improvements or corrections. For example, at Mark 8, 95 new routines were added to the 395 routines in the library at Mark 7. The implementation and example program suites, and the NAG library documentation, are supplemented in a similar manner.

Implementation

One of the tasks of the Central Office is to coordinate all the implementations of the NAG Library. The number of such implementations depends upon precisely what is counted; at the crudest level the library is available on 28 distinct major machine ranges and is being implemented on two more. But taking into account:

— minor variations in hardware;
— different precision versions;
— different compiler versions;
the numbers of distinct compiled versions of the Library are:

	Fortran	Algol 60
	Mk 4 1	
Already available	Mk 5 3	Mk 5 4
	Mk 6 2	Mk 6 1
	Mk 7 10	Mk 7 11
	Mk 8 32	
New implementations in train	2	1

There is a good deal of scope for reducing the total amount of work spent in implementation if we take advantage of common features of the various machine ranges. For example, for Fortran double precision implementations, a production version of APT (developed in the NAG Central Office) automatically performs most of the conversion from the single precision "Contributed Library" to a double precision version. This is then the common starting-point for all double precision implementations.

These divide into two subgroups: the "IBM 360 like machines" with hexadecimal arithmetic and the machines with binary arithmetic.

The predicted source texts for each of the machines in the two subgroups have common requirements. All of the byte machines require special modified subroutines in the Special Function chapter. By historical accident, many of the machines with binary arithmetic (e.g. Honeywell, Xerox 530 and Univac 1100 (with FTN compiler)) have Fortran compilers which do not include a Double Precision Complex facility. The feature is simulated by Double Precision arrays, with an extra leading dimension of 2, and the amended source text used on these machines.

Coordination of implementations requires the Central Office

— to supply the initial software;
— to advise about any anticipated difficulties (e.g. machine code);
— to help solve any problems which arise;
— to ensure that the implementation is of an acceptable standard (e.g. by examining the computed results).

Each implementation starts from its "Predicted Library" tape prepared by the Central Office.

The tape holds:

— the "Predicted Library" source text in the relevant precision or precisions;
— the example programs each with their input data and results (all in the relevant precision (s));
— the implementation programs, each with their input data and results (all in the relevant precision (s)).

The function of the implementor is to read the material into filestore, and then systematically to compile and to test the routines, example programs and implementation test programs. The activity is essentially one of file handling, file management and file comparison. Sophisticated programs have been developed for automatic comparison of results.

IMPLEMENTATION TREE (FORTRAN)

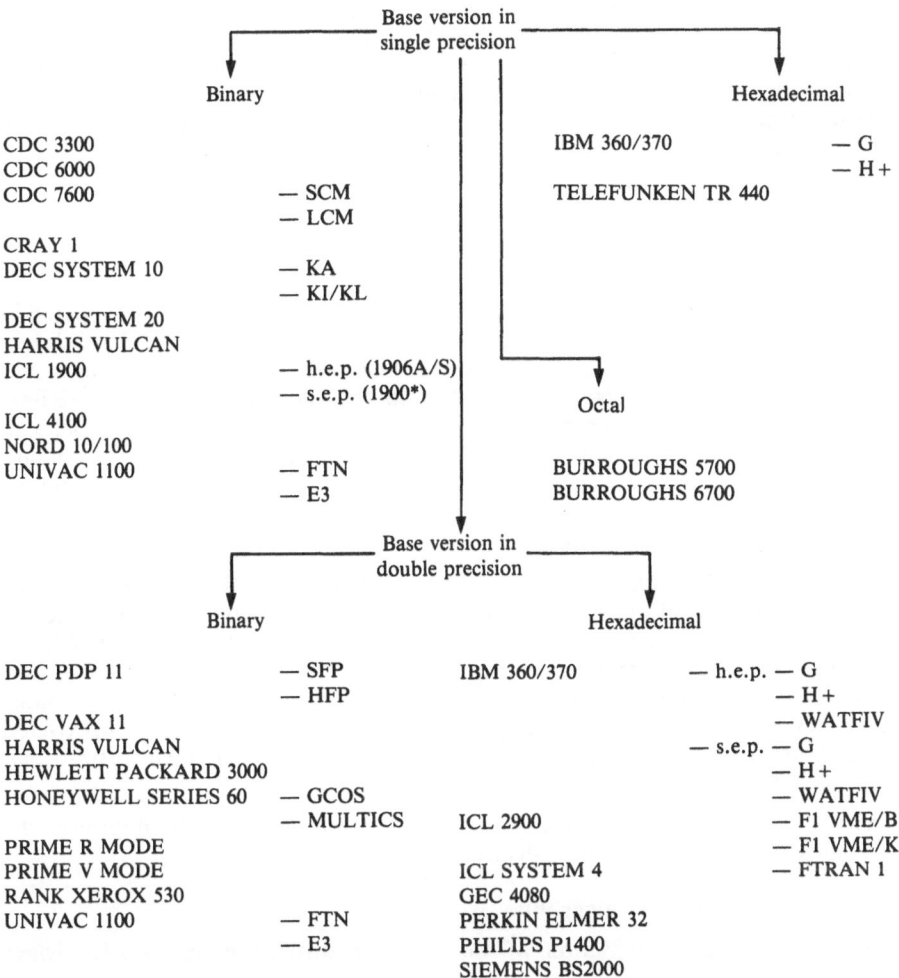

Base version in
single precision

Binary   Hexadecimal

CDC 3300   IBM 360/370   — G
CDC 6000   — H +
CDC 7600   — SCM   TELEFUNKEN TR 440
                     — LCM

CRAY 1
DEC SYSTEM 10   — KA
                     — KI/KL

DEC SYSTEM 20
HARRIS VULCAN
ICL 1900   — h.e.p. (1906A/S)
                     — s.e.p. (1900*)   Octal

ICL 4100
NORD 10/100
UNIVAC 1100   — FTN   BURROUGHS 5700
                     — E3   BURROUGHS 6700

Base version in
double precision

Binary   Hexadecimal

DEC PDP 11   — SFP   IBM 360/370   — h.e.p. — G
                     — HFP   — H +
DEC VAX 11   — WATFIV
HARRIS VULCAN   — s.e.p. — G
HEWLETT PACKARD 3000   — H +
HONEYWELL SERIES 60 — GCOS   — WATFIV
                     — MULTICS   ICL 2900   — F1 VME/B
PRIME R MODE   — F1 VME/K
PRIME V MODE   ICL SYSTEM 4   — FTRAN 1
RANK XEROX 530   GEC 4080
UNIVAC 1100   — FTN   PERKIN ELMER 32
                     — E3   PHILIPS P1400
                                  SIEMENS BS2000

Distribution

Each implementor prepares a certified library distribution tape. This contains a
precompiled version of the implemented library, the source text of the routines from
which it was prepared, and the example programs plus the input data and results
computed during its certification. The structure and format of the tape are chosen
to be optimum for the given implementation. The contents and form of the tape are
described in a Library Support Note, which also advise the Library site staff how to
read the software off the tape into filestore.

Service

The NAG project has always emphasised the importance of distribution, and basing its library service, on a tested, object module library. Each site simply reads the library software into filestore, and may then with confidence make it available immediately to their users. There is an annual update of the library mark (version) and intermediate correction of software and documentation errors, if required. A numerical and software advisory service by telephone, telex and letter is available from our two offices - and consultancy advice can also be arranged.

5. THE NEED FOR SEPARATE IMPLEMENTATIONS

It might be thought that once the base versions of the library had been prepared in accordance with our declared approach, a separate implementation phase should not be necessary, or should at most be a straightforward process of assigning values to the machine parameters, compiling the library and assessing the test results. However NAG has always emphasised the need, in real life, for a corrective phase in implementation (Hague and Ford, 1976), because we nearly always encounter unanticipated problems, which might be regarded as obstacles to transportability.

Errors in NAG Library Routines

It is not surprising that testing the Library on a very wide range of machine configurations should uncover some errors in it (even though it has been tested in three very different environments before it is released for implementation). What is perhaps surprising is that, of all the errors reported in the library over a two year period, 22 were discovered during the implementation phase (and the corrections immediately communicated to all implementors), compared with only 18 discovered by user sites. (Another four were discovered by contributors after their software had been included in the library.)

Therefore thorough testing during implementation significantly improves the reliability of the base version of the library.

Imperfect adaptability of algorithms

Although our parameterisation of the machine arithmetic has nearly always provided a satisfactory model for our contributors to work with, occasionally their algorithms have been shown not to adapt as well as possible to some subtler features of machine arithmetic. When one of our routines was tested on the Honeywell Series 60, the results for one problem were only accurate to 2 or 3 significant digits, whereas on other machines they were accurate almost to the precision of the machine. The cause proved to be this: for the Honeywell double precision implementation, the underflow threshold (2^{-129}) is not much smaller than the square of the relative machine precision (2^{-62}). During computation rounding errors introduced a value of about $0.01 \times$ machine precision which in exact arithmetic would have been zero; subsequent computation should have compensated for this perturbation, but the routine tested the square of the offending value: this underflowed, the compensating computation was skipped, and the errors festered. Again this was a fault in the base version of the Library which has now been corrected.

However in our experience the unanticipated problems of implementation have more often been caused by deficiencies in the computing configuration (hardware, Fortran compiler, link-editor, compiler library) than by deficiencies in the NAG Library - especially as the library is implemented on an increasing number of mini-computers.

Hardware Errors

Fortunately, these are very rare but we did encounter them in the initial stages of implementation on the ICL 2980 and the Prime 400. They have been corrected.

Compiler Errors

This is the most common cause of unanticipated problems; most implementations encounter at least one compiler error. Even with the CDC FTN compiler there has been a dwindling, but still nonempty set of routines which cannot be correctly compiled at the highest level of optimisation. There have been similar optimisation problems with the DEC 10 compiler.

Those problems can be avoided simply by recompiling at a lower level of optimisation. Others can only be avoided by modifying the source text, e.g. two types of error on the Burroughs 6700 connected with the use of subroutine-name parameters. On two machines the compiler proved to be so unreliable that the implementation could not be completed until a new version of the compiler became available.

Although our software cannot be guaranteed to exercise all the code in the Library — so that a compiler error might slip through — we do not know of any user site reporting an error in the NAG Library which has been traced to a compiler error. More than one manufacturer has asked to use the library and test programs to test their compiler.

Compiler Limitations

Some compilers have failed to compile the library because of poorly documented restrictions e.g. on the level of nesting of parentheses in expressions, or on the number of subroutine parameters; and in some cases these restrictions have been overcome merely by reconfiguring the compiler.

Link-editor Errors

(alias loader, binder, consolidator, composer etc.)

This is another area of poorly documented restrictions e.g. on the total number of library routines that can be linked to one main program or on the number of levels of library routines calling other library routines that can be permitted.

Errors in the compiler Library

The mathematical functions in the compiler library (e.g. SQRT, SIN, EXP) are nearly always taken on trust. Yet if they fail to perform to the required accuracy, they will degrade the performance of the NAG Library routines which call them. On the Prime 400, the test program for calculating eigenvectors by inverse iteration failed to produce an acceptable eigenvector: the cause was an insufficiently accurate eigenvalue which in turn was the result of inaccuracies in the DSQRT routine, which Prime has admitted. There is an obvious need for an independent test program to test the compiler library functions.

Thus, in the diagram at the head of the section, the feedback loops from the implementation phase are repeatedly being activated. Implementation problems prompt us sometimes to correct the base version of the library, sometimes to refine the standards that we impose, sometimes to tighten the checks that we make. To cure other problems, modifications to the source text are confined to the implementation concerned, especially when the problems arise from faults in the machine environment - in which case we hope that the modifications will be only temporary until the fault has been corrected.

Finally the fact that this corrective phase in implementation continues to be necessary justifies NAG's policy of always distributing to sites a compiled and tested version of the library (as well as the source text). Numerical software is not fully developed until it has been shown to perform satisfactorily in each computing configuration in which it is going to be used. Comprehensive testing in each configuration is essential to ensure:

a) that the algorithms adapt correctly to the configuration;
b) that the configuration is fit to support the software.

6. OPERATIONAL PRINCIPLES

1. Consultation: enables the Library to address problems met by users, and the NAG Project to serve the needs and requirements of all its parts.
2. Collaboration: gives access to the required expertise and knowledge.
3. Coordination: permits individual parts of the Library to be developed independently, within a unified structure.
4. Planning: permits overall design of individual chapter contents.
5. Standards: ensure the effectiveness and reliability of the product developed.
6. Mechanisation: minimises the cost of development, distribution and maintenance, and is the most reliable method of software processing.
7. Service: encourages wide and regular use of the Library.

7. CONCLUSIONS

A project such as the one we have described must, of necessity, involve staff with different abilities, background and interests. It has to combine its academic staff, responsible for library contents, and its commercial staff required for servicing the library. In our organisation this involves both volunteers, responsible in the main for providing up-to-date contents and indeed new language versions, and the full-time employees responsible for the coordination of the library activity and maintenance of the Library Service.

For the project to be successful there must be rigour, to ensure that quality and reliability are achieved and maintained, and yet there must be flexibility, to enable cooperation and to optimise the service for each and every implementation. We depend upon enthusiasm to broaden the coverage provided the library, and yet we require expertise in order to achieve a balanced, general-purpose numerical Library Service.

It is evident that the production of high quality numerical software is not an exact science but a branch of software engineering which must take account of the vagaries of a real and changing world. The approach which serves us well now will not necessarily continue to do so.

REFERENCES

Bentley J. and Ford B. (1977), On the enhancement of portability in the NAG project - a statistical survey, in Portability of Numerical Software (ed. W. Cowell), Berlin: Springer-Verlag.

Cody W.J. (1974), The construction of numerical subroutine libraries, SIAM Review Vol. 16 No. 1 pp. 36-46.

Dorrenbacher J., Paddock D., Wisneski D. and Fosdick L.D. (1974), POLISH, a Fortran program to edit Fortran programs, Dept of Computer Science, University of Colorado at Boulder, Ref. No. CU-CS-050-74.

Du Croz J.J. and Fosdick L.D. (1982), Incorporating a suite of routines into a library: a case history (in preparation).

Du Croz J.J., Hague S. and Siemieniuch J.L. (1977), Aids to portability within the NAG project, in Portability of Numerical Software (ed. W. Cowell), Berlin: Springer-Verlag.

Ford B. (1977), Preparing conventions for parameters for transporting numerical software, in Portability of Numerical Software (ed. W. Cowell), Berlin: Springer-Verlag.

Ford B. and Bentley J. (1978), A library design for all parties, in Numerical Software - Needs and Availability (ed. D.A.M. Jacobs), London: Academic Press.

Ford B., Hague S.J. and Smith B.T. (1982), Some transformations of numerical software (in press).

Fosdick L.D. (1974), BRNANL - a Fortran program to identify basic blocks in Fortran programs, Dept of Computer Science, University of Colorado at Boulder, Ref. No.: CM-CS-040-74.

Hague S.J. (1978), Software Tools, in Numerical Software - Needs and Availability (ed. D.A.M. Jacobs), London: Academic Press.

Hague S.J. and Ford B. (1976), Portability - Predicition and Correction, Software Practice and Experience Vol. 6, pp. 61-69.

Hague S.J. and Nugent S.M. (1980), Computer - based Documentation for a Multi-Machine Library, in Practice in Software Adaption and Maintenance (ed. Ebert, Luegger & Goecke), Amsterdam: North Holland.

Hooper M.J. (1976), TSSD, a typesetting system for scientific documents, AERE-R 8574, (13), London: HMSO.

Ryder, B.G. (1974), The PFORT Verifier, Software Practice and Experience Vol. 4, pp. 359-377.

Ryder B.G. (1975), The PFORT Verifier: User's Guide. Bell Telephone Laboratories, Technical Report No. 12.

TRANSPORTABLE USER DOCUMENTATION FOR NUMERICAL SOFTWARE

Brian Ford
NAG Central Office
Oxford, UK

1. INTRODUCTION: THE DEMAND FOR TRANSPORTABLE DOCUMENTATION

User requirements

It is a truism of the computing world that numerical software can only ever be as good as its user documentation. A programmer can only reliably learn of the contents of a package and of its user interface by consulting the documentation. This implies not only good presentation and information content; easy availability and access to the documentation is also essential. We have seen that in general we should aim to produce transportable software. If we are not to have a plethora of different (and therefore costly) documentation it should itself be transportable and be written to support transportable software. The programmer will prefer this because he may wish to use the same library or package:
(i) on different machines
(ii) in different precisions of computation.

He may also wish to use the same library in different computing languages. However, the varying semantics of languages require different calling sequences for the same algorithm realised in the different languages (or, less elegantly, calling compiled Fortran subroutines from user programs in other languages). A single library manual, for several languages, whilst feasible, would be most cumbersome and have few obvious advantages. Language specific documentation appears desirable. However the same structure, form and style should be used for each body of information so that the user having mastered one language manual (say) could easily find his way around all others.

D. T. Muxworthy (ed.), *Programming for Software Sharing, 225–234.*

Developer's Requirements

The developer has an interest in producing transportable documentation for he wishes to reach as wide an audience as possible with his software. Were he to produce machine-specific documentation for each machine the costs would be greater, the capital outlay larger and the problems of error-correction and administration increased. He is therefore much happier producing documentation which can be produced in volume, and can satisfy all of his customers.

The software developer also has demands that influence the design, structure and form of the documentation. The software may be:
(i)   expanded or modified to form a new version
(ii) implemented more widely
(iii) written into new languages.

This influences not only the structure, format and content of the documentation and the modes in which it is presented but also the fundamental technology by which it is prepared. The design of the documentation must provide the flexibility to accommodate these developments as easily as possible. This flexibility may not be secured by degrading the ability of the documentation to support the software in use. For example environment-specific information *should not contradict* earlier general comment. The documentation is designed so that specific information complements earlier general comments.

2. A MEANS OF WRITING TRANSPORTABLE DOCUMENTATION

The NAG Approach

Transportable documentation to support transportable software is achieved by focussing on the conceptual model of all computers and writing the documentation for that model. One avoids thinking about the idiosyncracies of any particular machine. Since the parameters of the model may be used freely, yet specifically, the documentation is tailored for each environment in which the software is ultimately installed once the specific values of the parameters for a given system are provided. Hence NAG's transportable documentation is achieved by writing generalised documentation, which focusses on our conceptual model of all machines, complemented by limited specific information for each individual machine range. The nature of the binding possible for different modes of presentation of information means that for printed documentation individual implementation documents are necessary to supplement the printed manual, whilst for on-line information — applicable for a specific machine — parameter keywords can be replaced by specific values.

3. THE DESIGN OF TRANSPORTABLE DOCUMENTATION

Documentation Design

If the software is to attract users from a wide variety of scientific disciplines then the user documentation should contain introductory material and general advice as well as specific information on individual pieces of software.

The specific information should provide algorithmic and performance aspects of the routine as well as the essential operational specification (purpose, calling sequence, parameter specification, error and warning indicators) and an example of use. Keywords for on-line use and for manual indexing are also important.

4. THE NAG APPROACH

The Use of the Documentation

Users approach documentation of software seeking answers to a variety of questions. The questions vary from the general to the very specific. For example for the Numerical Algorithms Group Library the questions include:

> What is in the Library? What does it cover?
> Will it solve my proplem?
> Is Curve and Surface Fitting in the Library?
> Can I understand the documentation?
> Will it help me learn what sort of fitting problem I have got?
> Will it tell me which routine to use?
> Does it have an SVD routine for band matrices?
> Will it show me how to use the routine?
> What are all these parameters for?
> What does IFAIL = 2 mean for E01BAF?

The user documentation must be designed to answer all of these questions (and many more). The solution adopted by NAG is to advise the new users to:

(a) read the whole of the ESSENTIAL INTRODUCTION;
(b) consult either the CONTENTS or KEYWORDS INDEX document to choose an appropriate chapter or routine;
(c) read the relevant *Chapter Introduction* document;
(d) choose a *routine*;
(e) read the approriate *implementation* document;
(f) read the *routine document*. If the routine does not after all meet his needs, return to steps (b) or (c);
(g) read the description of the IFAIL parameter in the *P01 Chapter Introduction* (if relevant);
(h) consult *local documentation* about access to the NAG Library on his computing system.

The user should then be in a position to include a call to the routine in a program and to attempt to run it. He may of course need to refer back to the relevant documentation in case of difficulties, for advice on assessment of results, and so on.

As the user becomes familiar with the Library some of steps (a) to (h) can be omitted but it is always essential to:

> be familiar with the Chapter Introduction document
> read the routine document
> refer to the implementation document.

Three distinct mechanisms may be used by the programmer, to reach the required routine document (which describes the software he hopes/believes will solve his problem). He goes in via the chapter introduction (with its flow charts for routine selection etc.) or the chapter index (list of routines in the chapter) or the keyword index. The more detailed his knowledge, the quicker he will be able to get to the routine document.

These three mechanisms are the same for all implementations of the Library. The price to the programmer of using documentation which supports transportable software is interpretation of the slightly generalised routine document, and the need always to read the appropriate implementation document.

Chapter Introductions

Most programs, packages and libraries can be broken down into constituent parts Each part is generally made up of a few, perhaps many, subroutines. The value of recognising constituent parts is that it allows examination and discussion of different functions or aspects independently of other factors. The unique problems and features of each part can be recognised. The effective usage of the package can thereby be significantly advanced. Self-teaching, which is essential in all computing, is immediately promoted.

For the NAG Library the division is by numerical areas, with each area given its own chapter. Further subdivision within each chapter follows the subdivision of the area of mathematics. Ideally there is one algorithm (the "best" algorithm) for each problem type within that area. The purpose of the Chapter Introductions is to help the programmer identify the numerical characteristics of his problem and lead him to the specific routine included in the Library to solve it.

Each Chapter Introduction consists of three sections:
1. Scope of the Chapter
2. Background of the Problems
3. Recommendations on Choice and Use of Routines.

The third section often includes decision trees, whose leaves consist of the names of specific routines, and an index, whose entries point to specific routines.

Each chapter also has a contents summary.

Routine Documents

Each routine document describes a routine of the same name and has 13 numbered sections with the following headings:
1. Purpose
2. Specification
3. Description
4. References
5. Parameters
6. Error Indicators
7. Auxiliary Routines
8. Timing
9. Storage
10. Accuracy
11. Further Comments
12. Keywords
13. Example

The sections on Purpose, References, Auxiliary Routines and Keywords are totally implementation-independent.

The sections on Descriptions, Error Indicators, Timing, Storage and Accuracy may refer to machine parameters (aspects of the conceptual machine) and include implementation-specific information. For example the section on Accuracy will often discuss the accuracy of the computed result and hence refer to the relative machine precision.

Timing varies widely between implementations. Section 8 may indicate how the timing varies as, for example, the order of a matrix varies.

The sections on Specification, Parameters and Example address the awkward problems that arise from transportable software. The precision of computation may be single or double. Many programmers will wish to run parts of their program in each of the two precisions to determine the accuracy of their results.

Repeated sections for Specification and Parameters in each routine document for each precision would make already substantial documentation too voluminous (and expensive). Hence italicised terms are used to indicate different interpretations in different implementations (e.g. *real* may mean REAL or DOUBLE PRECISION)

2. Specification
   SUBROUTINE D01BCF (ITYPE, A, B, C, D, N, WEIGHT, ABSCIS, IFAIL)
   C INTEGER ITYPE, N, IFAIL
   C *real* A, B, C, D, WEIGHT (N), ABSCIS (N)
5. Parameters
   A - *real*.
   on entry A must specify....

The example program in Section 13 of each routine document illustrates a simple call of the routine. In addition to modification of the program text to take account of issues of precision there arises the more fundamental question of the computed results. Whilst ideally the sample problem will return an identical result on all machines (through selection of a well-conditioned problem with simple input data and returning the result to limited accuracy), not all numerical areas easily provide such examples and appreciating when comparable results have been achieved may occasionally involve substantial numerical insight.

The discussion thus far has ignored what is perhaps the most difficult problem for transportable software available in different precisions, and hence for its documentation. We have seen that often a user will require to run his program in single and in double precision. Inevitably this will require two separate versions of the library software. However some auxiliary routines, to achieve single (double) precision results, will require their computations to be carried out to double (triple/quadruple) precision. For other auxiliary routines there will not be this requirement.

Under the ANSI Fortran 1966 Standard routine names could only have six characters. In a body of software with 466 primary routines and 436 auxiliary routines, where each of the first five characters is taken up with numerical area and problem type classification, unique identification of each routine becomes a challenge. In addition two sites with identical computing configurations might prefer to emphasise a different computing precision as the basis of their local service. Sites opted to have *annaa*F as their standard computing precision, and *annaa*E as the routine computing for the other precision. Hence a program calling the same routine by the same name on a similar system can achieve a different precision of computation. The precision of calculation computed on a given system when a routine *annaa*F is called is defined in the local documentation. Fortunately for the vast majority of implementations this problem does not arise and the precision of the standard library implementation is the same throughout the machine range.

Implementation Documents

For the flexibility of being able to run his program on many different machines, confident of access to the same library, the programmer must also read the appropriate implementation document. This document (revised at each release of the software) gives any necessary *additional* information which applies specifically to the implementation. In particular it notes the precision of the standard library implementation (*annaa*F) and advises the user of a specific implementation
— the interpretation of italicised terms
— the values of parameters of the conceptual machine
— how to modify the published example programs, and where to expect significant differences in results.

For most implementations of the NAG Library the implementation document is a few sides (4-10), complementing a manual of some 3000 sides. Due to the constant demand for the information in the document it is available on-line at most Library sites.

5. ON-LINE INFORMATION

Routine Summaries

Inevitably not all users will have easy or immediate access to the printed manual. Many will work via computer networks where much user documentation is provided on-line. Some programmers prefer to work solely or largely at their terminals rather than consulting libraries and completing preparatory work at their desks. A balance has to be struck between the cost of providing filestore and computing power to support on-line documentation and the level and amount of information users need and can effectively use via a terminal. For NAG an acceptable compromise appears to be to provide an extended summary of use on-line. This serves as:
— adequate, self contained documentation of a routine either where the routine is straightforward to use, or where the user is familiar with the subject area and understands the concepts and terms used;
— a reminder to the user of the role of a particular parameter or about the significance of an error indicator (where the user has previously consulted the full documentation);
— a detailed pointer to the suitability of a routine for a user's problem (the user then consults the printed documentation).

The summary of use is an operational specification of the routine describing the purpose of the routine, its calling sequence, specification of parameters and error and warning indicators. An example of use is also provided. The representation of the information inevitably depends on the breadth of character set made available upon a particular machine and via a given terminal. Whilst simple portability might suggest using a restricted character set available on all machines (72 ASCII Set - involving only upper case), use of a single data-base for extraction and preparation of copy for the various modes of documentation also permits the flexibility to use the broadest character set feasible on a given configuration. The presentation of the material also poses a significant challenge.

The operational specification includes all the sections that contain the generalised information to enable one information source to support different precisions of computation on different machines. However transformation of the generalised terms to become machine configuration specific is possible before the information is made available (for example complex or *complex* is of type COMPLEX*16 for IBM equipment and type COMPLEX*D for the ICL 2900 computed in double precision). Further, if machine resources permit, the on-line information can be provided in the various precision-specific versions with the actual routine names etc. for the local computing service.

The Need for Portability

We have seen that the material made available by NAG in on-line summaries is an extraction from the printed documentation. Due to the many different computing environments in which it is used its preparation requires careful attention to questions of representation and presentation. When we consider the availability of chapter introductions in printed, micromedia and on-line form we again recognise the need to extract certain essential information for the immediacy of on-line interrogation, leaving much of the background information for consultation at the desk or in the library. However if the on-line information is to be available in a reasonably portable and efficient form we must become concerned with the portable interfaces of our enquiry system and the integrity and extensibility of our information database.

Routine Selection

Selection of the desired routine to solve a user's problem by on-line techniques is apparently a straightforward problem. One simply takes the decision trees given in the chapter introduction of the printed manual and makes them available on-line. Unfortunately the matter is far from straightforward.

First it is evident that many people do not follow a single path through the flow charts by response to a series of binary questions. Programmers scan the decision trees to discern the types of questions they are being asked to respond to, seek broad answers (or simply develop impressions) to the questions raised, and then on the basis of this multi-level consideration select a particular path and hence a particular routine. Second in a number of instances the decision trees are not totally binary structures. There are iterative cycles included in the charts.

To achieve the ability to scan (at least to a limited extent) it is desirable to be able to backtrack when interrogating the information on-line. In general this requires a tree-processing based system. Such systems are the subject of active computer science research at the present time. Certainly the aim of an efficient and portable system is unlikely to be achieved by one system for use on many different machine ranges. An interesting attempt is NITPACK (Gaffney et al, 1981).

Foregoing the possibility of a portable system one can achieve perhaps the fundamental requirement of efficiency by defining a portable interface for the data, and building sufficient structure into the data to enable its handling to be implemented efficiently (if differently) on different machines. Further with careful repetition of some data, iterative elements within the decision trees can be eliminated so that an essentially binary reply system is achieved. A well tried approach is then the Cambridge HELP system (Hazel et al, 1980).

On-line information systems require many characteristics. Perhaps the primary one is that a system should be flexible. People rarely appear to agree what features an on-line information system should have. Hence we require a system that can accommodate itself to individual desires and requirements.

Requirements for on-line Documentation

Listing documentation at a terminal or printer means that a far more restrictive character set must be employed (as compared with the printed documentation) and minimal assumptions about carriage control made.

This is particularly so for documentation for transportable numerical software as it will be listed on a wide variety of printing and display devices. The on-line form of information can be viewed as a reduced form of the master files (from which the printed documentation is ultimately derived) in at least two senses:
(i) it must be a simpler, more restrictive representation of the information in the master files since it has to be capable of reproduction on a wide variety of devices including terminals with short line widths, no backspace or underline facility and little more than the Fortran 66 character set available;
(ii) some parts of the documentation, particularly mathematical expressions are very difficult to express clearly on a conventional terminal or printer. Moreover the slow speed of some devices and the limited storage available at some user sites indicate that the on-line form must have reduced information content (for example, for the NAG routine documentation only the operational specification of the routine is provided on-line).

6. MICROFICHE

Requirements of Microfiche

The same level of detail of information is required by the user from microfiche as from the printed documentation. The preferred format of the information on the fiche is different to that in the printed manual if we are to achieve the clarity of presentation necessary for users to extract information quickly and without ambiguity. Since the cost of preparing individual sets of microfiche is much less than printing manuals on paper, recovery of the capital cost of preparing the master documents is far more difficult (than for the printed manual) if the old technology of IBM golf-ball typewriter is employed. However suitable masters for fiche preparation can be made by transforming the machine-based document files and by selection of typesetting styles sensitive to microfiche requirements.

7. PRINTED DOCUMENTATION

Production

The traditional means of producing printed documentation was to type master documents using IBM golf-ball typewriters and prepare printing plates from them. What advantages does computer based documentation have over this approach?
— more compact printed forms are possible by employing a computer-based typesetting system
— there was only one set of typed masters whilst machine readable masters are reproducible
— machine-based documents are readily updatable
— there is greater scope for producing variant publications by transforming or selecting parts of the master document files.

Computer-based documentation introduces new skills for both clerical and technical staff. Clerical staff find it is more sympathetic to typing and transcription errors, and more flexible in its handling of layouts and formats than traditional methods, but have to learn the semantics of data-input and typesetting systems to be able to sustain the production of high quality masters over a long period of time. Technical staff are more easily able to submit author's corrections at late dates in production, and thus become more heavily involved in proof-reading.

Appropriate computing facilities (both hardware and software) must be available — some computers are not suited to text processing (e.g. ICL 1900) — supporting data input, typesetting data storage and maintenance systems. Finally the change to a new technology should ideally reduce overall costs, and provide a better quality product than the old technology.

Given machine-based document files typesetting offers the prospect of fine control over layout, a wide range of characters and different sizes and typefaces of script. An important element in scientific and technical documentation is the use of mathematical expressions, so any suitable computer-based typesetting system must provide powerful features for composing such expressions.

It must also have adequate facilities for general text processing e.g. vertical and horizontal spacing, indentation control, headings, footing, justification. Given such a system it should be possible to maintain or to improve upon the quality of conventionally produced masters; to achieve the clarity of presentation necessary for users to extract the information quickly and without ambiguity.

8. DOCUMENTATION AND DATABASES

The Possibility of Using Just One Database

Whilst each mode of presentation of the document has its own special needs and requirements it is evident that the material all derives from the same body of information. It is feasible, reliable and effective to create a single database of documentation from which copy for printed, micro-media and on-line forms is extracted and prepared.

The NAG Approach

The first reduction for preparation of the on-line information is a technical problem solved by writing an extraction program which maps the typesetting language into a simpler form for on-line publication. The second reduction is more philosophical in nature because we must ask ourselves what the role of on-line documentation is and how it should relate to the printed reference documentation.

If we conclude that the on-line form should provide programming information only about the software, as opposed to including algorithmic information too, or indeed requiring additional information specific to an on-line/interactive environment and hence not given in the reference documentation, then this may be extracted from the database of the document masters. The preparation of the database will be fundamentally geared to preparation of masters for the printed manual, and the copy for the other forms will be derived from them. Should additional information to that provided for the printed manual be thought necessary, a preferred strategy will require careful formulation, involving a single database, or a database augmented by additional material (directly or via pointers), or two separate bodies of information: and whether the basic information is to be held in the typesetting language or a form more suitable for the on-line information.

9. CONCLUSIONS

It is in both the users' and the software developers' interests to write transportable documentation. In this way costs can be minimised and the amount of documentation required by a user kept as small as possible.

Although documentation may be produced in three forms (printed, on-line and microfiche), which separately make special demands, it is possible to produce all from a single database.

REFERENCES

Gaffney P.W., Wooten J.W. and Kessel K.A. (1981), NITPACK - a Numerical Interactive Tree Package. Tech. Report ORNL/CSD - 89, Union Carbide Corp., Nuclear Division, Oak Ridge, Tennessee.

Hazel P. and O'Donohoe M.R. (1980), HELP Numerical: The Cambridge Interactive Documentation System for Numerical Methods - in Production and Assessment of Numerical Software, ed. M.A. Hennell and L.M. Delves. Academic Press.

DATA SHARING IN DISTRIBUTED COMPUTING SYSTEMS

Fabio Schreiber,
Università di Parma
Parma, Italy

In this chapter the different ways of sharing data through computer networks are reviewed, and attention is focused on distributed databases. The distribution features of a DDB are examined with respect to the application needs. Possible architectures for a DDB management system are considered and a quick mention is made of the problem of keeping data integrity.

1. INTRODUCTION

The availability of commercially operated computer networks has brought to an outstanding level the importance of software shareability and transferability among many different users, working on different computers. In fact, even if the efforts of achieving program portability from one machine to another are as old as programming itself, they have not achieved, to date, highly satisfactory results and everybody has undergone the frustrating experience of transferring a standard Fortran routine from one machine to a different one having to recode more or less extended parts of it. In a computer network, where software sharing by hundreds of users is standard and fundamental, the capability of a highly efficient and reliable transportability becomes vital; the possibility of on-line operation makes the request for efficiency much more dramatic than when sharing occurs by sending magnetic tapes around the world.

While other parts of this volume focus on the problem of program sharing, in this chapter we shall point out the major issues in sharing data among a community of users and we shall show, in particular, the architectures and the functions of Distributed Database Management Systems (DDBMS).

It is worth mentioning that, while the sharing of programs is mainly achieved by means of techniques which enhance their portability, the sharing of data is mainly achieved by techniques which access them where they are "naturally" stored. The rationale for that lies in the very large volume of many databases which makes it very expensive, if not impossible, to move them around the world.

D. T. Muxworthy (ed.), Programming for Software Sharing, 235–246.

Therefore, since the beginning of the distributed computing systems era, data have been considered one of the most interesting resources to be shared in the system, and a considerable number of studies have been made and prototype systems for distributed data management have been implemented in recent years. The reasons claimed for such an interest are many; among them the following can be mentioned:

— *Reliability*: a strongly centralized system is highly vulnerable to damage caused by hardware and/or software failures or by inadvertancy. Once damaged, operation is denied to everybody. On the other hand, a distributed system, even if suffering from failures, undergoes a graceful degradation, still allowing users to operate on it with a reduced functionality. Conversely recovery procedures, to reestablish data integrity in a distributed system after a failure, are more complex, as we shall see later on.

— *Load sharing*: computing centers having complementary utilization profiles can be connected into a distributed system in such a way as to better utilize existing resources by sharing the total load among them. Even the time difference between two computing centers placed far away from each other could be a reason for sharing computing power among similar loads but with peaks occurring at different "system absolute time".

— *Resource sharing*: one of the most popular reason claimed for distributed systems is the possibility of using very specialized resources ranging from entire computers (e.g. ILLIAC IV array computer), to special terminals (e.g. graphical plotters or displays, robot arms, etc) to specialized software (e.g. special compilers, application programs, etc), to common data (i.e. distributed databases), which are held in a common pool.

— *Efficiency*: handling very large masses of centralized data can result in a loss of efficiency of the system. For example, the unloading and reloading of a database to perform physical reorganization and maintenance can be a very long operation resulting in reduced availability. Also response times can be severely affected if the database grows above a critical size. In a distributed system these deficiencies can be overcome by a suitable distribution of data among the different machines allowing the optimization of several parameters.

— *Efficacy*: a distributed philosophy naturally allows the decomposition of a complex multifunction system into a set of simpler interconnected systems, each of them being specifically designed to perform at the best cost/performance level. Also a better service to the user is claimed for distributed systems, even if this factor cannot be easily defined and quantified.

— *Flexibility*: a distributed system, by its own nature, can grow and modify its structure without major restructuring efforts. Often, components of the system can be added or taken away only by modifying some system tables without disturbing the on-going operations. This fact allows a "physiological" fitting to the needs of the organization the information system works for.

— *Human engineering*: a very strong centralization of EDP services has proved harmful to the psychological attitudes of the employees and of the middle management; lots of misunderstandings arose between the end users and the system analysts placed far apart from each other, and in many cases they led to the rejection of the computing services by the end users themselves. Also, the sense of power associated with the possession of data contributed to the success of a decentralized philosophy for the EDP systems and data management.

— *Economy*: some authors claim also economical reasons in favour of distributed information systems. However, too little experience has been gained up to now on the economical dynamics of distributed systems to formulate conclusions. We can only point out that while the hardware costs are decreasing, the costs of software tend to rise (or to remain constant, at best) penalizing the considerably higher amount of complexity involved in the system software to control distributed systems. On the other hand, the costs of telecommunication facilities, the third component of distributed systems, are heavily affected by political factors, which mainly dictate the leasing tariffs.

2. DATA SHARING IN THE DISTRIBUTED ENVIRONMENT

When speaking of distributed computing systems we mean a collection of computing devices connected through telecommunication facilites. However the connection can be made in many different ways, giving rise to very different families of systems. In particular we shall mention three main classes:

a) Tightly coupled systems
   This class includes multiprocessor devices which communicate through one or more shared buses and/or one or more shared memories.

b) Loosely coupled/high bandwith systems
   This class includes those systems constituted by many processors connected through serial high-bandwith telecommunication lines such as coaxial cables or optical fibers. They are usually called *Local Computer Networks*.

c) Loosely coupled/low bandwith systems
   This class includes those systems constituted by many processors connected through serial low-bandwith telecommunication lines such as the telephone or the data networks. They are usually called *Geographical Computer Networks*.

The system architecture heavily influences the structure of the data management system. Systems of type a) can be usefully used in building database machines, i.e. special purpose computers entirely devoted to the management of large quantities of data. Systems of type b) tend to be used in connection with a distribution-by-function philosophy. In this case the machine devoted to data management is called a back-end computer, even if this name is not peculiar to such architectures. The back-end computer can be a general purpose machine on which the database management system runs as the only function, or it can be a database machine.

Finally, in systems of b) and c), data can be stored at different nodes in the form of local databases, which can be accessed by any other node through the computer network.

In the following we are going to examine this solution in more detail. Fig. 1 shows a computer communication network with several host (nodes) connected to it.

In such a structure many different ways of sharing data are possible, and have been described in the technical literature. In this section, we are going to mention very briefly those which are the most typical. Then, in the rest of the chapter, we shall focus our attention on the most evolved: the Distributed Database (DDB).

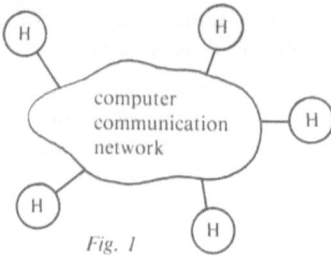

Fig. 1

Independent Databases Connected to a Computer Network

The development of commercial computer networks like ARPANET, DATAPAC, EURONET, INFONET, TELENET, TRANSPAC, and many others, allows network users to access remotely databases, existing on host computers connected to the network itself. These databases, however, are completely independent both as to their contents and as to their management systems (Fig. 2).

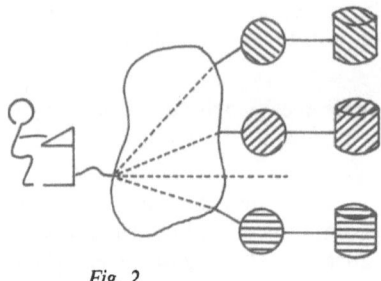

Fig. 2

What differentiates this system from a classical centralized teleprocessing (TP) system is the fact that the computer network allows a homogeneous connection with many different machines and, hopefully, lower operational costs.

Independent Databases with a Standard Command Language

This kind of system is a direct evolution of those described above. In this case it is still the task of the user to connect himself to the appropriate host computer and to ask it for access to the database he wants to interact with. However, the user is now freed from the need of knowing the details of the database itself and of its management system since he is provided with a standard command language which interfaces all the — possibly heterogeneous — local data management systems (Fig. 3).

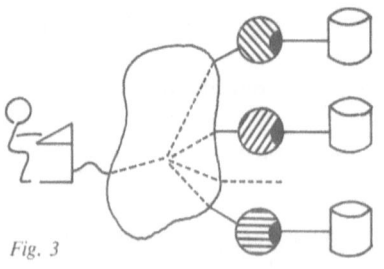

Fig. 3

Such a kind of system is represented by the DIANE service, which is offered by EURONET, interfacing as many as 300 Databases stored at 36 different Hosts (April 1982).

Distributed Database

For many years, database has been a synonym for a highly centralized data organization. This is not in contradiction with a physical partitioning of data among many different sites. In fact, what distinguishes a distributed database from the systems described in the preceeding sections, is that the data, even if stored at different sites, all belong to the same universe and are logically related with each other. Therefore the user is given only a global knowledge either of the whole database (network or global conceptual schema) or of part the database relevant to his application (global external schema), and an integrated access method which makes the physical data location transparent to him. Moreover, the integrity and consistency of the whole database must be preserved at all sites, in spite of possibly partially executed transactions aborted while operating on several sites simultaneously (Fig. 4).

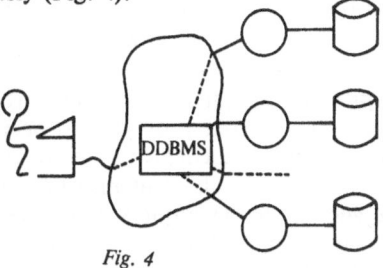

Fig. 4

3. DISTRIBUTION FEATURES IN A DDB

Necessary for the existence of a DDB are the distribution of the processing power (i.e., the existence of a computer network) and a physical distribution of data. However a third parameter, the *control* over the DDB, further partitions the DDB systems into two major classes:

— *Hierarchical DDB's*, when a master node exists in the system which controls the flow of the distributed operations in the whole DDB - exceptions being made for those operations belonging to a transaction which can be completely processed at a single site (local transactions). The control is kept over the update operations (e.g. for integrity, consistency, etc.) the locking conditions (e.g. for deadlock prevention and resolution), the recovery operations, etc. Even if such a control philosophy has many limitations, because the master node can easily become a bottleneck, it can be usefully used, taking advantage of the greater implementation simplicity, in those information systems which are hierarchical by their very nature or which are built on a hierarchical (star or tree-shaped) computer network.

— *Distributed control DDB's*, when the control over the DDB is distributed among the different nodes the system and is performed through an exchange of messages and parameters among them. The obvious advantages of the distribution are now balanced by a considerably higher complexity of the DDBMS software and, in general, by a lower efficiency.

As to data, they can be distributed in many different ways. In the simplest cases the distribution is made at the *file level*, that is the logical file is also the unit of physical distribution. However, in many applications it is convenient to consider a partitioning below the file level. In this case we can consider the logical file composed of many records subdivided into fields, and we can consider its partitioning into physical fragments in one, or in a combination, of the following two modes:

— *Horizontal partitioning*: all the fragments have the same logical structure (i.e., the same sequence of fields); records belong to a fragment according to some distribution criteria. This corresponds to making a selection on a field value which is characteristic of a particular node.

— *Vertical partitioning*: the structure of the distributed fragments is derived from the structure of the original file by subsetting (or projection) operations, i.e. by storing only some fields at each node. Each logical record is then fragmented into its vertical partitions and then stored in the DDB.

Until now we have not considered the possibility that data be stored in multiple redundant copies at different sites. Historically, this was one of the first forms of DDB to have been considered and the reasons in favour of data replication lie in an increased reliability, shorter response times to enquiries, and cost optimization. However the existence of multiple copies of a data item poses some problems as to the consistency of the different copies when updating operations occur, i.e. how much and how long the contents of the different copies can be different. Some applications ask for a very *tight consistency*, that is the contents of every copy must exactly the same at every moment in such a way as a query could not distinguish from which copy the answer came; other applications can require only a *weak consistency*, in the sense that only one copy of the data item is updated by a transaction, while all others are updated in a deferred mode by the DDBMS. More precisely, we can consider the DDB under the following aspects:

a) *Permanence*: data items can be *permanently distributed*, i.e. once loaded they have a life of their own, or *temporarily distributed*, i.e. a master data item exists and replicated copies are distributed when and where they are needed; possibly they must be refreshed from the master copy to keep consistency.

b) *Consistency*: the copies of a replicated data item are *fully dependent* on each other when tight consistency is required; they are *partially dependent* when weak consistency is sufficient; they are independent where updates on one copy do not affect the other copies of the data item. It must be noticed that independence does not necessarily imply the lack of interrelations among the different copies; since it is often used together with temporary distribution, consistency is kept only at the level of the master copy and hence by refreshment of the other copies.

Often the choice among the different features is dictated by the peculiarities of the applications the system is built for. In many cases queries are real distributed process, while updates are made only on local data. Also, the mode of operation — batch, real time, etc. — can influence the distribution feature of the DDB system.

4. ARCHITECTURES FOR DDBMS

Gross Architecture

In designing a DDBMS the first step is to define its gross architecture. In the field of the centralized DBMS a considerable popularity has been gained by the ANSI/SPARC model, which should allow a maximum of physical and logical data independence. It defines three layers, called schemata:

— The *Conceptual Schema* which represents the data belonging to the whole organization, as seen by the enterprise administrator;

— The *External Schemata* each of which represents the "view" of the organization as seen by a particular application program;

— The *Internal Schema* which represents the way data are physycally stored in the system.

When several DBMS have to cooperate in a distributed environment to constitute a DDBMS, a fourth level has to be added: the Network Schema (NS) or Global Conceptual Schema, mentioned before, which defines the data global to the whole distributed database. We shall not go into a detailed discussion of the possible different architectures arising from the level at which the NS is placed in the model, but we shall only show two of them which are the most general:

a) *The Integrated DDB* (Fig. 5). In this architecture the ownership of data stored in the local DDB belongs to the distributed computing system. All the external schemata are defined starting from the NS which represents the logical union of the logical conceptual schemata existing on the different nodes.

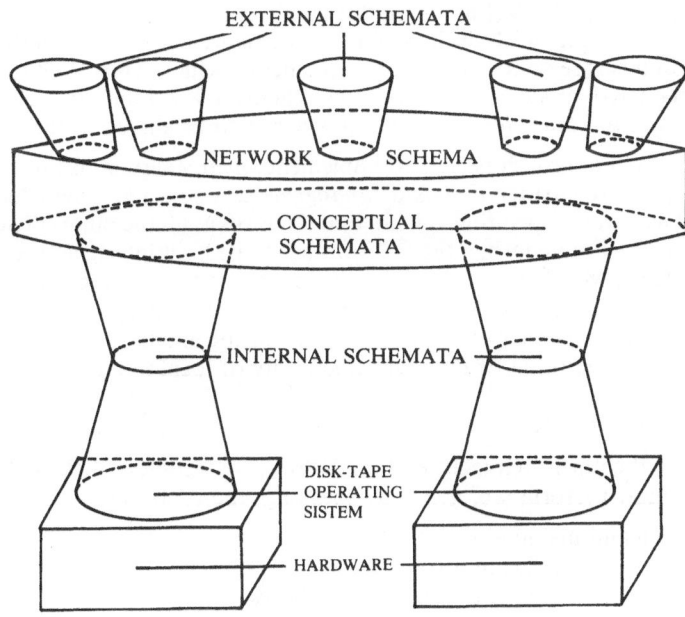

Fig. 5 - Logical Architecture of an Integrated DDB

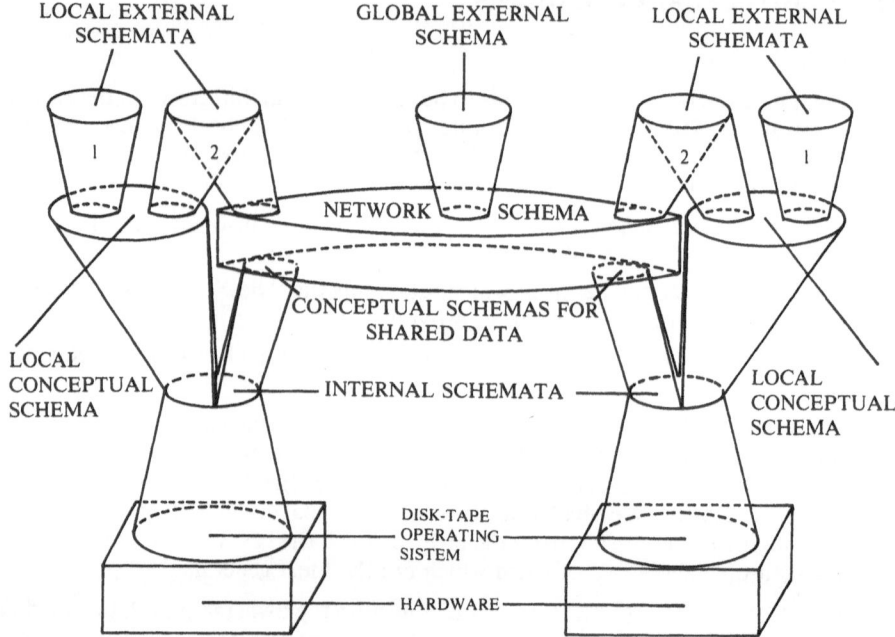

Fig. 6 - *Logical Architecture for an Aggregated DDB*

b) *The aggregated DDB* (Fig. 6). In this architecture the ownership of data belongs to the local system, which decides which of them are to be shared in the distributed system. In this case on top of the internal schema, which refers to physical data in a undifferentiated mode, two conceptual schemata are built, one for pure local information, the other for information which is to be shared in the network.

The integrated approach is easy to implement when a system has to be built from scratch, and even better if it is a *homogeneous* one - i.e., every local host has identical hardware, operating system, and DDBMS as all the others. The aggregated approach is well suited when the DDBMS has to be built interfacing several existing local systems, which very often are *heterogeneous* - i.e. they differ as to the hardware and/or as to the system software. However the aggregated approach can be used whenever privacy constraints are very strong and the amount of shared data is much lower than that of data which are only of local interest.

Software Architecture

Going into the inner architecture of a DDBMS, we recognize that the functions the software must perform are, generally speaking, the following:

— to create and maintain the DDB;
— to process the application transactions;
— to cope with hardware and software failures.

In the following we shall briefly discuss the mechanism of transaction processing, using the model of fig. 7. On the left hand side the logical levels are shown, in the center the evolution of the transaction and the relevant software functions and on the right hand side the additional information required to process it. We shall use a block numbering from the top to the bottom to identify each block.

Block 1

The first function performs the translation of the transaction from the external schema language, in fact in the most general case all the data models used in the different schemata can be different. The translation makes use of the mapping between the two schemata and some semantical integrity constraints can be checked at this level.

Block 2

Formal correctness and authorization constraints must be checked before going on. These operations are done with the aid of the data dictionary.

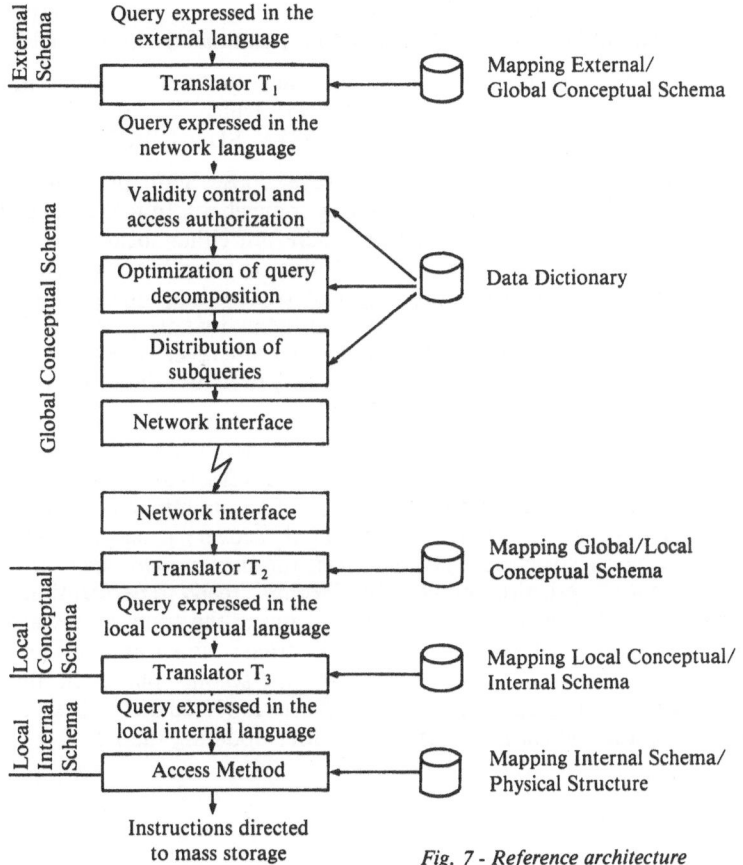

Fig. 7 - Reference architecture

Block 3

A complex transaction involving data stored at many different nodes must be decomposed into many simpler transactions. This operation is very critical and it can be done in many different ways. A lot of work has been done and is still in progress to obtain the maximum of efficiency by reducing the amount of data to be transferred through the network.

Block 4

The elementary transactions are sent to the execution node. This phase requires resource locking and synchronization mechanisms. Distributed concurrency control, distributed deadlock, and recovery are another area which stimulates much research.

Block 5

The network interface must offer a high level communication protocol for the colloquy among the local DBMS.

Block 6, 7, 8

These blocks correspond to the operations made by the local DBMS's where, by means of the mapping functions and of the file system, transactions expressed in a local conceptual language are translated into commands for the mass storage.

All these functions and the relevant software modules can be found, even if in different forms, in all the prototype DDBMS which have been developed and are under development (SIRIUS/DELTA, COSYS, SDD-1, POREL).

Processing distributed transactions, however, poses hard problems as to keeping data integrity when something goes wrong somewhere. In fact we saw that in Block 4 locking mechanisms can be set up; therefore either local or general deadlock conditions can arise somewhere and for this or for other reasons, an elementary transaction, belonging to a single global transaction, must be aborted. If the transaction was updating the database, all the actions triggered by the transaction must be aborted, and their effects cancelled wherever they took place, and the database must be restored to its original state to assure data integrity.

Therefore special protocols have to be designed to coordinate the actions of the elementary transactions on every involved site, in such a way as either all of them perform or all of them are aborted and their side effects are cancelled. Such a way of operation violates somehow the assumption of autonomy of local sites, however it is the only known way to obtain a distributed recovery procedure. These protocols have a two-phase structure; in a first phase the sites *prepare* themselves to perform the elementary transactions and send each other "ready to perform" messages. If all the sites are actually ready, in the second phase the transactions are performed. Otherwise, if at some site the elementary transaction was aborted, no "ready" message can be issued from it and in the second phase all the elementary transactions are aborted, and the local DB are recovered on the basis of "in doubt" back-up log files which had been built before updating the DB.

5. CONCLUSIONS

The purpose of this chapter was to give a simple introduction to the problem of data sharing in distributed systems, therefore many topics have been treated in a very concise way, while many others have been purposely left out. In the bibliography some papers are listed, out of a fast growing literature, which can help the reader to go deeper into the subject.

BIBLIOGRAPHY

A - *General Topics*

Adiba M., Chupin J.C., Demolombe R., Gardarin G., Le Bihan J. (1978) Issues in Distributed Data Management Systems: a Technical Overview. In Issues in Database Management, H. Weber and A.I. Wasserman (Ed.), North-Holland, pp. 127-153.

Aschim F. (1974) Data Base Networks: an Overview. Management Informatics, vol. 3, n. 1, pp. 13-27.

Baldissera C., Ceri S., Schreiber F.A. (1979) Basi di Dati Distribuite. Rivista di Informatica, vol. IX, n. 3.

Emery J.C. (1977) Managerial and Economic Issues in Distributed Computing, in Information Processing 77, Gilchrist (Ed.), North-Holland, pp. 945-955.

Rossetti A., Schreiber F.A. (1978) Architetture alternative del sistema di elaborazione per un sistema informativo aziendale. Automazione e Strumentazione, vol. XXVI, n. 1, pp. 7-17.

Spaccapietra S. (1978) Problematique de conception d'un Système de gestion de bases de données reparties. Thèse à l'Université Paris VI.

Schreiber F.A., Di Filippo C. and Zagolin M. (1980) Un processore per l'interfacciamento di sistemi eterogenei di Information Retrieval su una rete di calcolatori, Atti AICA 80, vol. 2, Bologna, Ott. 1980, pp. 1245-1263.

B - *Application Features*

Giovacchini L., Schreiber F.A. (1976) Some Considerations on Distributed Management Information Systems, Proc. Int. Symposium on Technology for Selective Dissemination of Information, IEEE Press, pp. 102-109.

Paolini P., Pelegatti G., Schreiber F.A. (1972) An Application Oriented Approach to Distributed Databases. Proc. Journées AFCET sur les bases de données répartities, pp. 139-151.

Rossetti A., Schreiber F.A. (1978) Architetture alternative del sistema di elaborazione per un sistema informativo aziendale, Automazione e Strumentazione, vol. XXVI, n. 1, pp. 7-17.

C - *Allocation Problems*

Casey R.G. (1972) Allocation of Copies of a File in an Information Network, Proc. Spring Joint Computer Conference, AFIPS Press.

Chu W.W. (1973) Optimal File Allocation in a Computer Network. In Computer Communication Networks, N. Abramson, F. Kuo (Eds.) Prentice Hall.

Levin D.K., Morgan H.L. (1977) Optimal Program and Data Location in Computer Networks, Communications of the ACM, vol. 20, n. 5.

D - *Architectures*

Adiba M., Chupin J.C., Demolombe R., Gardarin G., Le Bihan J. (1978) Issues in Distributed Data Base Management Systems: a Technical Overview. In Issues in Database Management, H. Weber and A.I. Wasserman (Ed.), North-Holland, pp. 127-153.

Baldissera C., Ceri S., Schreiber F.A. (1979) Basi di Dati Distribuite. Rivista di Informatica, vol. IX, n. 3.

Biller H., Neuhold E.J. (1977) POREL: A Distributed Database on an Inhomogeneous Computer Network. Proc. 3rd International Conference on Very Large Data Bases.

Rothnie J.B., Goodman N. (1977) An Overview of the Preliminary Design of SDD-1, a System for Distributed Data Bases. Proc. 2nd Berkeley Workshop on Distributed Data Management and Computer Networks.

Spaccapietra S. (1978) Problematique de Conception d'un Système de Gestion de Bases de Données Réparties. Thèse à l'Université Paris VI.

Toth K.C., Mahmoud S.A., Riordon J.S., Sharif O. (1978) The ADD System: An Architecture for Distributed Databases. Proc. 4th International Conference on Very Large Data Bases.

Tsichritzis D., Klug A. (Eds.) (1977) The ANSI/X3/SPARC DBMS Framework. Report of the Study Group in Database Management Systems, AFIPS Press.

E - *Query Processing*

Bracchi G., Baldissera C., Ceri S. (1979) Query Processing Strategies for Distributed Database Processing. EEC-CREST Advanced Course on Distributed Data Bases, Sheffield City Polytechnic.

Hever A.R., Yao S.B. (1978) Query Processing on a Distributed Database. Proc. 3rd Berkeley Workshop on Distributed Data Management and Computer Networks.

Pelagatti G., Schreiber F.A. (1979) A Model of an Access Strategy in a Distributed Database. In Database Architecture, G. Bracchi; G.M. Nijssen (Eds.); North-Holland.

Wong E. (1977) Retrieving Dispersed Data from SDD-1: a System for Distributed Databases. Proc. 2nd Berkeley Workshop on Distributed Data Management and Computer Networks.

F - *Data Integrity and Reliability*

Colliat G., Backman C. (1979) Committment in a Distributed DB. In Database Architecture, G. Bracchi, G.M. Nijssen (Eds.), North-Holland.

Lindsay G.B., Selinger P.G. (1979) Notes on Distributed Databases. EEC-CREST Advanced Course on Distributed Data Bases (Integrity), Sheffield City Polytechnic.

Martella G., Ranchetti B., Schreiber F.A. (1981) Availability Evaluation in Distributed Database Systems. Performance Evaluation. Vol. 1, n. 3, pp. 201-211.

FORTRAN IV DIALECT CONVERSION
A CASE STUDY: CDC TO IBM

Aurelio Pollicini
Joint Research Centre,
Ispra, Italy

1. INTRODUCTION

This case study fits into the more general problem area of making application software available on a computing system which is different from the one used for the development of the software.
The study is also intended to demonstrate a practical approach to managing a small scale project.

The purpose

The specific requirement is the conversion of programs written in Fortran and originally implemented on CDC computers, in order to run them satisfactorily on an IBM-compatible architecture.

The environment

The activities of the Joint Research Centre (JRC) of the Commission of the European Communities are mainly concentrated in the following areas:

— Nuclear Safety and the fuel cycle;
— New Energies;
— Study and Protection of the Environment.

The development of research activities in these fields requires a wide use of application software. Some of the products are developed in house, other are obtained from outside sources. In the second case the researchers are frequently faced with large Fortran programs developed on CDC computers. Such programs have to be adapted to the local mainframe which is, at present, an Amdahl 470/V8. The Fortran processors available are the IBM compilers Fortran IV H Extended and Fortran IV G1, running under the Operating System OS 370 MVT. In these circumstances, users need a specific procedure to carry the adaptation task through in a systematic way.

D. T. Muxworthy (ed.), Programming for Software Sharing, 247–262.
Copyright © 1983 ECSC, EEC, EAEC, Brussels and Luxembourg.

The project

Let us depict the worst situation by two hypotheses:

I : User A has to convert product P with the only guidance of compiler diagnosis (cumbersome task);

II: Hypothesis I applies simultaneously to n isolated users (inefficient approach).

The primary aim of the project was to prevent both "cumbersome task" and "inefficient approach". As an additional constraint, preliminary results which would have a practical impact were expected, within approximately, six months of the commencement of the project.
The objectives of the project were defined as follows:

— A preliminary analysis should produce a complete checklist of conversion problems. For every problem a proposal for code modification should be included; in case of alternatives the simplest one must be emphasized.
— A checklist of critical problems needing algorithm adaptation and reprogramming should be added with suggestions for tentative solutions.
— An analysis of software tools useful for computer-assisted conversion should develop in parallel with the dialect comparison. This should result in practical recommendations about the use of available tools.
— The specifications for a suitable converter should also be outlined.

The resources allocated to the project were:

— the local computing facilities;
— reference manuals of both Fortran implementations (CDC, 1981) (IBM, 1976 a);
— manpower allocation 6 man-months.

Of course, requirements and manpower allocation had a conflicting influence in defining the project schedule. It was planned to have:

— the checklists ready for review and comments by end September 1981;
— a progress report available by end October 1981;
— user guidelines ready for review and comments by end November 1981;
— a final report available by end 1981.

2. A METHODOLOGICAL SCHEME

If a single program has to be converted, the programmer involved can apply an "ad hoc" process. The level of difficulty is a function of the number and complexity of the conversion problems involved. If the same programmer is successively assigned another conversion task, his previous experience might be of little help because of the well known lack of generality of any "ad hoc" solution.

Therefore the first attribute of the solution proposed must be "generality".

Moreover, an additional purpose of the project is the harmonization of recommendations and use of programming aids so that the proposed conversion scheme may look like an organic procedure to face the task. The achievement of this intention relies on a careful integration of the different steps of the project as well as on the application of a consistent methodology.

Incompatibilities and Conversion Problems

Conceptually a conversion process consists of two interdependent actions: isolating the actual incompatibilities met in moving a software product between two different language processors and then providing a compatible form which gives an equivalent effect on the target processor. Every incompatibility is intrinsically a conversion problem. We recognize incompatibilities of two distinct natures.

Architectural incompatibilities regarding CDC and IBM systems are well known. They cause the general problems of range and precision of numeric data types and representation and handling of characters.

Language incompatibilities are the specific concern of the preliminary investigation of this project. They split into syntactical incompatibilities, in which syntax specifications do not match and semantic incompatibilities in which a form syntactically accepted by both processors behaves differently. Since both languages conform to the standard Fortran ANSI X3.9-1966 (ANSI, 1966), the comparison of the respective extensions to the standard is the quickest way of noting all syntactical incompatibilities. Moreover, from the comparative analysis of the implementation specifications, semantic incompatibilities may be discovered. The table in Annexe I gives an image of the comparison. The entries in the table are ordered according to the classification scheme of the standard. The same order has been adopted for the presentation of all listed subjects during the project. Notice that for any difference reported in the table, in which the CDC specification is a subset of the corresponding IBM feature, no conversion problem arises in moving from CDC towards IBM. In such cases the CDC form is, indeed, compatible in the IBM environment.

In the preparation of the checklists, the review technique was of primary importance. The draft versions were circulated among a group of qualified users to solicit comments, rectifications and possible extensions. The final version of the checklists as they appear in the Conversion Guide (Pollicini, 1982) is the result of fruitful review sessions. Most of the conversion problems are detected by the syntactical analysis of the source program.

In addition to compilers, other tools may be used to check the conformity to the syntax of the Fortran language. Those available in the environment considered are the PFORT Verifier (Ryder, 1974) and a SCAN option of the Editor invoked in time sharing under the TSO system (IBM, 1973). Moreover, some inconsistencies not recognized at the program unit level are detected by inter-unit checks when loading the program.

In order to test the actual responses of these tools the case program KAMIKAZE was set up. This allegorical name identifies a meaningless collection of Fortran statements which reproduce specimens of all recorded language incompatibilities. Such a collection was "sent into the fight" of syntax checking. The reactions of the tools are synthesized in the following table.

LANGUAGE INCOMPATIBILITIES		H Ext.		G1		SCAN		Link. Ed.		PFORT	
		n	%	n	%	n	%	n	%	n	%
SYNTAX	Unit level	45	84.9	45	84.9	41	77.3			47	96.2
(53 items)	Inter-unit level							4	7.5	4	
SEMANTICS (6 items)		—	—	—	—	—	—	1	16.7	4	66.7

Despite the high level of problem detection shown by PFORT, it is worthwhile noting that the figures reported in the table only represent the potential capabilities of the verifier. The purpose of PFORT is, indeed, checking conformity to a standard. It refers to a predefined subset of the Fortran language and certain severe violations of the accepted syntax may mask further diagnosis or even inhibit the completeness of the analysis. However, the aim of the conversion is to have a version of the original program running correctly on the target processor with the minimal effort. Attempting to produce a version which conforms to the PFORT standard is normally beyond this scope. Therefore, a balanced plan for application of the syntactical analysis as provided by the compilers and PFORT should be followed in order to detect as many conversion problems as possible before starting the test phase.

A plan aiming to achieve this goal is presented in the recommendations addressed to the users of the Conversion Guide previously mentioned. In this document information is also given regarding the library support software which has been developed. Logical operations can be applied, bit by bit, on scalar entities. Octal to decimal conversion is provided both for fixed and floating point representation. A set of primitives which hide character handling from the application program is available for the conversion of operations on strings.

Concerning the requirement of extending the accuracy of computation, the use of the Automatic Precision Increase Facility (IBM, 1977) provided as an option by the H Extended compiler has proved very helpful and is suggested as a useful conversion aid.

Source Modification

The necessary transformations of the text of a source program must be designed thoughtfully. Depending on the conversion problem, the context in which careful control is required to avoid introducing ambiguities or logic distortion may range from a single program unit to the entire program.

It is also important to agree on conventions regarding the practical way of modifying the statements to be revised. The fact that a converted program may be subjected to the reverse process after a local metamorphosis should also be considered. Therefore, the final version should appear as the symbiosis of the original product and its target image.

Only if the IBM compatible version conforms to the standard and the CDC implementation of that standard feature behaves identically may the modification become permanent. For all other modifications the following principles should be observed.

Principle of separation. Any rejected element needs to be separated from the body of the program and also any inserted element must not be materially embedded into the existing text. This is achieved by considering the Fortran statement as the smallest modifiable unit.

Principle of conservation. Any statement containing a rejected element must be transformed to a comment line to maintain a trace of CDC peculiarities.

Principle of identification. Any added statement must be unequivocally identified to allow an easy recognition of IBM peculiarities. This can be done by enclosing statements or segments of code in special comment lines.

Principle of restoration. Simple coded comments must be incorporated to make possible an automatic restoration of the source to CDC form.

Documentation

The converted version of a software product is in fact a distinct product. As such it needs a complete documentation. What must be provided is a conversion report which can be integrated with the existing documentation of the original product. Appropriate references to the relevant sections of the original documents will establish the necessary links. Such a report should be sized according to the extent of the program and the amount of conversion work. It should at least contain one section on each of the following subjects.

— Description of the conversion process with indications of difficulties and solutions. The inclusion of segments of code could help in the understanding of the transformations which have been performed.

— Restrictions on the application of the converted program. This concerns especially numerical applications which may cause underflow or overflow in special conditions as well as differences in the accuracy.

— Details about input preparation and output interpretation when they differ from the original version.

3. SEMI-AUTOMATIC CONVERSION

Integrated guidelines may assist users in overcoming the incompatibilities just as the use of a flexible context editor make program modification easier. However, much clerical work is still associated with conversion. Manual operations can represent too arduous a task in the case of large and complex nuclear codes of many tens of thousands of statements.

No doubt a specific converter is needed to make the conversion process reasonably simple, especially when dealing with such large systems. In any conversion exercise, i.e. language to language, dialect to dialect, it has been ascertained that fully automatic conversion is unrealistic. The use of a converter allows for a semi-automatic process. Usually the converter automatically provides a compatible form for simple problems. Additionally, it is able to recognize most of the remaining problems for which it may suggest a replacement to be checked in the context or just issue a warning with as much explanation as possible.

A subsequent step of manual refinement is required before the verification of the compiler and the testing of the new version.

General Requirements

To provide a good service a converter should completely fulfil some basic requirements. From such a software tool we expect above all a reliable performance. That is, if it is able to replace automatically a set A of problems and flag a set W of different problems, it must do this job for any problem a_1, a_2, ... a_i belonging to set A and w_1, w_2, ... w_n belonging to set W and do so in whatever circumstances such problems may occur. Secondly, the robustness of the tool should guarantee that unwanted actions and false messages will never arise.

Additionally, explanatory output should be limited to the essential, to avoid useful information being diluted by a flow of meaningless messages. It is also advantageous if the facilities offered by the converter and its applicability fit in with the devised conversion scheme rather than having to adapt the scheme to the tool. Finally, it is important to specify for what problems the automatic conversion is feasible. By analysing the characteristics of the items in the general checklist of conversion problems the ones collected in the following list appear to be automatically convertible.

— Different characters in the used character set;
— Use of asterisk or dollar sign as comment flag;
— Labelled and/or continued END line;
— Multiple statements per line;
— Seven character names (user control is needed, however);
— Octal constants, at least in executable statements;
— Hollerith constants used in expressions;
— Short forms of logical constants and logical operators;
— Implied unary subscripts;
— Relational operators applied on COMPLEX operands;
— Multiple assignment, both arithmetic and logical;
— Omitted comma in assigned and computed GO TO statements;
— Arithmetic expression controlling computed GO TO statement;
— COMPLEX expressions in arithmetic IF statement;
— Two branch arithmetic IF statement;
— Missing RETURN statement;
— Numbered COMMON block;
— Additional keyword TYPE in type statements;
— Shortened form DOUBLE in type and in FUNCTION statements;
— Parenthesized form of DATA statement;
— Asterisks enclosing character constants in FORMAT statements;
— Output of integer numbers with leading zeros;
— Output of real numbers with exponent length specification;
— Certain non-standard forms of the X editing;
— Editing of octal data;
— Implied parameter list in ENTRY statement;
— Named BLOCK DATA;
— PROGRAM statement.

Availability of Conversion Tools

The best solution for the user is to have an existing tested converter ready for use. In fact the availability of such a converter represents by far the cheapest solution, because of saving of effort, little dead-time before starting the application and immediate reliable production. These are, indeed, the advantages of sharing good software!

In practice the profile of the converter, as outlined in the previous section, makes it quite a specialized tool. Unfortunately, it is not so easy to find the required conversion tool. Two relevant references were found. The first one is reported in the catalogue of the SHARE Program Library (Gorsline, 1971). As summarized in the abstract, "CONVERT" translates some CDC Fortran statements into "compatible IBM Fortran IV, G level". The tool is available as a SNOBOL4 program and its main purpose is the saving of much of the manual work. Unfortunately, the target dialect is tailored to an out of date IBM compiler. Also, the requirement of a SNOBOL4 environment means that it is not immediately applicable in the frame of the described project. However, the analysis of the documentation has provided an interesting indication of the usefulness of SNOBOL4 as a tool for source manipulation.

The second reference is the IBM Installed User Program "Fortran Conversion Aid" (1976 b), the usefulness of which is to be evaluated in the forthcoming stage of the project.

Project Assessment and Future Plan

The results currently achieved by the project should have a positive effect in the environment described. The user guidelines can be seen as a local standard which may homogeneously increase the professionality of programmers regardless of their assignment to different scientific units. Therefore, the effort has represented a good investment. The benefits of education and training of scientific programmers are discussed in detail by Dowell (1982).

Nevertheless, it must be stated that this stage only represents a partial result.

The process needs to be improved soon by the use of a conversion tool. Consequently we consider that a delayed introduction of a powerful tool is the wrong approach. More preferable would be the introduction of a very simple tool in a short time. Such a tool should cover trivial problems which occur frequently. Thus, most of the time necessary for hand conversion could be saved and the users would then be allowed to concentrate on the intellectual aspect of the task. The possibility of using a more sophisticated tool could be envisaged for a later stage.

4. CONCLUSIONS

As final reflections on the overall subject one could attempt to answer two questions which arise.

"How can this case study improve sharing of software?"

"Can these specific aspects be seen as a contribution to a more general problem area?"

Concerning the first question, which is certainly a vital point, only an appreciable user feedback can give the affirmative answer we hope for.

For the second question our answer is "Yes!"

At the time in which standardization processes are focusing on Fortran 8X, this work may be seen as the ground-layer on which the move from Fortran IV to Fortran 77 can be modelled.

Four years after ANSI (1978) approved the current standard, practical schemes of conversion could contribute to give confidence in the existing implementations of Fortran 77 as well as to reward the efforts of compiler writers.

5. ACKNOWLEDGMENTS

The author is grateful to D. Lord and H. Renshall of CERN and H. Hultzsch of GSI who provided very useful information. Also appreciated is the help provided by J. Pire, M. Dowell, J. Donea, J.P. Halleux and W. Kolar who gave an active contribution as members of the review panel.

REFERENCES

American National Standard Institute (1966). ANS FORTRAN. ANSI X3.9-1966. ANSI, Inc. New York (1966).

American National Standard Institute (1978). ANS Programming Language FORTRAN. ANSI X3.9-1978. ANSI, Inc. New York (April 1978).

Control Data Corporation (1981). FORTRAN Extended Version 4 Reference Manual. Publication N°. 60497800 Revision G (January 1981).

Dowell M.D. (1982). Managing Software Development (This book).

Gorsline G.W.Jr. (1971). CONVERT-Source Conversion of CDC FORTRAN to IBM G Level. SHARE Program Library Agency. User's Guide and Catalog of Programs, SEAS (1979).

International Business Machines Corporation (1973). IBM System/360 Operating System: Time Sharing Option Command Language Reference. GC28-6732-4 Revision GN28-2531 (April 1973).

International Business Machines Corporation (1976 a). IBM System/360 and System/370 FORTRAN IV Language. GC28-6515-10 Revision GN26-0805 (April 1976).

International Business Machines Corporation (1976 b) Fortran Conversion Aid, IUP 5796-PFG, Description/Operation. SH20-1727 (June 1976).

International Business Machines Corporation (1977). IBM OS FORTRAN IV (H Extended) Compiler Programmer's Guide. SC28-6852-2 Revision SN20-9202 (February 1977).

Pollicini A.A. (1982). Converting CDC FTN4 to IBM FORTRAN IV. J.R.C. Ispra Computing Centre Newsletter, Handbook series (May 1982).

Ryder B.G. (1974). The PFORT Verifier. Software Practice and Experience, 4 pp. 359-377.

ANNEX I

EXTENSIONS TO THE STANDARD FORTRAN ANSI X3.9-1966

ANSI X3.9-1966 classification	CDC FORTRAN EXTENDED VERSION 4	IBM FORTRAN IV H EXTENDED
3.1 Character set	- additional characters ≠ ''	- additional characters ' & - $ belongs to alphabetic characters
3.2 Lines	- comment lines may also begin with $ or * in column one - END line may be labelled and continued - multiple statements may be written on one line, separated by $	
3.5 Symbolic names	- symbolic names may be up to 7 characters long	- symbolic names may contain $
4. Data	- octal data allowed	- hexadecimal data allowed - length specification is allowed for INTEGER, REAL, COMPLEX and LOGICAL data
5.1 Constants	- octal constants - Hollerith constants may also be expressed as: nR... (right justified) nL... (left justified) ≠...≠ (delimited string) - any form of Hollerith constant may appear in expressions - LOGICAL constants may also be expressed in short form: .T. .F.	- hexadecimal constants - Hollerith constants may also be expressed as: '...' (delimited string)
5.1.3 Arrays	- subscript expressions may be any arithmetic expression - if the number of subscript expressions is less than the number of dimensions, the omitted subscripts have value one	- up to 7 dimensions - subscript expressions may be any arithmetic expression of type INTEGER or REAL

Table 1. sheet 1

ANSI X3.9-1966 classification	CDC FORTRAN EXTENDED VERSION 4	IBM FORTRAN IV H EXTENDED
6.1 Arithmetic expressions	- for operators + — * / any combination from INTEGER to COMPLEX is allowed - for exponentiation INTEGER, REAL and DOUBLE PRECISION can be raised to exponents of any type - A**B**C** is interpreted as (A**B)**C - Typeless operands are allowed anywhere in arithmetic expressions	- for operators + — * / any combination from INTEGER*2 to COMPLEX*32 is allowed - for exponentiation INTEGER*2, INTEGER*4, REAL*4, REAL*8 and REAL*16 may be combined in any way - A**B**C is interpreted as A**(B**C)
6.2 Relational expressions	- combination of arithmetic expressions implies the conversion rules under 6.1 - COMPLEX entities may be compared using all the operators (.LT., .LE., .GT. and .GE. apply only to the real part)	- combination of arithmetic expressions implies the conversion rules under 6.1
6.3 Logical expressions	- shortened forms .N., .A., .O. are allowed for the logical operators - logical operators may be used with non LOGICAL operands to build masking expressions. Such expressions represent bit negation, conjunction and disjunction, respectively	
7.1.1.1 Arithmetic assignment	- the value of one expression may be assigned to several entities: V1 = V2 = ... = VN = E - an arithmetic expression of any type may be assigned to an entity belonging to any arithmetic type - the bit pattern of a masking expression may be stored into any arithmetic entity	- an arithmetic expression of any type may be assigned to an entity belonging to any arithmetic type
7.1.1.2 Logical assignment	- the value of one expression may be assigned to several entities: LV1 = LV2 = ... = LVN = LE	
7.1.2.1.2 Assigned GO TO	- the comma between the integer variable and the list of labels may be omitted	

Table 1. sheet 2

ANSI X3.9-1966 classification	CDC FORTRAN EXTENDED VERSION 4	IBM FORTRAN IV H EXTENDED
7.1.2.1.3 Computed GO TO	- any arithmetic or masking expression may be used in replacement of the control variable - the comma after the list of labels may be omitted	- if the value of the control variable is out of range, the execution continues in sequence
7.1.2.2 Arithmetic IF	- the use of a masking expression as well as an expression of type COMPLEX is allowed - a form with only two labels is allowed: IF (e) s1,s2 $e \neq 0 \rightarrow s1$ $e = 0 \rightarrow s2$	
7.1.2.3 Logical IF	- an alternative form is allowed: IF (e) s1,s2 $e = .TRUE. \rightarrow s1$ $e = .FALSE. \rightarrow s2$	
7.1.2.4 CALL statement	- a list of alternate return points may be specified in the form: CALL..., RETURNS (list) where list is a sequence of statement labels - use of the form CALL OVERLAY	- labels are allowed as actual parameters by using the prefix &: CALL... (...,&50,...)
7.1.2.5 RETURN statement	- RETURN may appear in a main program acting as a STOP - the form RETURN a is allowed in a SUBROUTINE, "a" is a symbolic name appearing in the RETURNS list. - RETURN may be omitted. In this case the END line implies a RETURN	- RETURN may appear in a main program acting as a STOP - the form RETURN i is allowed in a SUBROUTINE, the "ith" parameter is used as actual return
7.1.2.7.1 STOP statement	- the optional operand may be a character string	- the optional operand is expressed by decimal digits
7.1.2.7.2 PAUSE statement	- the optional operand may be a character string	- the optional operand is expressed by decimal digits or may be a character string

Table 1. sheet 3

ANSI X3.9-1966 classification	CDC FORTRAN EXTENDED VERSION 4	IBM FORTRAN IV H EXTENDED
7.1.3 Input output statements	- the format specification may also be a NAMELIST name. In this case the I/O list is omitted - the format specification may also be an asterisk implying list-directed input output - on output the I/O list may also contain Hollerith constants and arithmetic expressions	- the format specification may also be a NAMELIST name. In this case the I/O list is omitted - the format specification may also be an asterisk implying list-directed input output

7.1.3.2.2
Formatted
READ
	- short form
	    READ f, list
	for in-line input
		- short form
		    READ f, list
		for in-line input
		- END and ERR options

7.1.3.2.3 Formatted WRITE	- short form WRITE f, list for output to be printed	
7.1.3.2.4 Unformatted READ		- END and ERR options
7.1.3.2.5 Unformatted WRITE	- the form WRITE (u) without output list to create null records	
ADDITIONAL I/O STATEMENTS	- PRINT - PUNCH - BUFFERIN - BUFFEROUT - ENCODE - DECODE	- PRINT - PUNCH - Asynchronous READ - Asynchronous WRITE - WAIT - DEFINE FILE - Direct access READ - Direct access WRITE - FIND
7.2.1.1 Array declarator	- the specification of an array declarator may be omitted in a subprogram for a formal parameter which is not referenced as subscripted array in the subprogram, although associated with an actual array	- the number of dimensions may exceed three with a maximum of seven
7.2.1.1.2 Adjustable dimension		- the actual value of the dimension may also be passed in a COMMON block

Table 1. sheet 4

ANSI X3.9-1966 classification	CDC FORTRAN EXTENDED VERSION 4	IBM FORTRAN IV H EXTENDED
7.2.1.3 COMMON statement	- labelled COMMON blocks may also be identified by a number of 1 to 7 digits	
7.2.1.4 EQUIVALENCE statement	- an array name may appear without subscript to mean the first array element	
7.2.1.5 EXTERNAL statement		- a user-supplied subprogram may be used instead of the Fortran library subprogram of the same name if the name prefixed by & is included in an EXTERNAL statement
7.2.1.6 Type statement	- the word TYPE may optionally be used as prefix in type statements - the short form DOUBLE may also be used to mean type DOUBLE PRECISION	- use of length declarator to define some additional data types: LOGICAL*1 INTEGER*2 REAL*16 COMPLEX*16 and COMPLEX*32 in addition the standard data types may also be referred to as: LOGICAL*4 INTEGER*4 REAL*4 and REAL*8 COMPLEX*8 - initial values may be assigned in type statements
7.2.2 DATA statement	- an alternative form is allowed: DATA (vlist = dlist),... - array names as well as implied-DO loops may also appear within the list of names - a DATA statement which provides initial values for entities belonging to a labelled COMMON block, may be used in any program unit in which such a COMMON block appears REMARK. Extensions referred to under 4 (data types) and 5.1.1 (constants) apply to the constants used in DATA statements	- array names may also appear within the list of names REMARK. Extensions referred to under 4 (data types) and 5.1.1 (constants) apply to the constants used in DATA statements

Table 1. sheet 5

ANSI X3.9-1966 classification	CDC FORTRAN EXTENDED VERSION 4	IBM FORTRAN IV H EXTENDED
7.2.3 FORMAT statement	- additional field descriptors: Ow (octal data) Rw (right justified alphanumeric data) Zw (hexadecimal data) Tn (tabulation: null counter allowed) Vw.d (variable specification) - two delimiters are allowed to enclose character strings in addition to the H descriptor: $\neq \ldots \neq$ $* \ldots *$ - the descriptor Aw causes string truncation if $w < 10$ - leading zeros may be output with the I descriptor - exponent length may be specified with E and D descriptors - X descriptor also allowed in any of the forms: X, 0X, $-$nX, $+$nX - Use of equal sign for delayed specification of an integer constant in any edit descriptor	- additional field descriptors: Qw.d (quadruple precision) Zw (hexadecimal data) Tn (tabulation) - apostrophes may be used to enclose character strings in addition to the H descriptor - the G descriptor is extended to INTEGER and LOGICAL data - the descriptor Aw causes string truncation if $w < 4$
ADDITIONAL NON EXECUTABLE STATEMENTS	- NAMELIST - IMPLICIT - LEVEL - ENTRY - OVERLAY	- NAMELIST - IMPLICIT - GENERIC - ENTRY
8.3 Intrinsic functions	- additional intrinsic functions: AND OR XOR COMPL SHIFT MASK RANF LOCF	- additional intrinsic functions: QABS HFIX DIMAG QMAX1 QSIGN QIMAG QMIN1 DDIM QEXT DINT QDIM QEXTD QINT SNGLQ DCMPLX IQINT DBLEQ QCMPLX QMOD DREAL DCONJG DFLOAT QREAL QCONJG QFLOAT IMAG

Table 1. sheet 6

ANSI X3.9-1966 classification	CDC FORTRAN EXTENDED VERSION 4	IBM FORTRAN IV H EXTENDED
8.3.2 Referencing external functions	- Hollerith constants may be used as actual parameters	- Hollerith constants may be used as actual parameters - to force any scalar parameter to be referenced by location, it must be enclosed in slashes in the FUNCTION statement: ...,/a/,... "a" is the symbolic name of a formal parameter used as scalar in the FUNCTION subprogram
8.3.3 Basic external functions	- additional entries: DTANH SINH DSINH COSH DCOSH ERF ERFC SIND COSD TAND ATANH ACOS DACOS ASIN DASIN TAN DTAN	- additional entries: LOG QARCOS COSH QLOG QATAN DCOSH CDLOG QATAN2 QCOSH CQLOG QSIN DTANH QLOG10 QCOS QTANH QEXP CDSIN CDABS CDEXP CQSIN CQABS CQEXP CDCOS ERF QSQRT CQCOS DERF CDSQRT TAN QERF CQSQRT DTAN ERFC ASIN QTAN DERFC ARSIN COTAN QERFC DARSIN DCOTAN GAMMA QARSIN QCOTAN DGAMMA ACOS SINH LGAMMA ARCOS DSINH ALGAMA DARCOS QSINH DLGAMA
8.4 Subroutines	- the specification RETURNS (list) may follow the parameter list in a statement SUBROUTINE. Each element of the list is a variable name associated to an actual parameter providing a label value	- an asterisk is allowed as formal parameter to mean an alternate return - all scalar parameters are referenced by value instead of by location; to force any scalar parameter to be referenced by location, it must be enclosed in slashes in the SUBROUTINE statements: ...,/a/,... "a" is the symbolic name of a formal parameter used as scalar in the SUBROUTINE subprogram
8.5 Block Data	- BLOCK DATA subprograms may be named - IMPLICIT and LEVEL statements may appear within a BLOCK DATA subprogram	- IMPLICIT statements may appear within a BLOCK DATA subprogram

Table 1. sheet 7

ANSI X3.9-1966 classification	CDC FORTRAN EXTENDED VERSION 4	IBM FORTRAN IV H EXTENDED
9.1.5 Main Program	- the first statement of a main program must be a PROGRAM statement which assigns a name to the program and allocates external files if necessary	
10.1.1 Restrictions on symbolic names	- a symbolic name used as COMMON block name can also be used as the name of a subprogram in the same executable program	
10.2.3 Status of entities	- all undefined entities are initially in a uniform status since they are allocated in a previously zeroised storage	

Table 1. sheet 8

USERS' EXPERIENCE: INTRODUCTION

Martyn Dowell
Joint Research Centre
Ispra, Italy

Software sharing may be considered as an import-export trading system. There are software producers who export their products to others and consumers who import the products which they use. Many sharers begin their work thinking that they are totally self-sufficient. They produce their own software for their own needs and do not think of exporting it or importing other people's software. Often, however, they find either that the product which they are developing is in demand by other groups or that they themselves could make use in their work of a software product provided by another group. Frequently persons drift into both import and export sharing in this way although obviously many others plan their involvement from the start.

Many scientific computer users are software import-exporters; the vast majority of them being software importers. In many cases they are applied scientists or engineers for whom computer science represents simply a peripheral part of their more important scientific activities. For them the lure of the software package, already written, requiring no effort to use, is overpowering. The idea that using a package already written and tested by others which will allow them to present their data and receive results in terms which can easily be related to their physical problem is an extremely attractive one. Alas, in the real world all too often the reality is much more complicated and difficult.

Often a particular package is the only one available to perform a certain type of analysis and, therefore, the need to have access to it is all important. Thus, the fact that extensive and difficult conversion work may be necessary to adapt in to the user's local computing environment is far outweighed by the fact that its availability is considered indispensible. Quite often the alternative of constructing an equivalent system locally, although perhaps requiring less manpower, is unacceptable because the original program is in some way the certified or approved means for resolving a particular problem. In such case the conversion although expensive and difficult may have to be performed.

D. T. Muxworthy (ed.), Programming for Software Sharing, 263–264.
Copyright © 1983 ECSC, EEC, EAEC, Brussels and Luxembourg.

Conversions of such types are commonplace and persons involved in the work often accumulate considerable experience in the task. These persons take a very pragmatic approach to their particular problems. They see nothing of the generality, the overview, the concepts of software sharing or conversion. They see only their problems and the need to resolve them. Their problems are real and the gulf between their needs and the methodologies of the more theoretical approach to the problems of software sharing is evident. The gulf must be narrowed by making the ideals work in practice and by making the users aware of the appropriate methodologies to follow.

In the following two papers the experience of two groups of computer users is presented. The papers point to the severe practical problems encountered by the users in acquisition and implementation of software packages which were originally developed on a computing system different from the one on which they must execute the packages. Their problems are caused by the incompatibilities between the hardware and software of the two systems. These problems are often exacerbated by the scant thought given to transferrability by the software developers and the lack of tools and systematic techniques for adapting the software at their own site.

They have a microcosmic view of the field of software sharing but still they have practical problems which they need to resolve. More effort should be made by the computer science community to provide assistance, education, techniques and tools in a form which will allow such computer users to resolve more readily their software transfer problems.

EXPERIENCE WITH THE RELAP CODE

Walter Kolar, Stuart Duffield, Reinier Nijsing, Gerhard de Vries
Joint Research Centre
Ispra, Italy

1. RELAP CODE OVERVIEW

Purpose

RELAP is a reactor safety system code capable of simulating certain types of transients which may occur in light water reactor (LWR) nuclear power plants. The primary function of RELAP is to describe a loss-of-coolant accident (LOCA). This accident, produced by a rupture in the high pressure circuit (ca. 160 atmospheres), is characterized by a sudden reduction of system pressure, flashing of water to steam and blowing of the steam-water mixture through the break. RELAP is aimed at providing information on the time history of flow, pressure and temperature in the nuclear core as well as in the coolant circuit.

Code models

Key modelling features of the RELAP code regard

— transient thermohydraulic coolant behaviour in the coolant circuit
— coolant flow and heat transfer in the core region
— transient conduction in structural materials (pipe walls) and fuel rods
— fuel deformation
— reactor kinetics for computing the power behaviour during accident conditions.

The thermohydraulic coolant model

This model, which is the most important one in the RELAP code, is based on mass and energy balances on "control volumes" that are connected by "junctions" (see Fig. 1). Momentum balances are applied to the junctions. Actually the equations solved are one-dimensional in nature; this holds not only for the circuit but also for the core with many parallel coolant channels. The two-phase description of the coolant is one where the mass, momentum and energy relations are applied to the two-phase mixture, assuming thermodynamic equilibrium between vapour and liquid (homogeneous model). In the latest code RELAP5 of the RELAP series a

D. T. Muxworthy (ed.), Programming for Software Sharing, 265–274.

more detailed modelling is applied involving a separate description of the 2 phase allowing for thermodynamic non-equilibrium (two-fluid model).

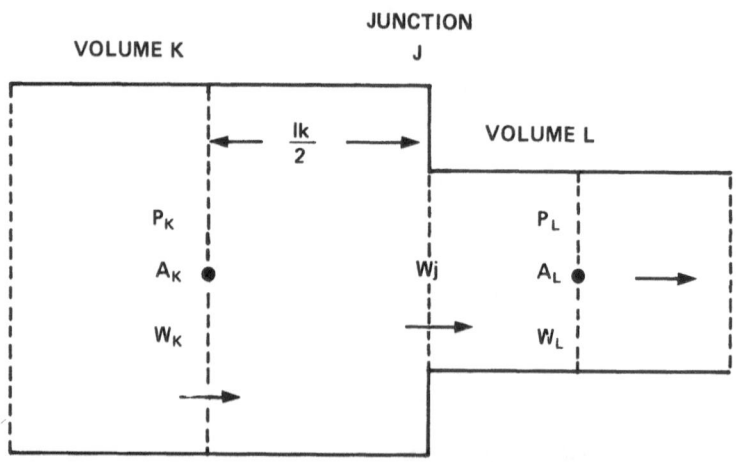

Physical properties constant over each control volume and centred at the volume centre

Pressure drop occurs across junction

P Pressure
A Area
W Mass flow rate

Fig. 1 - Flow path control volume

Heat transfer to coolant

The temperature at the walls of piping and fuel rods are governed by heat fluxes, coolant temperature and "heat transfer coefficients". The latter depend markedly on the "heat transfer regime", e.g. liquid coolant flow without boiling, different boiling regimes (e.g. subcooled boiling, saturated nucleate boiling, film boiling), flow of coolant vapour. The code contains a package of empirical heat transfer relations, derived from experiments. A special logic is needed for selecting a specific relation at a given location and given time.

Transient conduction model

This model solves the transient conduction equations pertaining to structural materials and fuel rods. It computes the temperature distribution in these materials and the heat flux into the flowing coolant. An important aspect is the thermal coupling between the solid materials and the coolant.

Special models

RELAP contains a number of special models required for describing special processes and for predicting the behaviour of components. These models are essentially related to hydrodynamic aspects. Examples are: (a) critical flow, needed to compute the mass discharge through the break, (b) transient two-phase flow through passages with abrupt changes, (c) interaction of transient coolant flow with a pump, (d) simulation of flow in pressurizers and accumulators.

RELAP history

It may be helpful to describe the development of the RELAP program as an example of how a large engineering code evolves under the constraints of time, money and the constant pressure of producing results which are relevant to outside phenomena, such as Three Mile Island.

In May 1966 predictions for design work on the LOFT test facility (LOFT is a nuclear test facility in Idaho, U.S.A. designed to simulate the major components of a pressurized water reactor during a LOCA) were needed and a Westinghouse version of the FLASH code was modified and used, and became RELAPSE-1. This was the beginning of the RELAP program. The code had only three control volumes, equilibrium thermodynamics, lumped physical parameters, simple heat transfer and it could self-initialise, something which it does not do now. This work was done using an IBM 7040 with 32 K word core.

By March 1968 the code was modified to model BWR geometries and became RELAP2, but essentially the code was similar to the earlier version and had still a coarse description of the reactor system.

RELAP3 arrived by 1970; this allowed the modelling of piping arrangements and the reactor core, initially with a maximum of twenty control volumes but soon this was extended to two hundred. The program structure had become modular and was made up from 75 subroutines. Originally, the work was performed both on an IBM 7044 and the Univac; later on the Univac version was dropped, the IBM computer was changed to an IBM 360/75 and work was initiated on a CDC 6600.

Many unpublished additions to RELAP3 were made in the next few years, implicit numerics were incorporated, the whole heat transfer portion of the code was changed giving the possibility of detailed fuel rod modelling, and eventually the code RELAP4/MOD3 update 36 was released in May 1971. This had approximately 30,000 statements, 150 subroutines and used 500 K bytes of storage. By now the code was being used to study many thermohydraulic problems not necessarily nuclear, and was being continuously used in a production mode to predict each Semiscale and Loft experiment. Special versions were developed to extend its versatility; these included RELAP4/FLOOD for refill and reflood analysis, RELAP4-EM for the N.R.C. Evaluation model, RELAP4-CONTAINMENT and RELAP4/MOD4 (never published) for small break analysis. Parts of FRAP, a detailed fuel rod model covering metal water reaction, fuel-cladding gap heat transfer, cladding deformation and rupture were added to the code and by the end of 1976 a code including all these options, RELAP4/MOD5, was released. At this stage the code had grown to 45,000 statements with some 200 subroutines and 1 million bytes of storage requirement, and both an IBM and a CDC version were available.

Of course, life is never perfect and difficulty was experienced with reflood calculations and the heat transfer packages. This stimulated the development of RELAP4/MOD6 and some eighteen thousand statements and fifty new subroutines were added to the code. A CDC version and an IBM version were available, but the majority of the work and the checking was done with the CDC version.

The code was further developed so that an entire accident sequence could be run continuously and this was released as RELAP4/MOD7, but only in a CDC version. A RELAP4/MOD8 version was scheduled to clean up and do some optimization of the code, but this was not given priority.

In parallel with this development (from about 1977) was that of RELAP5. The need for a simpler cleaner code with basic improvements in the physics had been appreciated so that non-homogeneous problems could be tackled with confidence. High priority was given to this work after the Three Mile Island incident in March 1979 when the emphasis of LWR safety was switched from the large break to the small break type of accident. RELAP5/MOD0 was released in CDC version in May 1979 and in the following March the most up-to-date version RELAP5/MOD1 was released.

Example of a RELAP4/MOD6 Application

Figure 2 shows the LOBI test facility at JRC-Ispra which is an out-of-pile facility to simulate a loss of coolant accident in an LWR reactor. This is a typical application

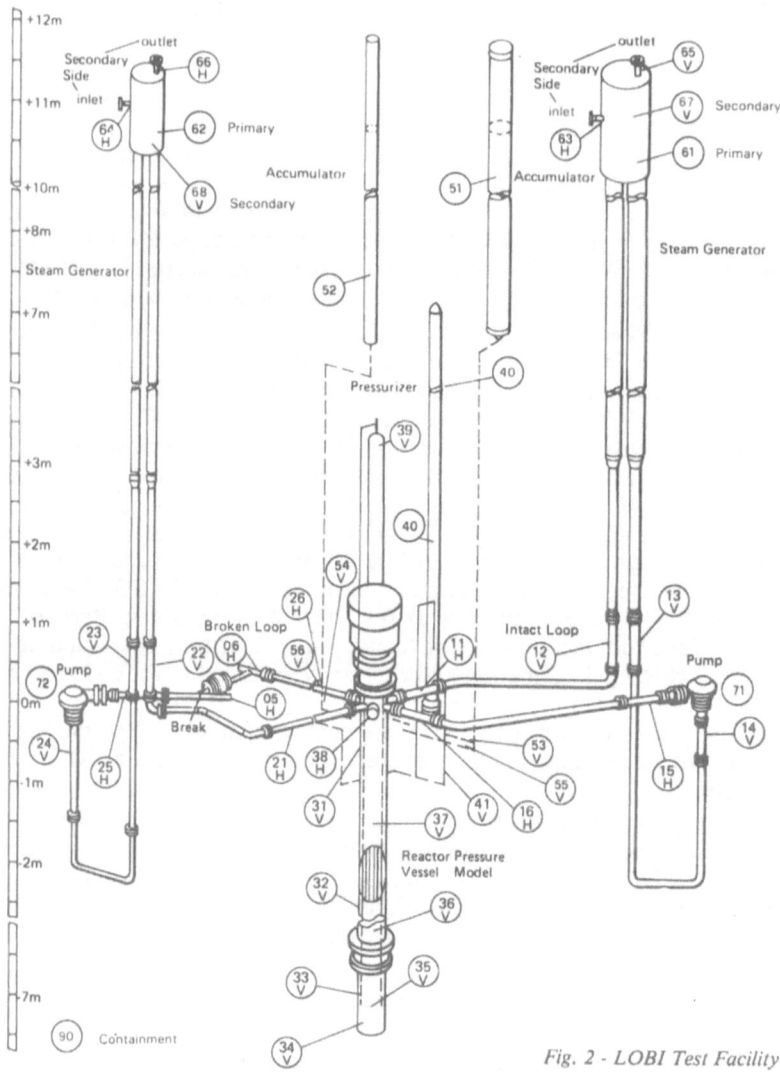

Fig. 2 - LOBI Test Facility

of the RELAP code. Fig. 3 shows the nodalization scheme with both volumes and junction shown. For each volume or junction, parameters such as pressure, temperature, void fraction, heat transfer coefficients, mass flow rate etc. are calculated at each time step through the transient and stored on tape. Later this data is processed to give graphical output, examples of which are shown in Figs. 4 and 5.

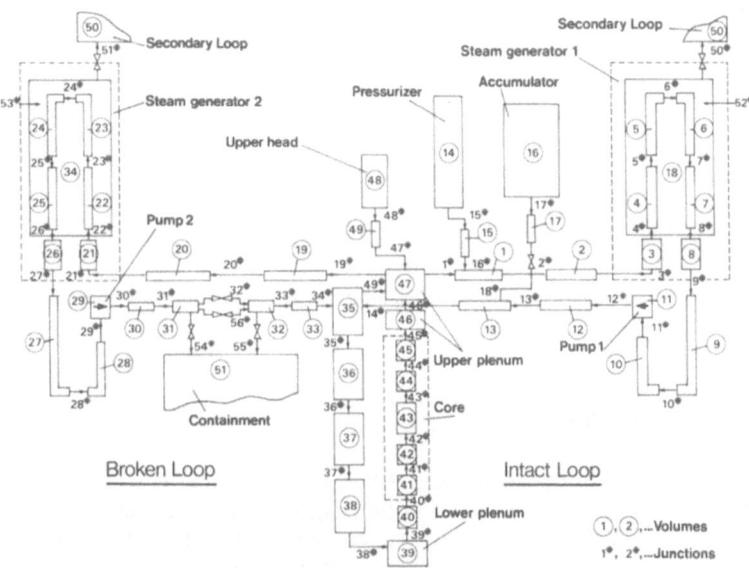

Fig. 3 - RELAP4 nodalization for LOBI large cold leg breaks
(used for post-test prediction)

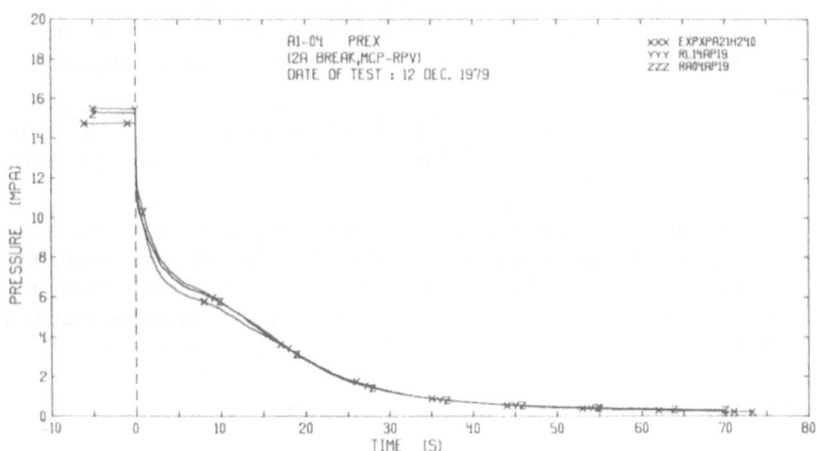

Fig. 4 - Pressure in broken loop hot leg, vessel outlet

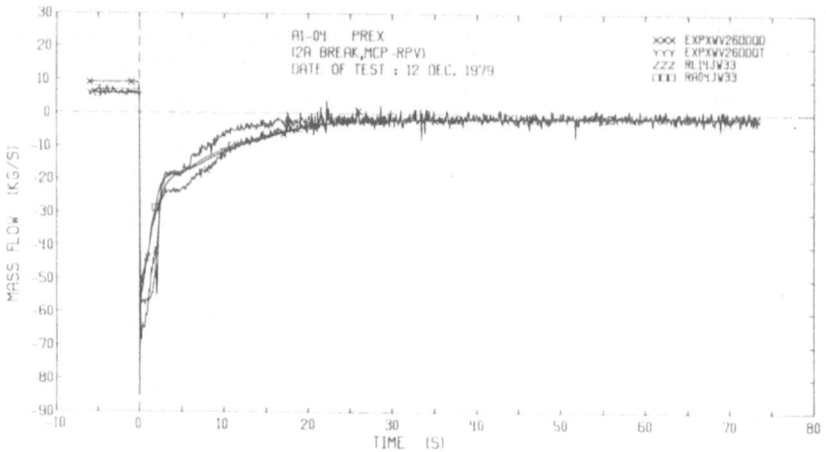

Fig. 5 - Mass flow in broken loop cold leg, vessel inlet near vessel side break

2. IMPLEMENTATION

The conversion of codes like **RELAP, TRAC, SIMMER** which are developed in a CDC environment, or to say it in more general terms on word oriented computer systems, to IBM or byte oriented computer systems raises many problems at different levels. These problems may be grouped together according to their nature into:

— problems due to the differences of the Fortran compilers
— problems due to the computer environments and operating systems
— problems due to the different lengths of a computer word.

As an example the code RELAP5/MOD1 (Ramson et al, 1981) has been chosen in order to illustrate in more detail the different problem areas an implementor is faced with.

Originally, the code RELAP5/MOD1 had been written on a CDC-7600 at INEL (Idaho National Engineering Laboratory). At present it is implemented on the Amdahl 470/V8 at JRC-Ispra.

There are two main reasons for choosing this code, which is a typical and the most recent of the RELAP code family. First the RELAP codes are probably the most used codes world wide in Light Water Reactor Safety Analysis; second, this code is a good example, that in spite of its wide dissemination no effort has been made by the code developer to increase the portability of new code versions.

Problems due to differences in the Fortran compilers

Many problems at this level can be easily solved. They are of a syntactical nature and are therefore recognized by the IBM Fortran compilers, which indicate the erroneous statements and the type of errors. Table I contains a list of the most often detected incompatibilities.

TABLE I - List of the most often encountered compilation "errors" of RELAP5/MOD1

1. Variable names with more than 6 characters
2. Inconsistent names of the double precision in-line functions
3. Quotation marks enclosing literals
4. Computed GO TO with no comma after closing parentheses
5. Multiple assignments
6. Data initialization, truncation or spill
7. Data initialization in labelled common blocks
8. Improper boundary alignments in common blocks
9. Illegal use of logical operations
10. Coding of Hollerith strings in statements.

Some of the incompatibilities of the compilers, however, necessitate much more conversion effort or even create severe problems. Typical examples are the initialization statements. Due to the different number of characters which can be stored in a CDC and an IBM word truncation occurs on IBM systems. Therefore the corresponding variables have to be dimensioned or the dimensions have to be increased. The data initialization statements have to be practically always recoded. A further problem arises when variables which are contained in a COMMON block are to be initialized. In this case the IBM compiler demands the creation of a block subprogram, in which only initialization is possible.

Another big problem exists when within a COMMON block, integer and real variables are mixed and when at the same time this COMMON block is equivalenced with a double precision real array. The result is incorrect boundary alignment of the variables, which will lead to incorrect storage allocations.

A very severe conversion problem, at least in RELAP5, is posed by the use of two CDC functions, MASK and SHIFT. These two functions in combination with the logical operators, AND and OR, give access to the bits of a word. They are used frequently throughout the program in order to store more than one piece of information in one word. On the IBM these two functions do not exist, versions may be provided but simulation has to be in double precision in order to be as close as possible to the 60 bits of a CDC word. But this demand conflicts with the IBM compilers which allow only the combination of logical variables/constants or relational expressions with logical operators (logical quantites are normally represented by a 4 byte word).

Problems due to the computer environments and operating systems

In implementing RELAP5 at the INEL laboratory the project group used as much as possible two in-house software systems which facilitate

— the input data processing
— the data file allocation.

Both systems originally developed for the CDC-6600 computer series represent sophisticated program packages allowing in the case of the input processing format free data coding, automatic card replacement, free order of the input card sequence and arbitrary use of comment cards.

The file allocation system permits the dynamic allocation and deletion of data files, for which space is reserved in the memory or on disk.

Fortunately there exist already IBM versions of these sofware systems (partly written in Assembler), because earlier versions of RELAP have also been implemented on IBM computers. Therefore it is hoped that only minor changes will be necessary in order to adapt the programs to the present situation.

If no IBM versions of these special purpose systems existed, this would represent a severe bottleneck for the implementation of RELAP5.

At this point an interesting CDC feature which does not exist on IBM computer systems should be mentioned. Although it concerns the Fortran compilation it is discussed here, because it is more directed towards the operating system. In a CDC environment one can put all labelled COMMON blocks in front of the program source. By coding special commands within the programs, the compiler will at their occurrence replace them with the desired COMMON block. The advantage is that updating of COMMON blocks is done only once and does not result, as on IBM systems, in the tedious work of changing in each subroutine the corresponding COMMON blocks.

Problems due to the different lengths of computer words

Here one encounters the biggest problems, because one needs a thorough understanding of the code. They are in reality the consequence of the basic design features of CDC and IBM computer systems.

To illustrate the problems let us assume that in a CDC integer word several integer values and literal constants are stored. On an IBM system the CDC integer word has to be declared real double precision. If one now, by MASK and SHIFT operations, extract the different values, they will be real double precision variables and not integers. One has to ensure that the IBM code version interprets them in the original sense.

This is especially important if two literals are compared where one has been extracted (by MASK and SHIFT operations) and the other one has been initialized by a DATA statement. If the types (integer/real) of the variables containing the literals are not the same, the comparison (with relational operators) will give wrong answers and direct the program at execution time in wrong directions. It should be noted for this case that the compiler does not generate any error diagnostics.

3. USER EXPERIENCE WITH RELAP4/MOD6

Code Organization

Primary goals in developing large and widely used code systems like RELAP ought to be
(a) user convenience
(b) minimization of problems related to maintenance and possible future extension of the code
(c) ease of implementation at other centres and/or computers.

Ad (a) - User convenience for a code like RELAP means that the code should be easily understandable to personnel with experience in thermohydraulic analysis and LWR safety. It further means ease of input preparation implying minimization of the number of options and of variables to be specified.

Ad (b) - Easy maintenance and code flexibility allowing code modifications (possibly by the user) and further code extensions is achieved by:

— good documentation, both external (i.e. manuals) and internal (i.e. comments inside the program);
— modularity (qua function and qua components) as far as the physico-mathematical model allows this;
— a good description of theoretical models with flowsheets of the computation (if possible also indicating in which subroutines relevant computations are made).

Ad (c) - Implementation aspects have already been discussed in section 1.
The above requirements are only partially fulfilled by the code version RELAP4/MOD6.

The main problems in this program arise because of its size. As already mentioned, the code consists of about 250 different subroutines which are interconnected in a rather complex manner. RELAP4/MOD6 is a code with a modular structure. Owing to its history (see above), it is not a very transparent code which allows modifications to be introduced by the user. It may, however, be said that the code is sufficiently clear for an experienced user to follow its logic. The further discussion of RELAP4/MOD6 requires some specific comments on documentation and input preparation.

Documentation

The importance of good documentation is underlined in Gaggero (1982).

External documentation of RELAP4/MOD6 (Fischer et al, 1978) is extensive, although frequent reference is made to the previous RELAP4/MOD5 (Katsma et al, 1976) manuals. These volumes are a compromise between reports containing everything (which nobody would probably read), and a quick look, providing little understanding or control of the program running. They are written in a way which allows the user to drive the program.

With regard to internal documentation (i.e. documentation inside the program) the following remarks may be made. The subroutines are ordered alphabetically, which allows the user to find them easily. The attempt was made to select subroutine names which describe their functions. In general there is a short comment at the top of each subroutine describing its purpose, and very often the quantities which are calculated inside the routine are indicated. The common blocks are well documented not only in the main program, but also within the subroutines. The code RELAP4/MOD6 exists in two versions, one for the IBM and one for the CDC computer series. The differences of the corresponding Fortran compilers necessitate duplication of certain statements and slightly different coding in order to avoid compilation errors. In the IBM version the CDC statements are contained as comments. This reduces somewhat the readability of the program and sometimes may guide an analyst in wrong directions.

Input and output

One of the most time consuming elements of using the RELAP4/MOD6 code is the input preparation. Generally this is overspecified and typically 2000 to 5000 input variables are necessary to describe a problem. However, it is of great importance that the input description is physically correct since different input will give consequently different output. The code in its present state has the severe drawback of not having a steady state solution, so extensive hand calculations are needed to specify the correct initial pressure and temperature distributions. The situation is not quite as bad as this would suggest since the input checking of the code is very extensive and the error messages are instructive, and if desired it is always possible to obtain conservative results with the use of the Evaluation Model version RELAP4/MOD6-EM. It can be generally stated though, that it takes someone who is familiar with thermohydraulic problems from six months to a year before consistently good input data are produced.

4. CONCLUSIONS

The RELAP codes are probably the most commonly used codes world wide, for LWR safety analysis. Over the past few years the later versions have been increasingly tailored around the INEL computing facilities, resulting in a somewhat low degree of portability. This has been the natural consequence of financial and time limitations. Also owing to the way in which the RELAP codes have developed or probably more correctly, evolved, it is extremely difficult to decouple parts of the program so that modifications to the program can be made.

However, it can be generally said that the codes are rather user dependent, since as the input description of a system is not unique, different modelers will produce different input with consequent different output.

Thus, engineering decisions required in preparing the input are as important in the final code results as the code itself. This means that code user should have competence in the fields of engineering and numerical solution procedures and should have some software experience.

It therefore seems not unreasonable that a training period of 6 months is necessary before a new user will get results.

REFERENCES

Fischer S.R. et al. (1978), RELAP4/MOD6. A Computer Program for Transient Thermal Hydraulic Analysis of Reactions and Related Systems. User's Manual, CDAP TR 003.

Gaggero G. (1982), Program Documentation (This book).

Katsma K.R. et al. (1976), RELAP4/MOD5. A Computer Program for Transient Thermal Hydraulic Analysis of Nuclear Reactors and Related Systems. Vols. 1, 2 and 3 - ANCR-NUREG-1335.

Ransom V.H. et al. (1981), RELAP5/MOD1 Code Manual - Vols. 1 and 2 NUREG/CR-1826.

EXPERIENCE WITH THE SIMMER II CODE

Alan Jones
Joint Research Centre
Ispra, Italy

1. INTRODUCTION

Programming for software sharing, even in a language as well-known and standardised as Fortran IV, is a nuisance for the individual programmer. He will certainly be forced to eschew the use of very convenient extensions to the language granted by his local version of Fortran. Local software which is not readily packaged with the code, such as graphics routines, must be replaced by cumbersome and circumlocutory calls to subroutines with simple functions (e.g. draw a line between two points passed as arguments) which can be readily substituted by the recipients' local routines, and perhaps worst of all, any machine-dependent features of the code design must be foregone. Users of machines designed for scientific calculations (CDC, Cray) must learn to rethink their use of fast cache memory or of vectorisation and discover rough equivalents on the business oriented machines so prevalent even in scientific establishments, no matter how clumsy and inefficient such rough equivalents may prove.

This said the conclusion is obvious. Only in the most favourable circumstances will programmers write shareable software as a matter of habit, and for local applications such coding will not be the most efficient or convenient to use. The decision to write a particular code or software package in a shareable style is one for management to take, based on the intended future use of the software, and taking full cognizance of the extra time and costs both in writing and in testing which will be incurred.

2. SIMMER-II CODE

SIMMER-II is a multi-component, multiphase coupled hydrodynamics/neutronics code developed for fast reactor safety applications at Los Alamos National Laboratory. The machine for which it was originally programmed was the CDC 7600, and the language was Fortran throughout. The code made use of local

D. T. Muxworthy (ed.), Programming for Software Sharing, 275–278.

graphics routines, and had options for microfiche and movie output. The structure of the code made extensive use of the CDC UPDATE facility, and required a post-processor to create further graphical and other output from the numerical output files written on disc by the main code.

The function of UPDATE was as follows: since many options of the SIMMER-II code were possible (e.g. no phase changes permitted in the hydrodynamics, point-kinetics for neutronics or, at the other end of the scale, the more sophisticated of the two phase change models to be used in the hydrodynamics, transport theory for neutronics), the code was written in the form of a monolithic block of source from which the segments required for the option desired could be selected by commands written in UPDATE language. Once the segments had been selected they could be compiled, linked and run in the usual manner.

When the decision was made to release the code to the wider world the Nuclear Regulatory Commission insisted that an IBM version of the code be produced by LANL. This must have involved considerable work, especially since at LANL no IBM machine was available to test the resulting converted software. The source was edited to eliminate overlong identifiers, two statements on the same line and other CDC Fortran features, and double precision was programmed in everywhere to compensate for the shorter wordlength of the IBM machines. The UPDATE facility presented more difficulties since no equivalent could be assumed to exist on IBM computers. The decision was taken to write a Fortran program, the preprocessor, which would accept the UPDATE commands and perform the segment selection accordingly. A set of commands were defined for this preprocessor which would specify a restriction of the range of SIMMER options available so that the resulting preprocessed code would always be IBM compatible - the cache memory size was always defined as zero, for example. Certain combinations of input variables to the code itself (e.g. those specifying the colour of film output or giving details of the movies required) were prescribed.

As for the postprocessor, the LANL graphics routine calls were left unchanged, and only the most obvious CDC Fortran extensions were modified. The code was then released, and reached Ispra in the closing days of 1979.

Implementation at Ispra

The code was received in the form of a magnetic tape containing the various component parts of the SIMMER package, source code, pre- and post-processors, and the various data files for the neutronics and equation of state sections of the code, together with abundant documentation on the physics of the code and upon the numerical algorithms used to solve the sets of partial differential and algebraic equations involved. There were also input descriptions for the code and the post-processor, and a few pages of typescript describing how the specification for the preprocessor should be made, and the input and output files required by the preprocessor. The preprocessor also needed a number of logical functions to be supplied by the user, which operated upon variables at bit level, and other routines to provide the clock time, time remaining since the job began execution, etc. It was found to be necessary to program the logical functions in assembler and link them in with the compiled version of the preprocessor, while most of the clock routines appeared to have local equivalents. Considerable difficulty was encountered in identifying the cause of link-edit failures before it was realised that an Ispra routine, STCLOK, contained a call to a subroutine TIME, while the preprocessor called a routine, also called TIME, which itself called a subroutine which had been replaced by STCLOK.

A further difficulty with the preprocessor was that it used a routine FORQTS to define, allocate, open and write to a direct acess dataset. In IBM Fortran, no way of allocating a direct access dataset directly by using a Fortran statement was found. Also, in IBM Fortran, the channel number to be used for direct access transfer may only be defined as a constant integer parameter to the DEFINE FILE statement, whereas in CDC Fortran the equivalent parameter may be a integer variable. In the end a longish routine had to be written which used the parameters of FORQTS to branch to one of its subsections in which the correct opening or writing instructions were provided for the dataset FTxxF00y which was defined in job control language statements. Once the program had been connected to the right dataset by this means, a further problem was encountered with over-long records being written to the direct-access files. The correct block-size for the dataset had to be determined by trial and error in some cases.

When the preprocessor was compiled and running, it was necessary to test it. A number of sample problems and specimen output were published with the code, and the simplest of these, a point-kinetics problem, was tried using the newly created preprocessor to assemble the desired option of SIMMER and the input data supplied on tape. Very luckily the output furnished by LANL (on microfiche) and the output printed out by our IBM corresponded closely. If they had differed significantly, it would have been a conundrum to discover whether the difficulty lay in the source or in the selections from it made by the preprocessor or in both. The lack of compilation and other difficulties with this option of SIMMER are a testament to the conversion job performed by LANL on the code itself.

For the postprocessor a sheet or two of typescript was supplied which described the actions of the various LANL graphics routines. It was necessary to write new routines for the local plotting command set available at Ispra. Like the preprocessor the postprocessor also made use of logical functions and of routines of the FORQTS type to be supplied by the user, and the same sorts of expedients had to be employed. Coding and testing took some time, but acceptable plots were eventually produced as a matter of routine.

The next obstacle was encountered when attempts were made to run the SIMMER test cases using more advanced neutronics methods, such as diffusion or transport theory, which needed nuclear cross-section data. Unshielded microscopic cross-section data were to come from a standard interface file ISOTXS, while the shielding factors were to be input from the interface file BRKOXS. It turned out that although both sets of data were already available at Ispra, where they had been used for shielding and neutronics calculations, neither was in the format required by SIMMER. For their conversion to this format it was necessary to employ the code LASIP-3, which was not available at Ispra. Although it had been developed at LANL (originally for the CDC again) this code was found to have been installed in the N.E.A. code library at Saclay in an IBM-compatible version. It was ordered from there and when it eventually arrived, the files ISOTXS and BRKOXS were created without problems. Sad to say, by this time the manpower which had been temporarily available to handle the software aspects of the code SIMMER had been transferred to other work, and the more advanced neutronics test problems have still not been tested at Ispra.

As a postscript to this little history, it should be mentioned that in December 1980 a new version of SIMMER arrived from LANL, complete with new versions of the preprocessor and postprocessor, and the whole conversion/installation process has had to be recommenced, with reduced manpower.

3. CONCLUSION AND LESSONS LEARNED

The transfer of codes which are not initially designed for sharing is laborious, time-consuming and seemingly Sysiphean task. Were it not for the considerable work already put in on this job by LANL (in the translation to IBM Fortran of the SIMMER source and the pre- and post-processors) and elsewhere (in the conversion of the LASIP-3 code and the original data-bases which led to ISOTXS and BRKOXS), Ispra would have been unable to make use of SIMMER at all with the limited quantities of time and manpower it was willing to devote to its conversion. If SIMMER had been originally designed for sharing it would not have made use of the UPDATE facility but would have been designed in another way or would have grown up together with its preprocessor. The postprocessor would have had all graphics functions in a separate subset of subroutines, and the task of each subroutine would have been simple enough for a direct equivalent to be available at any establishment with graphics software. Thirdly, there would have been no place for subroutines of the type of FORQTS for which no equivalent exists on IBM machines. The problem of bit-string handling routines and of clock routines seems to have been handled in the only possible way, that is of separating these routines in special-purpose subroutines or function definitions, specifying their actions clearly, and leaving it to the recipient to find or develop the equivalents on his own machine. There is also a little lesson for bodies which act as paymasters: if they ask the original programming team to convert the code to a form compatible with another machine, they should make sure that the team contains someone who is familiar with the new machine, and that the team has access to the new machine to test its conversions and modifications as it goes along. Even very full machine documentation is no substitute for a procedure of continuous modification and testing.

SUBJECT INDEX